I0761609

The Pamphlets of Lewis Carroll

Charles Lutwidge Dodgson. Miniature portrait by E. Gertrude Thomson, undated.

The Political Pamphlets and Letters of Charles Lutwidge Dodgson and Related Pieces

A Mathematical Approach

COMPILED, WITH INTRODUCTORY ESSAYS, NOTES,

AND ANNOTATIONS, BY

Francine F. Abeles

Published by the Lewis Carroll Society of North America, New York,
and distributed by the University Press of Virginia,
Charlottesville and London

2001

This volume and series is funded in part by the
Morton N. Cohen Publishing Trust for the Benefit of
the Lewis Carroll Society of North America

First published 2001

Library of Congress Cataloging-in-Publication Data
Dodgson, Charles Lutwidge, 1832–1898.
The political pamphlets and letters of Charles Lutwidge Dodgson and related pieces : a mathematical approach / compiled, with introductory essays, notes, and annotations, by Francine F. Abeles.
p. cm. — (The pamphlets of Lewis Carroll; v. 3)
Includes bibliographical references and index.
ISBN 0-930326-14-8 (alk. paper)
1. Letters to the editor—England. 2. Carroll, Lewis, 1832–1898—Correspondence. 3. Authors, English—19th century—Correspondence. 4. Mathematicians—Great Britain—Correspondence. 5. Great Britain—Politics and government—1837–1901. 6. Tennis. 7. Voting. I. Abeles, Francine F. II. Title.

PR4611.A4 A24 2001
828'.809—dc21

2001022448

The Pamphlets of Lewis Carroll

SERIES EDITOR

CHARLIE LOVETT

VOLUME 3

The Political Pamphlets and Letters of
Charles Lutwidge Dodgson and Related Pieces
A Mathematical Approach

In Remembrance of
Joseph A. Brabant
and Stan Marx

Contents

Illustrations

Series Preface

Between 1860 and 1897, Charles Lutwidge Dodgson wrote and had printed some 185 pamphlets, booklets, leaflets, form letters, and instruction manuals. They varied in format from a single leaf to booklets of more than 40 pages. Some he signed with his given name, others as Lewis Carroll, and others with some other suitable pseudonym. Some were not signed at all. Taken together, they constitute a unique body of work in the history of English literature.

Their uniqueness is manifested in the broad range of Dodgson's interests, his readiness to challenge any authority, and his unlimited creativity, which flourished up to the time of his death. A churchman who loved the theater (frowned upon at the time); a mathematician who could make his subject an instrument of fun; a logician; a photographer; a creator of games, puzzles, and brain twisters—Dodgson had a mind that was constantly at work. In the pamphlets he emerges as a Victorian activist, a University man, and a moral crusader. These works additionally reveal layers of character and personality in this eminent Victorian that are not evident in his other publications.

In his pamphlets and related material even more than in his better-known works—the *Alice* books, *The Hunting of the Snark,* volumes of poetry, books on mathematics and logic, and his prolific letters—one most easily comprehends the seemingly unending limits of his mind.

We have only to look at his very first separate publication, *Rules for Court Circular,* issued in 1860, to catch a glimpse of what would follow. Invented in 1858, according to his diary, the game of Court Circular has some resemblance to Rummy. The pamphlet, a forerunner of many others of similar format, was printed on four pages, in size slightly smaller than 5" by 8". Also in 1860, he printed up his *Notes on the First Two Books of Euclid,* as well as a list of photographic portraits he had taken. This pattern of varied interests continued throughout his life. Most years would see three or four items on a wide range of subjects, until the last fifteen years of his life, when even more per year would be issued. Beginning in the mid-1880s his interests fastened on logic, and it was during this later period that all 26 of his pamphlets on that subject were written and printed. His growing interest in a field often combining mathematics and philosophy coincided with his revised edition of *Euclid and his Modern Rivals* and his release of *A Tangled Tale, Curiosa Mathematica,* and the

Sylvie and Bruno books, the most seriously philosophical of his stories. Months before he died, he notes on November 12, 1897, in his diary, his intention of bringing out "my Games and Puzzles and Part III of *Curiosa Mathematica* . . . in paper cover," and he was indeed working on these projects in his final days.

Over the years insufficient attention has been paid to Carroll's pamphlets and ephemeral pieces, in contrast to the wealth of interest shown in the *Alice* books. A number of pamphlets were reprinted in various editions of his collected works, but many more were little known or lost. Dodgson's nephew, Stuart Collingwood, even mentions several in *Life and Letters of Lewis Carroll* that have not been seen in this century.

The Pamphlets of Lewis Carroll will provide a scholarly annotated collection of the pamphlets and related material, brought together for the first time. Each book in the series—six are projected—will deal with a particular area: Oxford; Mathematics; Games and Puzzles; Elections and Parliamentary Procedure; Logic; and *Alice* and Miscellaneous.

For their enthusiastic assistance in the early days of organizing this series, the Lewis Carroll Society of North America would particularly like to thank the late Dr. Alexander Wainwright of the Princeton University Library for providing copies of the rare pamphlets in the Parrish Collection; Dr. Morton Cohen and Dr. Selwyn Goodacre for their many suggestions and guidance; Dr. Frank Walker of the Bobst Library at New York University; Mary Lou Ashby of the Pierpont Morgan Library; and Dr. Sandor Burstein and the late Joseph Brabant for their assistance in providing materials and information. The Society appreciates the patience and enterprise of the many people who are contributing to this project.

Finally, the initial series editors must be thanked for their prodigious efforts over many years. From the days when Morton Cohen suggested the project and Stan Marx worked diligently to secure the support of the LCNSA and began obtaining copies of each pamphlet, through the editing and preparation of the manuscripts for each volume, the general editors have brought dedication and cooperation to this monumental task. General editorship for the series through volume II was a collaboration between the late Stan Marx and Edward Guiliano. Charlie Lovett has assumed responsibility for volume III and subsequent volumes.

In the process of producing the first three volumes, the scope of the project has continually expanded. We have discovered that the "related pieces" which we include with the pamphlets are often as important or more important than the pamphlets themselves. Collections of Carroll's shorter works on mathematics and parliamentary procedure, for instance, could not be considered complete without the inclusion of his many contributions to periodicals on those subjects. So, while the original number of items projected in the six volumes of the series was 185, after only three volumes we have reprinted 146, most of which were available only in rare-book libraries prior to their publication in this series. When the series is complete, we hope to have published all of Carroll's works that were not originally issued in hardcover, with the exception of his poetry and fiction.

CHARLIE LOVETT

Editor's Preface

Charles L. Dodgson's publications on political subjects offer a very different view of Lewis Carroll, the man made famous by the *Alice* books. Better known for his whimsical and nonsense writings, Dodgson wrote on the entire spectrum of voting theory. He brought his prodigious abilities in mathematics and logic to bear in matters of local governance at Christ Church College in Oxford University, where he was employed all of his professional life, and to issues of national politics. Although Dodgson's contributions brought a fresh perspective to what then was the embryonic school of politics, his work in this area fell into obscurity after his death. The sophistication and complexity of his theories were not truly appreciated until the second half of the twentieth century.

This third volume of *The Pamphlets of Lewis Carroll* is a comprehensive account of Dodgson's publications on voting. Drawing together all of his pamphlets, letters, diary entries, and other pieces on this subject, we trace the development of Dodgson's theory of voting, from its beginnings in the academic affairs of Oxford University, to his attempts to influence the outcome of bills before the British Parliament. It also brings together letters from correspondents to London newspapers, especially the *St. James's Gazette,* who carried on a lively exchange of ideas with Dodgson on issues of national importance.

Collected together for the first time, these writings deal with such topics as ranking methods, voting anomalies, sophisticated voting, proportional representation, apportionment, and applications of game theory to voting strategies. They also address objectivity and fairness in such sports as horse racing and lawn tennis, which Dodgson considered to be governed by several of the same principles as political elections.

Each chapter of the book is preceded by an introductory essay that provides background information, analyses, and context for the general reader and the specialist.

The abbreviations listed below refer to the collections housing the items included in this volume, as well as the standard sources relating to Lewis Carroll's work that are cited here.

Bodleian	The Bodleian Library, Oxford University.
Colindale	The Newspaper Library of the British Library, Colindale Avenue.

LCAT	*Lewis Carroll at Texas: The Warren Weaver Collection and Related Dodgson Materials at the Harry Ransom Humanities Research Center,* compiled by Robert N. Taylor (1985).
LCH	*The Lewis Carroll Handbook,* S. H. Williams, F. Madan, and R. L. Green; revised edition by D. Crutch (1979).
Lindseth	Jon A. Lindseth, private collection.
Lovett	Charlie Lovett, private collection.
NYU	The Alfred C. Berol Collection of Lewis Carroll, Bobst Library/ Fales Library.
Princeton	The Morris L. Parrish Collection of Victorian Novelists, Princeton University Library.
Wakeling	Edward Wakeling, private collection.
Woking	The Dodgson family collection at Woking.

FRANCINE F. ABELES
NEW YORK, N.Y.

Acknowledgments

Gathering the items for this volume required the assistance of many librarians, collectors, and admirers of Charles Dodgson. Charlie Lovett obtained almost all of the pamphlets and letters, several from his own collection and many others which required sustained efforts to secure. For this service, I owe him a considerable debt. For assistance acquiring these items, Charlie thanks as well the staffs of the Newspaper Library of the British Library at Colindale Avenue, the Dodgson family collection at Woking, the Bodleian Library of Oxford University, and Edward Wakeling.

I am grateful to Kimberly Fraone, Shirley Horbatt, and Sean Mara of the Kean University Library, who helped locate items and supplied needed information about published pieces; and to Jon A. Lindseth and Edward Wakeling for providing rare items.

For their help in obtaining illustrations, I wish to thank the members of the Prints and Photographs Division of the Library of Congress; Marvin Taylor and Mike Kelly of the Fales Library in the Bobst Library at New York University; Linda Briscoe of the Department of Photography and Film at the Harry Ransom Humanities Research Center, the University of Texas at Austin; James Kilvington, the Picture Library of the National Portrait Gallery, London; Anna Lou Ashby, the Pierpont Morgan Library; Jonathan Harrison, the Library of St. John's College, Cambridge University; Jon A. Lindseth; Jonathan Smith, Trinity College Library, Cambridge University; Janet McMullin, Christ Church Library, Oxford University; and Charlie Lovett.

Gerald E. Lenz and Stanley H. Lipson served as manuscript critics, reading the first complete draft of the volume, identifying errors, and offering useful suggestions.

Without financial support for travel and time away from teaching duties, I could not have undertaken this project. That support was provided by the state of New Jersey through its Research Awards for Travel and Released Time, and my colleagues at Kean University who were instrumental in having these grants awarded to me. I am particularly grateful to Mark M. Lender and John E. Kmetz for their trust and encouragement during the extended period of time when I did this challenging work.

Finally, I wish to express my gratitude to Morton N. Cohen, who allowed me to use material from his personal library and supplied elusive information; and to my husband Ernest, who cheerfully took over family responsibilities when I was preoccupied with this project; and to my editor, Cornelia B. Wright, who has worked with me as colleague and muse to create this book.

F.F.A.

The Political Pamphlets and Letters of Charles Lutwidge Dodgson and Related Pieces

A Mathematical Approach

The Lobby of the House of Commons, 1886, *by Liberio Prosperi, 1886. The members of Parliament represented in this group portrait include Inspector Denning, Archibald John Scott Milman, John Bright, Sir William Vernon Harcourt, Ralph Allen Gossett, Henry du Pré Labouchere, Charles Bradlaugh, Joseph Chamberlain, and Charles Stewart Parnell.*

Introduction to the Political Pamphlets and Letters

> The *Perpetuum Mobile* is discovered! We may confidently expect that a clock will shortly be exhibited which, as often as it runs down, is able to wind itself up again. The discoverer of this marvellous principle—the mere details of construction being trifles that any watchmaker can arrange—is no less a person than Mr. Gladstone, on whose great mind it has dawned, for the first time in the world's history, that a body of men *can confer on themselves* rights, over another body of men, which they do not already possess.[1]

Charles L. Dodgson's publications on political subjects add a new dimension to our understanding of the eccentric figure best known as Lewis Carroll, who amused children with such whimsy as *Alice in Wonderland* and *The Hunting of the Snark*. The reserved bachelor was quite an activist—he was involved in both issues of local governance at Christ Church College and Oxford University, where he spent all of his adult life, and problems of national politics at the highest level. To address the issues that captured his interest, Dodgson combined his extraordinary ability to reason logically with simple mathematical techniques in algebra, probability, and statistics. Using an approach all his own, he produced novel solutions to the processes shared by all democratic political systems—voting and elections.

Systematic work on voting theory began in France in the thirty years before the Revolution. The great voting theorists of that century were Jean-Charles de Borda (1733–1799) and Marie-Jean-Antoine-Nicolas de Caritat (1743–1794), better known as the Marquis de Condorcet, who was considered the best of that era's theoreticians. A member of the Academy of Sciences and later of the French Academy and the Legislative Assembly, he was one of the Encyclopédists whose emphasis on rationalism and scientific determinism formed part of the intellectual preparation for the French Revolution. In his quest to develop a science of politics, Condorcet also wrote about the theory of juries and legislative assemblies.[2]

1. Untitled letter to the editor, the *St. James's Gazette,* 23 March 1882, 4.

2. See Isaac Todhunter, *A History of the Mathematical Theory of Probability from the Time of Pascal to That of Laplace* (1865; reprint, Bronx, N.Y.: Chelsea, 1965).

It was Condorcet who discovered one of the chief flaws in voting theory: a cyclical majority, or the voting paradox as it is now called. Where there is a cyclical majority, no candidate or issue can achieve a majority over each of the others when compared in pairs.

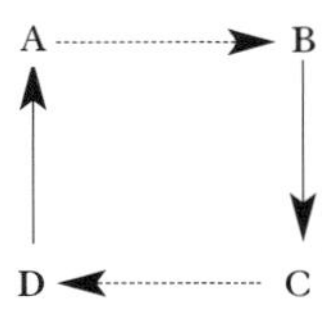

A cyclical majority is most easily explained through the example of a tournament. Represented as a directed graph in which any two nodes are connected by exactly one arc, a tournament is a model of the pair-comparison voting method. For example, the tournament on the left represents a four-point cycle: A is preferred to B, B is preferred to C, C is preferred to D, but D is preferred to A.

In democratic governments, voting is the chief mechanism for making group decisions. Of the many different voting methods, perhaps three are best known: majority rule, plurality rule, and proportional representation. In single-member districts, seats can be awarded according to majority or plurality rule. With majority rule, the winning candidate obtains more than 50 percent of the vote; with plurality rule, the winner receives the greatest number of votes of any one candidate. Proportional representation is used in plural-member districts, where seats are distributed among the political parties in proportion to the vote each party receives.

A natural question to ask in choosing a voting method is whether a best system exists. The answer could never be determined until 1951, when Kenneth Arrow published *Social Choice and Individual Values.*[3] Arrow proved the startling result that it is impossible to obtain a group ranking based on individual preferences, a finding for which he shared the 1972 Nobel Prize in Economics. The answer is, unfortunately, no.

The plurality rule voting method uses a version of Borda's method of marks, in which only first-place preferences are counted. The runoff method, which uses a second election between the most preferred two candidates if plurality voting does not produce a clear winner, uses the Condorcet pair-comparison method to select the winner.

What election method is used has an effect on a political system over time. In the context of electing a single member to represent a district (by a majority or a plurality), the choice of Borda's method of marks or Condorcet's pair-comparison method influences political parties to put up candidates who are not viewed by the electorate as extremists. The reason for this is that the winner will be that candidate whom the voters place highest on their preference lists, on average. Borda's method interprets "on average" as scoring the highest total mark, while Condorcet's method

3. For an analysis of this result, the reader should consult Kenneth Arrow, *Social Choice and Individual Values* (New York: John Wiley, 1951).

interprets "on average" as standing highest in the preference lists. However, should public opinion turn toward one party, these systems can produce a landslide in favor of that party.

If the proportional representation system is used in multimember districts, with the desideratum of having the members of the legislative body reflect the political opinion of the electorate, some mathematical method must be used to decide how seats should be divided among the parties, and which of each party's candidates should occupy those seats. Two of the many proportional representation methods are the single transferable vote method and Dodgson's proposed method, described in Chapter 3. A weakness of the proportional representation method is that more political parties may form over time. However, a strength of this method is that it is almost impossible, in a situation where public opinion favors one of the parties, for that party to win a majority of the votes in a free election.

DODGSON'S POLITICAL INVOLVEMENT

Dodgson's membership on the Governing Board of Christ Church from 1867 to the end of his life involved him in such academic political matters as the election of Students (Fellows, in modern parlance), physical alterations to the College's buildings and grounds, and in university professorships. His pamphlets and related letters from 1872 to 1876 reflect his attempts to find the best method of voting on these matters to ensure the selection of the best candidate or proposal, a method determined by reason and fairness.

In the period from 1881 to 1885, Dodgson involved himself in the important political issues of his day: the extension of the voting franchise, the redistribution of seats in the House of Commons, and methods of achieving proportional representation in the House. These issues applied to Ireland as well, especially relating to the concern over allotting Ireland additional seats in the House. Dodgson's pamphlets and related letters of this period reflect his interests in guaranteeing minority representation and ensuring just outcomes in elections, eliminating, as much as possible, chance events and outside influences from the voting process.

In July 1881, Dodgson decided to resign his mathematical lectureship at Christ Church effectively at the end of the year, after twenty-six years in that demanding position. The *Alice* books had given him sufficient financial independence, and he wanted more time for writing. He wrote in his diary on 14 July 1881,

> My chief motive for holding on has been to provide money for others (for myself I have been for many years able to retire) but even

> the £300 a year I shall thus lose I may fairly hope to make by the additional time I shall have for book-writing.[4]

Dodgson remained a Student, which allowed him to continue living in Christ Church and retain his position on its Governing Body. Just short of his fiftieth birthday, he now would have all his time to himself. Curiously, Dodgson's increased attention to national politics and to matters affecting the public interest date from this time.

Dodgson had established friendships with several government figures early in his career. In a diary entry of 22 September 1857, we first read of his acquaintance with James Garth Marshall (1802–1873), M.P., and his family. Marshall, a Liberal very much involved in electoral reform, was an influential writer on this issue.

Dodgson first met Gathorne Gathorne-Hardy (1814–1906), Home Secretary, on 8 April 1867 when Gathorne-Hardy helped him enter the House of Commons for the second reading of the Reform Bill. (Passed in 1867, the bill added about 938,000 voters to the electorate, an 88 percent increase.) Gathorne-Hardy helped Dodgson enter the House of Commons again on 28 June 1872 for the debate on the House of Lords' amendment to the Ballot Bill, which introduced secret voting. Prior to this bill, passed in 1872, a political party was able to poll within 5 percent of its pledged vote, since printed lists of voters and their votes were available after an election.

On the same day he met Gathorne-Hardy, Dodgson also met George Ward Hunt (1825–1877), M.P. and a Christ Church alumnus; they dined together in the Members' room. The following year, on 3 April, Hunt, who was now Chancellor of the Exchequer, helped Dodgson gain entrance to the House of Commons to hear the debate on the resolution to disestablish the Anglican Irish Church, which was introduced by William Ewart Gladstone (1809–1898), Leader of the Liberal party. This resolution would free Roman Catholics from having to pay tithes to support a Church that included only a small part of the Irish population. On 24 April, again with Hunt's help, Dodgson listened to the debate in the House on this issue. The bill passed in 1869.

Dodgson's most important and enduring friendship with a political figure and his family was with Robert Arthur Talbot Gascoyne-Cecil (1830–1903), third Marquess of Salisbury (1868), who served as Prime Minister from June 1885 to January 1886, from July 1886 to 1892, and again from 1895 to 1902. Their social relationship began in 1870 and lasted throughout Dodgson's life. Salisbury helped Dodgson gain entry to

4. Roger L. Green, ed., *The Diaries of Lewis Carroll,* 2 vols. (New York: Oxford University Press, 1954), 397.

Gathorne Gathorne-Hardy (1814–1906), Home Secretary and first Earl of Cranbrook, by George Richmond, 1857.

Lord Salisbury (1830–1903).

the House of Lords on 8 July 1872 so that he could hear the debate on amendments to the Ballot Bill.

Salisbury became Chancellor of Oxford on 22 June 1870. The next day, Dodgson took several photographs of his family: Salisbury, his two sons, his two daughters, and all four children. Two weeks later, he dined at Salisbury's house in London on Arlington Street. Dodgson frequently stayed at Hatfield House, Salisbury's country house, enjoying social gatherings and visiting with the children. From 1872, New Year's Day at Hatfield House became a regular occurrence. (Dodgson had been invited for 1871 but couldn't go.)

William Ewart Gladstone (1809–1898).

BACKGROUND TO THE PAMPHLETS

Between March of 1871 and February of 1885, Dodgson wrote two sets of pamphlets on voting theory, ranking processes, and election procedures that are remarkable both politically and mathematically. Singular achievements, they contain some of his best and most creative mathematical work.

The work of the earlier period, 1871 to 1876, was motivated by matters of governance at Christ Church, Oxford, while that of the later period, 1881 to 1885, dealt with the problem of election reform in Great Britain. These two contributions to the embryonic school of politics are knit together in extraordinary ways and provide the reader with the opportunity to follow Dodgson's thinking as it developed over these years.

From the beginning, Dodgson's main concerns were selecting the most preferred candidates to hold office, conducting elections properly, promoting minority representation, and achieving fair representation. He wrote his pamphlets at critical moments in an attempt to influence the outcome of the events that caused him to write them in the first place.

Almost a hundred years after Condorcet first identified them, Charles Dodgson independently rediscovered cyclical majorities in the course of his work as a member of numerous committees and the Governing Body of Christ Church. During the period preceding an election of Students at Christ Church, he developed a method to avoid cyclical majorities, publishing it in 1876 as the third of three pamphlets, *A Method of Taking Votes on More Than Two Issues* (item 3). Dodgson's need to establish a rational basis for decision making in situations where he believed it might not exist was of the utmost importance to him.

To accomplish his purposes, he distributed his pamphlets to members of the Governing Body of Christ Church, to members of Convocation of Oxford University, and to Members of Parliament, and he wrote letters to newspapers, particularly to his two favorites, the *Pall Mall Gazette* and the *St. James's Gazette.* In a paper distributed a week and a half before he completed the third and most remarkable pamphlet of the first set, *A Method of Taking Votes on More Than Two Issues,* he wrote,

> [P]artly from the fear of being left in a small, and therefore conspicuous, minority, it seems likely that many of the dissatisfied will abstain from voting. . . . I propose then, if thirty names at least are sent to me, by 4 P.M. on Monday, of Members of Convocation prepared to vote against this Decree, to print the names I receive (excepting any who may express a wish to the contrary) and to circulate the pa-

per. . . . Such a paper would be an assurance to all wishing to vote against the Decree that they will not be singular in so doing.[5]

The protection of minority opinion that he expressed here blossomed into a scheme for proportional representation in his writings of the later period. Dodgson wrote *The Principles of Parliamentary Representation* in 1884 to influence the outcome of two electoral reforms of concern to Salisbury, the leader of the Conservative party, who worried that an extension of the franchise without a redistribution of seats in the House of Commons would end the viability of his party in Parliament. As Dodgson saw it, and he was right, using Salisbury's proposed plurality voting method in single-member districts, with roughly an equal number of supporters for the two political parties among districts, would not guarantee that the Conservative party would receive the number of seats in the House of Commons proportional to the vote the party got.

A later pamphlet drew upon the works of the earlier period, this one on scheduling tennis tournaments. *Lawn Tennis Tournaments: The True Method of Assigning Prizes With a Proof of the Fallacy of the Present Method* (item 4) was published in 1883. Dodgson considered the standard single-elimination or knockout tournament used to select the top three winners to be faulty in the selection of the second and third winners. He used his understanding of cyclical majorities to construct a mechanism to avoid them: if player A beats player B and B beats player C, then A is not scheduled to play C, A being assumed the winner.

Game-theoretic ideas are present in most of Dodgson's political pamphlets. In *A Method of Taking Votes,* Dodgson recommended an approach to choosing a winner that permitted voters to change their votes when cycles were present in order to produce a consensus ranking based on inversion. This approach matured into the coalition strategies he advocated for allotting seats to candidates in an ordered list in *The Principles of Parliamentary Representation* (item 30), which Duncan Black (1908–1991), the Scottish economist and political theorist, described as "the most interesting contribution to Political Science that has ever been made."[6] Dodgson corrected and refined the ideas in this pamphlet in a *Supplement* (item 31) and *Postscript to Supplement* (item 32) of the following year.

5. Dodgson produced three short papers on "The Professorship of Comparative Philology," dated 4, 12, and 14 February 1876. The quotation is from the paper of 12 February. The papers are reprinted in Edward Wakeling, ed., *The Oxford Pamphlets, Leaflets, and Circulars of Charles Lutwidge Dodgson* (Charlottesville: University Press of Virginia, 1993), 121–26.

6. Duncan Black, "The Central Argument in Lewis Carroll's *'The Principles of Parliamentary Representation,'" Papers on Nonmarket Decision Making* 3 (1967), 1.

What is extraordinary about Dodgson's first three pamphlets is their complete originality. Black believed he was probably not familiar with the work of the great voting theorists of the previous century, Borda and Condorcet, and his familiarity with another of these, Pierre Simon, Marquis de Laplace (1749–1827), did not have a direct bearing on his work.[7]

The only other English mathematicians writing on voting methods were E. J. Nanson (1850–1936), a high honors graduate in mathematics from Trinity College, Cambridge, who became Professor of Mathematics at the University of Melbourne in 1875. His article "Methods of Election," read in Australia in 1882, was not published until 1907, after Dodgson's death, and could not have influenced his work. Isaac Todhunter (1820–84), who graduated first in mathematics from St. John's College, Cambridge and became a fellow there, had analyzed the views of Borda, Condorcet, and Laplace in one of his books, *A History of the Mathematical Theory of Probability from the Time of Pascal to That of Laplace* (1865). Dodgson had this book in his personal library, but Black believed he had not read Todhunter's book.[8]

Further, in an earlier letter to Dodgson dated 24 March 1876, in reply to his letter on some probability problems discussed by Todhunter in one of his books, Todhunter touched on topics that could possibly be linked to voting theory. The book referred to was not the history book, but a textbook, *A Treatise on Algebra* (1858, 6th. ed., 1871), and it does not contain topics on voting methods.[9]

Analyzing Condorcet's *Essai sur l'application de l'analyse* in his work on the history of the mathematical theory of probability, Todhunter commented on Condorcet's example of a cyclical majority, apparently without

7. Black based his conclusion that Dodgson was not familiar with the writings on election theory by Borda and Condorcet on two pieces of evidence. First, the pages of the copy of the *Histoire de l'Academie Royale des Sciences* containing Borda's article, "Mémoire sur les élections au scrutin" (1781), in the library of Christ Church were uncut. Secondly, one of the pages in the section on elections of Condorcet's *Essai sur l'application de l'analyse à la probabilité des décisions rendues à la pluralité des voix* (1785), in Oxford's Bodleian Library (Christ Church did not own a copy) was uncut. However, Black was reasonably certain that Dodgson had read Laplace's more literary and nonmathematical book dealing partly with elections, *Essai philosophique sur les probabilités* (1814), when he found a similarity between Dodgson's description of the method of marks in his 1874 pamphlet and a passage in Laplace's book. See Duncan Black, *Theory of Committees and Elections* (London: Cambridge University Press, 1958; reprint, 1968), 192–94.

8. Black, *Theory of Committees and Elections,* 192–94.

9. Morton N. Cohen supplied me with a copy of Todhunter's four letters to Dodgson, and I used W. Johnson, "Isaac Todhunter (1820–1884): Textbook Writer, Scholar, Coach and Historian of Science," *International Journal of Mechanical Science* 38 (1996), 1231–70, to identify the book.

recognizing its significance. Todhunter wrote, "Unfortunately these propositions are not consistent with each other." He then stated, "Condorcet treats this subject of electing out of more than two candidates at great length. . . . His results however appear of too little value to detain us any longer."[10] We may add that if Dodgson had read Todhunter's book, the Oxford scholar's negative opinion of Condorcet's work might have led Dodgson to drop the topic, since Dodgson admired and respected Todhunter. Dodgson later included an essay by Todhunter on geometry and diagrams from his edition of Euclid in *Euclid and His Modern Rivals* (1879).

Black has an entirely different opinion about the later pamphlets. In a recent book, he claims Dodgson was heavily influenced by James Garth Marshall and Walter Baily (1837–1917), a high honors graduate in mathematics of St. John's College, Cambridge, member of Lincoln's Inn, and Government Inspector of Schools.[11] Black cites Marshall's pamphlet, *Minorities and Majorities; Their Relative Rights—A Letter to the Lord John Russell, M.P. on Parliamentary Reform* (London: James Ridgway, 1853), as the source of the two-person zero-sum game with maximin criterion that Dodgson used to formulate his theory of parliamentary representation.[12] More specifically, Black points to section 1 of chapter III of *The Principles of Parliamentary Representation* as Dodgson's simplification of Marshall's work.

From Baily's pamphlet, *Proportional Representation in Large Constituencies* (London: James Ridgway, 1872), Black asserts that Dodgson borrowed the concept of wasted votes—one candidate getting more votes than he needs to be elected while another candidate has fewer votes than he needs for election—that underlies Dodgson's notion of the number of voters unrepresented, essential to his theory of proportional representation. Specifically, Black claims that table III in chapter III, section 1 of

10. Isaac Todhunter, *A History of the Mathematical Theory of Probability from the Time of Pascal to That of Laplace,* 375.

11. Iain McLean, Alistair McMillan, and Burt L. Monroe, eds., *A Mathematical Approach to Proportional Representation: Duncan Black on Lewis Carroll.* Boston/Dordrecht/London: Kluwer Academic Publishers, 1996, 112–20.

12. Dodgson assumes each of the two political parties will act to maximize the number of seats it receives in an election. The parties will decide how many candidates will run in a district and will provide instructions to their voters on how to arrange their voting preference orders for the party's candidates. One party's gain is the other's loss—hence the description, zero-sum game. Since most districts at this time were represented by two to four members in Parliament, the strategic decisions taken by one party to return its candidates took into account the possible choices available to the other party to elect its candidates—hence the term maximin (more properly, minimax) criterion.

Dodgson's pamphlet is directly derived from Baily's work. Black adds that Dodgson also took his "method of desiderata" in the first chapter from Baily.

Unlike the 1870s, when Dodgson was a lone voice writing on voting theory, the 1880s were filled with writings about proportional representation. Given Dodgson's keen interest in the topic, he naturally would have kept abreast of developments. Certainly the letters he wrote to the *St. James's Gazette* on aspects of proportional representation and redistribution attest to this. But to state that Dodgson made direct borrowings without attribution is not correct.

Interestingly, nowhere in his pamphlets, letters, or diary entries did Dodgson mention Marshall's or Baily's pamphlets. In the case of Marshall, this is somewhat strange since Dodgson knew him well, having first met his family on 22 September 1857 in the Lake District when he went to visit Alfred Tennyson. Dodgson recorded his many engagements with the Marshalls in his diary.

Neither Marshall's nor Baily's pamphlets are mathematical or politically theoretical in nature, nor does either attempt a comprehensive approach to the twin issues of proportional representation (that the proportions of political parties in Parliament should be nearly the same as in the electorate), and apportionment (that each member of Parliament should represent the same number of electors). If Dodgson did use these important ideas from Marshall's and Baily's pamphlets, what he did with them transcends the roles Marshall and Baily gave them. Then too, Marshall's work was widely known, and his ideas were picked up by advocates of proportional representation; attributions are not given for ideas in the public domain.

In chapter II, section 3 of *The Principles of Parliamentary Representation,* Dodgson does use a form of the widely accepted Droop quota, which minimizes the number of wasted votes, although without naming it. This formula, which specifies the number of votes needed for a candidate to be elected, was introduced in 1868 by Henry R. Droop (1832–1884), a high honors graduate in mathematics of Trinity College, Cambridge, a member of Lincoln's Inn, a Fellow of Trinity College, and Baily's brother-in-law. There is no doubt that Droop's ideas influenced Baily's writings on election methods.

Dodgson utilized a form of the Droop quota modified for two political parties as the basis of his theory of proportional representation. And his innovation, a constant Droop quota, or number of votes needed to allocate members in proportion to the number of voters, he used as the basis of his theory of apportionment. Dodgson achieved a logically consistent complete theory, one that would ensure not only proportionality of represen-

Henry R. Droop (1832–1884), developer of the Droop quota, which specifies the number of votes needed for a candidate to be elected.

tation between the parties, but also among the districts; at this time, he was the first and only person to accomplish this feat.[13]

13. McLean, McMillan, and Monroe, in the introduction to *A Mathematical Approach to Proportional Representation,* xxv, point out that Dodgson made an error in the statement of the second principle in chapter I of his pamphlet: "That each Elector . . . should be represented by the same fraction of a Member. Or (which is the same thing) that each Member should represent the same number of Electors." They assert correctly that these two are not the same because an arithmetic mean divisor rule is needed to minimize the first, while a harmonic mean divisor rule is required to minimize the second.

BACKGROUND TO THE LETTERS OF A PUBLIC AND POLITICAL NATURE

Dodgson showed a keen interest in matters affecting the public interest. He expressed this interest in his diary and in both public and private letters. According to Charles Lovett, Dodgson spent over fifty years writing for the press; his pieces appeared in more than three hundred issues of forty periodicals, using, in addition to his own name and his best-known pseudonym, Lewis Carroll, the pseudonyms B.B., The Lounger, K., R.W.G., Rusticus Expectans, and Dynamite.[14] From 1882 to the end of his life, 28 percent of these items, excluding the word puzzles he wrote for the magazine *The Lady,* were on political topics and issues affecting the public interest.

Letters written between 1857 to 1893 offer evidence that from the beginning of his career, Dodgson was an active, well-informed citizen who took a serious interest in public matters he considered important. In many of these letters Dodgson used his considerable logical and mathematical abilities to expose fallacious reasoning. In others he raised issues that ultimately led to legislative acts.

The first of these public letters appeared in *The Illustrated London News* on 18 April 1857 on the subject, "Where Does the Day begin."[15] He noted in a diary entry of 23 February that he had actually written about this idea in the Dodgson family magazine, *The Rectory Umbrella,* several years earlier. Dodgson wrote in response to other correspondents who were discussing the paradox of two places within an hour's time of each other having different names for the same day (other than at midnight). The idea certainly was not a new one. Portuguese navigators more than three centuries earlier were puzzled about the gain of a day on the western journey around the world, and the loss of a day on the journey east. In fact, the French scientist Nicolas Oresme (1320?–1382) explains in his treatise, *Traitié de l'espere,* that traveling east, a traveler will have a shorter than twenty-four-hour day, while traveling west he will have a longer one.[16]

The problem was resolved in 1884 when an international conference called by President Chester A. Arthur in Washington, D.C., established

14. Charles Lovett, *Lewis Carroll and the Press: An Annotated Bibliography of Charles Dodgson's Contributions to Periodicals* (New Castle, Del. and London: Oak Knoll Press and the British Library, 1999), 1, 14.

15. The letter is reprinted in Green, *Diaries,* 104–5. Green adds (*ibid.,* 160) that Dodgson gave a lecture on the subject to the Ashmolean Society in November 1860.

16. Cora E. Lutz, *Essays on Manuscripts and Rare Books* (Hamden, Conn.: Archon, 1975), 63–70.

the Prime Meridian, located at Greenwich, England. All longitude would henceforth be calculated east and west from this meridian to the zero meridian, a line in the Pacific 180 degrees from Greenwich. Together with the acceptance of a universal day, a mean solar day beginning at midnight at Greenwich and counted on a twenty-four-hour clock, the International Date Line was created.

Dodgson wrote several letters criticizing vivisection under the alias of Lewis Carroll. "Vivisection as a Sign of the Times," a letter that appeared in the *Pall Mall Gazette* on 12 February 1875 was Carroll's answer to a letter that had appeared in the *Spectator* a week earlier. He argues that education without the moral dimension supplied by religious teaching is deficient.

> The enslavement of his weaker brethren—"the labour of those who do not enjoy, for the enjoyment of those who do not labour"—the degradation of women—the torture of the animal world—these are the steps of the ladder by which man is ascending to his higher civilization. Selfishness is the keynote of all purely secular education; and I take vivisection to be a glaring, a wholly unmistakable case in point.[17]

He wrote another letter on vivisection that appeared on 16 February in response to a correspondent's letter published the day before. Again writing as Carroll, he followed up with an article, "Some Popular Fallacies About Vivisection," but the *Pall Mall Gazette* turned it down. Still as Carroll, on 8 May Dodgson wrote again to Frances Power Cobbe (1822–1904), Joint Secretary of the Anti-Vivisection Society, who had written to him in February in connection with his earlier publication, both to thank her for quoting it in an article she authored in the *New Quarterly Magazine,* and to ask her assistance in placing his article in the same magazine.[18] She gave it to *The Fortnightly Review,* where it appeared on 1 June.[19] In it, Carroll used logical reasoning to build a case against vivisection.

But Dodgson wanted not only public debate, but legislation restricting vivisection. To this end, he wrote on 9 May 1875 to his friend and Member of Parliament, Lord Salisbury, calling his attention to Cobbe's article and enclosing his own piece from the *Pall Mall Gazette* as well as an item

17. The letter is reprinted in Stuart Dodgson Collingwood, *The Life and Letters of Lewis Carroll* (London: T. Fisher Unwin, 1898), 167–71; the quoted passage appears on p. 170.

18. Morton N. Cohen, ed., *The Letters of Lewis Carroll;* two vols. (New York: Oxford University Press, 1979), 223.

19. *The Fortnightly Review,* vol. xvii n.s. (1 June 1875), 847–54.

printed by the Society for the Prevention of Cruelty to Animals. A Royal Commission to study the problem was established the following month. It delivered its report in January 1876, resulting in the passage of the Cruelty to Animals Act of 1876, which established regulations governing experiments involving live animals.

Carroll returned to this topic again ten years later when he responded to a dramatic sketch in the *St. James's Gazette* that he thought presented an incomplete picture of the current situation. His letter, "Vivisection Vivisected" appeared on 19 March 1885.[20]

In 1877, on 18 August, 8 September, and 22 September Dodgson published letters on the subject of vaccinating children in *The Eastbourne Chronicle.* These were replies to letters written by William Hume-Rothery, a committed opponent of compulsory vaccinations who also responded to each of Dodgson's letters. In his letters Dodgson questioned the statistics used by Hume-Rothery to discredit the value of vaccination in preventing smallpox. Dodgson correctly claimed that just using the percentage of deaths among vaccinated patients, without comparing it with the percentage of deaths among the nonvaccinated, proves nothing. However, when Hume-Rothery finally supplied all the necessary statistics, Dodgson was forced to the conclusion that if the reported statistics were correct, vaccination did increase the likelihood of smallpox infection.

He returned to the topic of the faulty use of statistics again in 1882 when he responded to a letter printed in the *Guardian* on 1 February that reported the increased number of men who had to leave Oxford because they could not answer the questions on Euclid I, II in the Responsions examination, the first of the three examinations for the B.A. degree. Dodgson saw the situation quite differently, showing with the proper analysis of the numbers, that the pass percentage had not changed significantly. His letter was published one week later, and he also wrote a short pamphlet, *An Analysis of the Responsions Lists From Michaelmas 1873 to Michaelmas 1881,* dated 9 February.[21]

In "Whoso Shall Offend One of These Little Ones," a letter published in the *St. James's Gazette* on 22 July 1885, writing as Carroll, Dodgson questioned the inclusion of explicit details regarding child prostitution in the first of four articles on the topic that were being published in the *Pall Mall Gazette.* The series was written by that newspaper's editor as part of a campaign to rouse public opinion against the practice. Carroll saw that the revelations had implications for pornography; he thought that reading

20. This letter is omitted in the bibliography of Carroll's letters to the *St. James's Gazette* in Roger L. Green, "Lewis Carroll and the *St. James's Gazette." Notes and Queries,* 7 April 1945, 134–5.

21. Both are reprinted in Wakeling, ed., *The Oxford Pamphlets,* 130–32, 132–35.

the vivid descriptions of vice in the *Pall Mall Gazette* articles would excite the imagination of young men and boys and lead them to ferret out such material elsewhere.[22]

Earlier, on 7 July, Dodgson had written to Lord Salisbury, now Prime Minister, calling his attention to a matter of "great national importance" and asking him to look at the 6 July issue of the *Pall Mall Gazette,* in which the first of the four articles on organized child prostitution appeared. Dodgson objected to its appearance in a daily paper where it could be read easily by boys and young men, and urged that legal steps be taken.[23]

On 22 August a large rally was held in Hyde Park, the largest of the many meetings organized to put an end to the prostitution of children. Two days later Parliament passed the Criminal Law Amendment Bill which included, among other provisions, increasing the age of consent from thirteen to sixteen, and making the exportation of minors for the purpose of prostitution illegal.

Dodgson wrote again to Salisbury on 31 August to clarify the meaning of the legal steps he asked for in his previous letter, which Lord Salisbury had answered. Dodgson wanted legal steps to be taken against other similar publications whose salacious material was "now flooding the streets."[24]

Writing as Lewis Carroll, Dodgson addressed the issue of children in the theater. On 19 July 1887, in a letter to the *St. James's Gazette,* "Children in Theatres," Carroll responded to an account of a large meeting of ladies recommending that children under the age of ten should not be permitted to act professionally on the stage, a point of view he vigorously disputed.[25]

This issue continued to simmer until August 1889, when the House of Commons passed a bill forbidding children under the age of ten to appear on the stage. Dodgson noted in his diary on 4 August,

> Mr. J. Coleman, who is bringing out a book on 'Stage Children' . . . had asked for my letter about 'Brighton Pier' ['Children in Theatres']. I sent it, and a new one which he has printed in today's *Sunday Times,* of which he has sent a copy to every member of the Lords![26]

22. This letter is partially reprinted in Morton N. Cohen, *Lewis Carroll: A Biography* (New York: Knopf, 1995), 432.

23. Cohen, *Letters,* 586–87.

24. *Ibid.,* 599–600.

25. This letter is partially reprinted in Collingwood, *Life and Letters,* 180–81, in Green, "Lewis Carroll and the *St. James's Gazette,*" 134 (where it is mistitled "Children in the Theatre") and in Green, *Diaries,* 452–53.

26. Green, *Diaries,* 472–73; excerpts from the letter follow.

In the letter published in the *Sunday Times* on 4 August, titled "Stage Children," Carroll criticized the House's bill and offered several recommendations of his own for the legislation of employment in the theater, including the licensing of children under sixteen years of age, limiting the number of hours a child can work, and providing for formal schooling during theatrical engagements. The Children's Protection Bill passed by Parliament in 1889 required that children engaging in public performances for profit at night should be placed in the care of their friends or other persons the Court deemed fit.

Clement Scott, editor of the *Theatre* magazine, reprinted Dodgson's letter from the *Sunday Times*. In a letter dated 3 December 1889 thanking him, Dodgson pointed out that he had never intended the letter for the newspaper, which had a poor reputation, but rather for Coleman's proposed pamphlet, which was never published.[27]

A short letter to the *Standard,* published on 19 August 1890 under the title "The Eight Hours Movement," was Carroll's reaction to a highly publicized five week dock strike by unskilled workers in 1889. He argues, logically but naively, for an understanding between employers and workers that would prevent disastrous strikes in the future.[28] By the 1870s the work week ranged from fifty-four to sixty-four hours, including Saturday half-days, but the forty-eight-hour work week did not become law until 1919.

Three years later, on 30 November 1893, Dodgson sent a letter of congratulations to one of his former pupils at Christ Church, Lord Rosebery, who had recently settled a sixteen-week strike of coal miners.[29]

In addition to the topics discussed in the public letters, in his private correspondence Dodgson addressed a variety of other topics in the public interest. All of them can be found in Morton Cohen's 1979 edition of Lewis Carroll's letters. Many are written to Lord Salisbury, with whom Dodgson corresponded from 1874 to 1897.

Dodgson wrote to Salisbury on 30 August 1895 in reaction to a disastrous fire at a restaurant in London; he recommended that there be lookout stations at the highest accessible points in the city, manned around the clock, and in electrical communication with the fire-truck stations. Dodgson added that some foreign cities had already done this. Salisbury replied the next day, saying he would inform someone in authority in the Fire Brigade Department. [30]

27. Cohen, *Letters,* 766.

28. This letter is reprinted in Collingwood, *Life and Letters,* 293.

29. Cohen, *Letters,* 997–98.

30. Dodgson's letter is reprinted in Cohen, *Letters,* 1069; Salisbury's response is in the Berol Collection, item 270, section VII, p . 224.

On 3 September 1895, after thanking Salisbury for sending along the suggestion about early fire detection, Dodgson proposed two ideas to strengthen and popularize the House of Lords. The first is that members of each House should be free to appear in the other for the purpose of discussions and questions; the second is that certain bills normally initiated in Commons could instead be initiated in the Lords. Salisbury responded on 6 September suggesting that although his ideas were good ones, they were not consistent with the *amour propre* of the House of Commons.[31]

Dodgson replied to Salisbury's letter on 17 September with an improved version of his first suggestion, i.e., that the House of Commons should have the right to require a member of the House of Lords to appear and to speak, and it would follow that the Lords should then have the same right. He added that Salisbury need not bother to respond again on this subject.[32]

Home Rule was an important issue in the last quarter of the nineteenth century. Dodgson had followed Irish affairs closely, recording events in his diary: Gladstone's 1868 bill to disestablish the Irish Anglican Church and his failed attempt in 1873 to establish a university for Irish Roman Catholics, Charles Stewart Parnell's unsuccessful attempts to have a Home Rule Bill passed in 1881, Parnell's arrest in 1881, the Dublin murders of the Secretary and Under Secretary for Ireland in 1882, and Gladstone's Home Rule Bill which failed and brought down his government in 1886, restoring Salisbury to power. Dodgson wrote on 29 November 1890,

> History is moving briskly just now! First, Parnell's disgrace as co-respondent in a divorce suit. Then Gladstone's letter, calling on him to resign the leadership of the 'Home Rule' party. And this morning Parnell's Manifesto to the Irish People, revealing Gladstone's negotiations with him, and the sham 'Home Rule' Bill he proposed to bring in when next in power, offering Parnell the Irish Secretaryship as a sop![33]

On the subject of Ireland, Dodgson wrote to Salisbury on 7 June 1897 expressing the naive notion that if Queen Victoria had visited Ireland, the two Home Rule bills would never have been proposed. Now Dodgson wants Salisbury to bring this suggestion to the Queen's notice, and he enclosed an article from the *St. James's Gazette* supporting the idea that the average Irish citizen wanted a royal residence in Ireland.[34]

31. Cohen, *Letters,* 1070. Berol, item 271, Section VII, p. 224.
32. Cohen, *Letters,* 1072–73.
33. Green, *Diaries,* 481.
34. Cohen, *Letters,* 1124–26.

Gladstone's Cabinet of 1868, *by Lowes Cato Dickinson, 1869–1874. Gladstone's advisers represented here include Robert Lowe, Viscount Sherbrooke; Spencer Cavendish, 8th Duke of Devonshire; John Bright; George Douglas Campbell, 8th Duke of Argyll; Chichester Samuel Fortescue, Baron Carlingford; and William Wood, Baron Hatherley.*

In his reply, Salisbury could not support the establishment of a royal residence in Ireland, so on 11 June Dodgson wrote again asking him to bring to her attention the need for an occasional royal visit.[35] Queen Victoria did visit Ireland, but not until 1900.

CONCLUSION

Charles Dodgson's publications on the mathematics of voting, the three pamphlets from the 1870s and the 1884 pamphlet on parliamentary representation, constitute his most significant legacy to the mathematics

35. *Ibid.*, 1126.

of politics. His independently original pamphlets on majority rule and those on the central concepts of proportional representation and apportionment establish him as the only nineteenth-century writer who completely understood the fundamental issues of the entire spectrum of voting theory. Yet this work remained entirely unknown at his death; not a single obituary notice mentions any of these pieces. In only one, *The Critic,* a New York publication, is a related pamphlet listed, *Lawn Tennis Tournaments.*[36]

Fifty-four years after his death, Duncan Black discovered Dodgson's work and in his 1958 book established his profound reputation in the theory of majority rule (social choice).[37] After first dismissing Dodgson's pamphlet on proportional representation and apportionment,[38] in a set of articles appearing between 1967 and 1970, he arrived at a very different evaluation, writing in a short essay that "the booklet incorporates something of Carroll's genius."[39] The first publications to describe and analyze the contents of *The Principles of Parliamentary Representation* from a mathematical standpoint were the work of this author.[40]

Black belatedly recognized Dodgson as a major figure in the development of the theory of proportional representation and apportionment after he discovered that Dodgson had used game-theoretic concepts in his pamphlet. Game theory is used to analyze conflicts of interest in order to determine optimal behavior. Early work in this field, which was not systematized into a formal theory until 1928 by John von Neumann (1903–1957), began in the nineteenth century. Von Neumann presented the first general theory for a zero-sum two-person game with an associated minimax condition.

Dodgson actually had showed an earlier interest in game theory, a fact not appreciated by Black. In his 1876 pamphlet, *A Method of Taking Votes on More Than Two Issues,* he wrote,

36. The reader should consult August A. Imholtz, Jr., and Charles Lovett, *In Memoriam: Charles Lutwidge Dodgson 1832–1898. Obituaries of Lewis Carroll and Related Pieces* (New York: Lewis Carroll Society of North America, 1998), 28–30.

37. In his article "Discovery of Lewis Carroll Documents" (*Notes and Queries,* Feb. 1953, 77–79), Duncan Black describes this discovery. In *The Theory of Committees and Elections,* Black stated that Dodgson attended the debates in Parliament only in 1872, relating to the Ballot Bill (p. 201). But Dodgson had also attended in 1867 on the Reform Bill, and again in 1868 on the bill to disestablish the Anglican Irish Church.

38. Black, *Theory of Committees and Elections,* 192.

39. Black, "Evaluating Carroll's Theory of Parliamentary Representation," *Jabberwocky* 1 (1970), 19.

40. Francine Abeles, "C. L. Dodgson and Apportionment for Proportional Repre-

> Suppose A be the candidate whom I wish to elect, and that a division is taken between B and C; am I bound in honour to vote for the one whom I should *really* prefer . . . or may I vote in whatever way I think most favorable to A's chances?
>
> This principle of voting [sophisticated voting to induce a cyclical majority] makes an election more of a game of skill than a real test of the wishes of the electors, and . . . [it is] my own opinion that it is better for elections to be decided according to the wish of the majority than of those who happen to have most skill in the game.[41]

Dodgson's description of sophisticated voting in this pamphlet is, I believe, the first to appear in print on this topic.

Along the way, political events gave Dodgson the opportunity to produce pieces that indulged his sense of humor, and he discovered that his penchant for rule-based methods could also be applied to popular games of sport.

---

sentation, *Ganita-Bhāratī* 3 (1981), 71–82; and "The Mathematical-Political Papers of C. L. Dodgson," in *Lewis Carroll: A Celebration,* Edward Guiliano, ed. (New York: Clarkson Potter, 1982, 195–210.

41. Dodgson, *A Method of Taking Votes on More Than Two Issues,* 1876, 18–19 (pp. 56–57 in this volume).

Fairness in Elections

Unattributed photograph of Christ Church Cathedral and Quadrangle, Oxford, from the 1860s, before the changes to the belfry and the quadrangle.

Introduction

In the 1870s, Dodgson wrote three pamphlets applying his mathematical skills to the political procedures at work in the committees that are ubiquitous in academic life. As a member of the Governing Body of Christ Church from 1867 to the end of his life, Dodgson became involved in many local college issues. In diary entries beginning November 1870 through June 1871, and in a short publication in March 1871, *Suggestions for Committee appointed to consider the expediency of reconstituting Senior Studentships at Christ Church,* we first learn of his serious interest in the election of Senior Students and in the terms and conditions of their employment. In the period from June 1872 to November 1874, Dodgson was involved in the controversies over the restoration of Christ Church Cathedral, the proposed alterations to the Great Quadrangle, and the design of the new belfry. During this period he confided many of his thoughts on these issues to his diary, publishing three pamphlets about them and sending two letters on these architectural matters to the *Pall Mall Gazette,* which were published 3 and 5 November 1874. In February 1876, Dodgson brought out three short papers, each titled "The Professorship of Comparative Philology."[1] He commented on the circumstances surrounding this University Chair six times in his diary.[2] These issues of university governance provided the setting for his attempts to solve some of the thorny problems they raised—those that were amenable to voting.

Issues of fairness, such as minority representation, intrigued Dodgson. The first set of three pamphlets on this issue, published from 1873 to 1876, reflect the changes in his thinking about how a committee should select the best candidate or proposal. On the strength of these completely original pamphlets, Dodgson is now generally considered second only to the great eighteenth-century French social scientist and philosopher, the Marquis de Condorcet, as a voting theorist.

In the first pamphlet published in December 1873, *A Discussion of the*

1. The pamphlets are *The New Belfry of Christ Church, Oxford* (June 1872); *The Vision of the Three T's* (March 1873); and *Objections, submitted to the Governing Body of Christ Church, Oxford, against certain proposed alterations in the Great Quadrangle* (May 1873). These pieces are reprinted in Wakeling, ed., *The Oxford Pamphlets,* 62–108, 119–26.

2. The diary entries for 3, 5, 12, and 15 February 1876 are in Green, *Diaries,* 349–50; entries for 11 and 14 February are from the unpublished manuscript diaries.

New Buildings of Christ Church, Oxford, from an 1868 engraving.

Various Methods of Procedure in Conducting Elections (item 1), Dodgson describes several election methods that were in current use: simple majority, absolute majority, elimination (two versions), method of marks (a form of cumulative voting in which each elector can assign any number of a previously agreed-upon total number of votes to any one or to several candidates), and nomination (printed as a separate sheet). He goes on to critique how each fails. His own suggestion is to adopt a version of the method of marks equivalent to Borda's.

As an example, consider four electors voting on three candidates A, B, C; each elector has three votes that can be assigned to any of the three candidates. Two electors assign two votes each to A; the other two give no votes to A. Each of three electors give B one vote; the other elector gives B no votes. Two electors assign two votes each to C; one elector gives C one vote; the other elector gives C no votes. The method of marks creates the preference schedules ACB, ABC, CBA, CBA. Dodgson's and Borda's method assigns 2 marks to the highest ranking candidate in each schedule, 1 to the next, and 0 to the lowest ranking candidate. Here C has received 5 votes, A has received 4 votes, and B has received 3 votes, making C the winner.

Robert Edward Baynes (1849–1921), Lee's Reader in Physics from 1873 and Senior Student at Christ Church from 1875 until his death.

Dodgson wrote this pamphlet for the Governing Body in connection with the election of a Lee's Reader in Physics and of a Senior Student at Christ Church. His method was used in the first stage of the Lee's appointment, involving three candidates, but was ultimately rejected. He wrote in his diary on 13 December 1873, "Began writing a paper (which occurred to me last night) on 'Methods of Election', in view of our election of a Lee's Reader in Physics and a Senior Student next Wednesday." On 18 December 1873, the day the pamphlet was printed, he wrote, "Election of Baynes and Paget: we partly used my method." And on 29 December 1873 he added, "I have been engaged writing about Elections very constantly lately."[3]

3. Green, *Diaries,* 324.

Dodgson's second pamphlet, *Suggestions As to the Best Method of Taking Votes, Where More Than Two issues Are to Be Voted On* (item 2), was published in June 1874. In its preface he wrote, "In the immediate prospect of a meeting of the Governing Body, where matters may be debated of very great importance, on which various and conflicting opinions are known to be held, I venture to offer a few suggestions as to the mode of taking votes." Here Dodgson abandoned the modified method of marks, embracing instead the Condorcet principle that the best candidate is the one who beats every other candidate in all pairwise comparisons. Why did he change his approach? The selection of the Lee's Reader had required a runoff election because the eventual winner, Robert Edward Baynes, with 47 marks, was in a near tie with another candidate, who got 48 marks. Obviously, the Governing Body was unwilling to let the method of marks determine the winner.

Dodgson proposed that when a first ballot does not produce an absolute majority for one candidate, all candidates should then be compared in pairs, which corresponds in sports terminology to a round-robin tournament. Generally, a tournament is a model of the pair-comparison method. A round-robin tournament requires that each player play every other player once. Seven years later, Dodgson was to return to the topic of tournaments, this time the knockout or single-elimination type, when he criticizes the scheduling of tennis tournaments. The pair-comparison method was used by the Governing Body to choose the architect from the group of four finalists who had submitted designs for the new belfry of Christ Church.[4]

A Method of Taking Votes on More Than Two Issues (item 3), published in March 1876, is the last pamphlet on the theory of committees and the most important one. It was distributed with a cyclostyled cover letter (item 3a). The setting for this piece is Dodgson's disagreement with the conditions of a plan to retain the distinguished Oxford professor of philology, Friedrich Max Müller. Dodgson's papers on "The Professorship of

4. In his discussion of the outcome of the election for the design of the new belfry in the collection of his papers (see McLean, McMillan, and Monroe, eds., *A Mathematical Approach to Proportional Representation,* 25–26), Black makes two contradictory statements. Using two tables, he first shows that of the four proposals submitted (two of which are by Mr. Bodley), the winner is Bodley's Gateway design. Then he claims the fresh design Bodley will create has the support of the majority in pairwise comparisons.

In the discussion of Dodgson's 1874 pamphlet, Black claims in error that Dodgson ultimately advocated the use of his modified method of marks if the pairwise comparison method failed to produce a winner (*Theory of Elections,* 190). Dodgson did not mention any other method in the final section of his pamphlet.

Comparative Philology" criticize the University's proposal to pay the future holder of the chair half the amount of Müller's salary (the other half to be allocated as the retiring professor's pension). The plan was presented to Convocation at Oxford on 15 February 1876 and Dodgson spoke against it. *The Times* reported the next day, "Mr. DODGSON wishes that the defenders of the decree would address themselves to the point attacked, which was not the merits of the Professor, but the mode of procedure."[5]

Dodgson explained in his diary, "I had not meant to speak, but the advocates of the Decree persisted so much in praising Max Müller, and ignoring the half-pay of the Deputy, that I rose to ask them to keep more to the point. The Decree was carried by 94 to 35."[6]

Dodgson proposed a method of ranking candidates in an election in the presence of "cyclical majorities," situations where no candidate can achieve a simple majority over each of the others. A cyclical majority, also known as the voting paradox, generally results from pairwise comparisons, the method he introduced in his 1874 pamphlet, and rarely from weighted ranking systems like the method of marks that he discussed in his 1873 pamphlet. Dodgson is now asking the natural question, when are sets of pairwise comparisons consistent with a unique ranking of the candidates? He proposes that when no candidate gains a simple majority over each of the others, then by a simple inversion scheme, the closest Condorcet winner may be selected. However, when cyclical majorities persist, Dodgson recommends no election should be the result.

Here is an example of his inversion method where fifteen electors are to choose one of four candidates A, B, C, and D. The first number in each pair is the number of votes for that candidate; the second number is the number of votes against. Reading downward, we see that A is preferred to B by 8 votes, to C by 6 votes, and to D by 4 votes.

	A	B	C	D
A		7/8	9/6	11/4
B	8/7		6/9	11/4
C	6/9	9/6		7/8
D	4/11	4/11	8/7	

None of the four candidates has a majority of the votes over each of the others: A fails to win 8 votes when paired with C and D; B fails to win 8 votes when paired with A and D; C fails to win 8 votes when paired with B; D fails to win 8 votes when paired with C. To choose the closest Condorcet winner, we count the number of changes (inversions) needed for each

5. *The Times,* 16 February 1876, 10.

6. Green, *Diaries,* 350.

candidate to achieve 8 votes in each pair. A needs six; B needs five; C needs two; D needs one. Clearly, D should be declared the winner.

In the context of voting as a game of skill, Dodgson goes on to discuss voter manipulation schemes that can defeat the majority will, stating,

> I think it desirable that all should know the rule by which this game may be won. It is simply this:– 'In any division taken on a pair of issues neither of which you desire, vote against the most popular. There *may* be some one issue which, if all voted according to their real opinion, would beat every other issue when paired against it separately: but, by following this rule, you *may* succeed in getting it beaten *once,* and so prevent its having a clear victory, by introducing a cyclical majority. And this will give, to the issue you desire, a chance it would not otherwise have had.'[7]

Dodgson has stated, I believe for the first time, a concept in game theory known as sophisticated voting, where a voter does not vote for his first choice issue in the hope of obtaining a cyclical majority in order to defeat a perceived favored issue that he does not want to become the winner.[8]

Years later, when writing about tennis tournaments, Dodgson draws explicit parallels between a game of skill, like chess, and the proper way to schedule a tennis tournament so that the best players win the top prizes. Similarly, he links the proper way to vote in an election with the goal of satisfying the will of the majority.

Dodgson wrote three entries in his diary concerning the 1876 pamphlet.

> *18 December 1875.* Election of Senior Students. After the usual dispute as to the way in which votes should be taken (a most complicated problem, which I still hope to work out some day) we elected Dalton, of C.C.C., and Payne Smith, of Trinity.[9]

> *9 February 1876.* G.B. meeting—The question of a system for taking votes at an election was again postponed—Afterwards I arranged with Bayne [Thomas Vere Bayne (1829–1908), Christ Church Governing Body Secretary] that we should try to get information as to the rules adopted in the other Colleges. Lawrence's opinion [C.W. Lawrence, Christ Church Chapter Clerk], given today, that, "the greatest number of votes does not necessarily mean an absolute majority," gives us the means of a final settlement of the

7. Dodgson, *A Method of Taking Votes on More Than Two Issues,* 1876, 18–19 (p. 57 in this volume).

8. The terminology of sophisticated voting and related ideas was first introduced by Robin Farquharson in *Theory of Voting* (Oxford: Blackwell, 1969).

9. Unpublished manuscript diaries.

matter, when there is a "cyclical majority" that will yield to no other remedy.[10]

23 February 1876. Spent the afternoon in writing out a new *Method for taking Votes* which I sent to the Press to be set up in slip.[11]

Dodgson would go on to apply several of these ideas and schemes, the modified method of marks from the 1873 pamphlet and pairwise comparisons from the 1876 pamphlet, in his pamphlets on proportional representation written in 1884 and 1885.

It appears that Dodgson was contemplating writing a book that would include the pamphlets. As he wrote in his diary on 3 July 1874, "I hope to . . . do a good spell of work in the Isle of Wight, including [a list of items] . . . and book on *Elections.*"[12]

Michael Dummett, the esteemed Oxford political philosopher, remarked in his book, "It is a matter for the deepest regret that Dodgson never completed the book that he planned to write on the subject. Such were his lucidity of exposition and his mastery of the topic that it seems possible that, had he ever published it, the political history of Britain would have been significantly different.[13]

VOTING METHODS

There is good reason to choose a voting system that meets theoretical standards as closely as possible. What has prevented the use of the Condorcet principle (among other accepted modern standards) in general elections is the technical difficulty of computing the results. It would require a complete schedule of the preferences of each voter. This can now be done using voting machines that are computer readable.

In two recent articles, the method in the 1876 pamphlet has been analyzed from the perspective of its computational complexity. Computational complexity deals with questions like this one: for a given problem, is there an effective procedure that a computer can carry out in a polynomial number of steps to solve this problem? If the answer to the question is yes, the problem is in *P*. If the answer is no, but a proposed solution can be checked in polynomial time, the problem is in *NP*.

In the first article, Bartholdi, Tovey, and Trick answer the question about the computational complexity of Dodgson's inversion method to determine the winner in an election.[14] Most natural election methods can

10. *Ibid.*
11. Green, *Diaries,* 350.
12. *Ibid.,* 330.
13. Michael Dummett, *Voting Procedures* (Oxford: Clarendon Press, 1984), 5n.
14. J. Bartholdi, C. A. Tovey, and M. A. Trick, "Voting Schemes for Which It Can

be computed easily using polynomial-time algorithms, but Dodgson's method is computationally prohibitive, i.e., *NP*-hard. But any fair voting scheme must, in the worst case, require excessive computation to determine the winner.

The authors of the second article, Hemaspaandra, Hemaspaandra and Rothe, extend the analysis of the inversion method and conclude that Dodgson's method is complete for parallel access to *NP;* i.e., all the queries necessary to solve the problems can be asked in parallel. They determine, among other things, that the computational complexity of checking if a candidate is the winner is greater than the complexity of *NP* problems, the next class in the complexity hierarchy after *P,* problems that run in polynomial time. Problems that are apparently not in *P,* but have efficient nondeterministic algorithms, are in the class *NP.* Complete problems are the hardest problems in their class. They write,

> it is somewhat curious finding 'parallel access to *NP*'-complete . . . problems that were introduced almost one hundred years before complexity theory itself existed [1972]. In addition, [the decision problem] **DodgsonWinner,** which we prove complete for this class, is extremely natural when compared with previously known complete problems for this class.

They go on to comment,

> Dodgson was before his time in more ways than one. His definition [the smallest number of exchanges of two adjacent candidates in the voters' preference orders] is closely related to an important concept that is now known in computer science as 'edit-distance'—the minimum number of operations (from some specified set of operations) required to transform one string into another.[15]

Although Dodgson could not have anticipated the computational capability of the modern computer, his approach in the 1876 pamphlet to finding the best voting method to select the best candidate necessarily involves an extraordinary amount of computation. That approach, based on principles of reason and fairness, and including the possibility of sophisticated voting, has an uncannily modern flavor.

Be Difficult to Tell Who Won the Election," *Social Choice and Welfare* 6 (1989), 161–62.

15. Edith Hemaspaandra, Lane A. Hemaspaandra, and Jörg Rothe, "Exact Analysis of Dodgson Elections: Lewis Carroll's 1876 Voting System Is Complete for Parallel Access," *Journal of the Association for Computing Machinery* 44 (1997), 808, 810–11.

1. A Discussion of the Various Methods of Procedure in Conducting Elections

[1873: LCH 96: Princeton]

This is the first of three pamphlets on election procedures. This copy contains corrections and notes in Dodgson's hand. After accidentally omitting the Method of Nomination, Dodgson had it printed as a separate sheet; it follows the text of the original pamphlet as item 1a. The complete pamphlet is reprinted in Duncan Black, *Theory of Committees and Elections,* 214–22, and Iain McLean and Arnold B. Urken, eds., *Classics of Social Choice,* 279–86.

❦

The following paper has been written and printed in great haste, as it was only on the night of Friday the 12th that it occurred to me to investigate the subject, which proved to be much more complicated than I had expected. Still I hope that I have given sufficient thought to it to escape the commission of any serious mistake.

I commence by considering certain known Methods of Procedure, in the case where *some* candidate *must* be elected, proving that each Method is liable, under certain circumstances, to fail in giving the proper result.

I then consider the question of 'Election or no Election?' proving that the two ordinary Methods of deciding it are unsound.

And I conclude by describing a Method of Procedure (whether new or not I cannot say) which seems to me not liable to the same objections as have been proved to exist in other cases.

C. L. D.

Ch. Ch., Dec. 18, 1873.

Oxford: E. B. Gardner, E. Pickard Hall, and J. H. Stacy, 1873.

CONTENTS.

CHAPTER I.

On the failure of certain Methods of Procedure, in the case where an Election is necessary.

CHAPTER II.

On the failure of certain Methods of Procedure, in the case where it is allowable *to have 'no Election.'*

CHAPTER III.

On a proposed Method of Procedure.

CHAPTER IV.

Summary of Rules.

CHAPTER I.

On the failure of certain Methods of Procedure, in the case where an Election is necessary.

§ 1. *The Method of a Simple Majority.*

In this Method, each elector names the *one* candidate he prefers, and he who gets the greatest number of votes is taken as the winner. The extraordinary injustice of this Method may easily be demonstrated. Let us suppose that there are eleven electors, and four candidates, *a, b, c, d;* and that each elector has arranged in a column the names of the candidates, in the order of his preference; and that the eleven columns stand thus:—

CASE (α).

a	*a*	*a*	*b*	*b*	*b*	*b*	*c*	*c*	*c*	*d*
c	*c*	*c*	*a*	*a*	*a*	*a*	*a*	*a*	*a*	*a*
d	*d*	*d*	*c*	*c*	*c*	*c*	*d*	*d*	*d*	*c*
b	*b*	*b*	*d*	*d*	*d*	*d*	*b*	*b*	*b*	*b*

Here *a* is considered best by *three* of the electors, and second by all the rest. It seems clear that he ought to be elected; and yet, by the above method, *b* would be the winner—a candidate who is considered *worst* by *seven* of the electors!

§ 2. *The Method of an Absolute Majority.*

In this Method, each elector names the *one* candidate he prefers; and if there be an absolute majority for any one candidate, he is taken as the winner.

CASE (β).

b	*b*	*b*	*b*	*b*	*b*	*a*	*a*	*a*	*a*	*a*
a	*a*	*a*	*a*	*a*	*a*	*c*	*c*	*c*	*d*	*d*
c	*c*	*c*	*d*	*d*	*d*	*d*	*d*	*d*	*c*	*c*
d	*d*	*d*	*c*	*c*	*c*	*b*	*b*	*b*	*b*	*b*

Here *a* is considered best by nearly half the electors (one more vote would give him an absolute majority), and never put lower than second by any; while *b* is put last by *five* of the electors, and *c* and *d* by three each. There seems to be no doubt that *a* ought to be elected; and yet, by the above Method, *b* would win.

§ 3. *The Method of Elimination, where the names are voted on by two at a time.*

In this Method, two names are chosen at random and proposed for voting; the loser is struck out from further competition, and the winner taken along with some other candidate, and so on, till there is only one candidate left.

Case (γ).

a	*a*	*a*	*a*	*a*	*b*	*b*	*c*	*d*	*d*	*d*
c	*c*	*c*	*c*	*d*	*a*	*a*	*b*	*b*	*b*	*b*
b	*d*	*d*	*d*	*c*	*c*	*c*	*a*	*a*	*a*	*a*
d	*b*	*b*	*b*	*b*	*d*	*d*	*d*	*c*	*c*	*c*

Here it seems clear that *a* ought to be the winner, as he is considered best by nearly half the electors, and never put lower than third; while *b* and *d* are each put last by *four* electors, and *c* by *three.* Nevertheless, by the above Method, if *(a, b)* were put up first for voting, *a* would be rejected, and ultimately *c* would be elected. Again, if *(a, c)* were put up first, *c* would be rejected, and if *(a, b)* were put up next, *d* would be elected—but if *(a, d), b* would be elected.

Such preposterous results, making the Election turn on the mere accident of *which* couple is put up first, seem to me to prove *this* Method to be entirely untrustworthy.

§ 4. *The Method of Elimination, where the names are voted on all at once.*

In this Method, each elector names the *one* candidate he prefers: the one who gets fewest votes is excluded from further competition, and the process is repeated.

CASE (δ).

b	*b*	*b*	*c*	*c*	*c*	*d*	*d*	*d*	*a*	*a*
a	*a*	*a*	*a*	*a*	*a*	*a*	*a*	*a*	*b*	*c*
d	*c*	*d*	*b*	*b*	*b*	*c*	*c*	*b*	*d*	*d*
c	*d*	*c*	*d*	*d*	*d*	*b*	*b*	*c*	*c*	*b*

Here, while *b* is put last by *three* of the electors, and *c* and *d* by *four* each, *a* is not put lower than second by any. There seems to be no doubt that *a*'s election would be the most generally acceptable: and yet, by the above rule, he would be excluded at once, and ultimately *c* would be elected.

§ 5. *The Method of Marks.*

In this Method, a certain number of marks is fixed, which each candidate shall have at his disposal; he may assign them all to one candidate, or divide them among several candidates, in proportion to their eligibility; and the candidate who gets the greatest total of marks is the winner.

This Method would, I think, be absolutely perfect, if only each elector wished to do all in his power to secure the election of *that candidate who should be the most generally acceptable,* even if that candidate should *not* be the one of his own choice: in this case he would be careful to make the marks exactly represent his estimate of the relative eligibility of *all* the candidates, even of those he *least* desired to see elected; and the desired result would be served.

But we are not sufficiently unselfish and public-spirited to give any hope of this result being attained. Each elector would feel that it was *possible* for each other elector to assign the entire number of marks to his favorite candidate, giving to all the other candidates zero: and he would conclude that, in order to give his *own* favorite candidate any chance of success, he must do the same for him.

This Method is therefore liable, in practice, to coincide with 'the Method of a Simple Majority,' which has been already discussed, and, as I think, provided to be unsound.

CHAPTER II.

On the failure of certain Methods of Procedure, in the case where it is allowable *to have 'no Election.'*

§ 1. *The Method of* commencing *with a vote on the question 'Election or no Election?'*

This Method has the strong recommendation that if 'no Election' be carried, it saves all further trouble, and it *might* be a just method to adopt, provided the electors were of two kinds only—one, which prefers 'no Election' to *any* candidate, even the best; the other, which prefers *any* candidate, even the worst, to 'no Election.' But it would seldom happen that *all* the electors could be so classed: and any elector who preferred certain candidates to 'no Election,' but preferred 'no Election' to certain other candidates, would not be fairly treated by such a procedure. He might say 'It is premature to ask me to vote on this question. If I knew that *a* or *b* would be elected, I would vote to *have* an election; but if neither *a* nor *b* can get in, I vote for having none.'

Let us, however, test this Method by a case—representing 'no Election' by the symbol 'o.'

Case (ε).

a	*a*	*b*	*b*	*c*	*c*	o	o	o	o	o
o	o	o	o	o	o	*a*	*a*	*b*	*b*	*c*
c	*c*	*a*	*a*	*b*	*b*	*d*	*d*	*c*	*c*	*b*
d	*d*	*d*	*d*	*d*	*d*	*b*	*c*	*a*	*a*	*a*
b	*b*	*c*	*c*	*a*	*a*	*c*	*b*	*d*	*d*	*d*

Here there seems no doubt that 'no election' would be the most satisfactory result: and yet, by the above Method, an Election would take place, and in all probability *b* would be elected—a candidate regarding whom *nine* of the electors would say 'I would rather have had no Election.'

§ 2. *The Method of* concluding *with a vote on the question 'Shall* x *(the successful candidate) be elected, or shall there be no Election?'*

Here again a voter who preferred certain candidates to 'no Election,' but preferred 'no Election' to certain other candidates, would not be fairly treated. He might say 'If you had taken *a* or *b,* I would have been content, but as you have taken *c,* I vote for no Election,' and his vote might decide the point: while the other electors might say 'If we had only known how it would end, we would willingly have taken *a* instead of *c.*'

But let us test this Method also by a case.

Case (ζ).

b	*b*	*b*	*b*	*b*	o	*a*	*a*	*a*	*a*	*a*
a	*a*	*a*	*a*	*a*	*b*	o	o	o	o	o
c	*c*	*c*	*c*	*c*	*a*	*b*	*b*	*b*	*b*	*b*
d	*d*	*d*	*d*	*d*	*c*	*c*	*c*	*c*	*c*	*c*
o	o	o	o	o	*d*	*d*	*d*	*d*	*d*	*d*

Here there seems to be no doubt that the election of *a* would be much more satisfactory than having no Election: and yet, by the above Method, *b* would first be selected from all the candidates, and ultimately rejected on the question of '*b* or no Election?' while *ten* of the electors would say 'We would rather have taken *a* than have no Election at all.'

The conclusion I come to is that, where 'no Election' is allowable, the phrase should be treated exactly as if it were the name of a candidate.

CHAPTER III.

On a proposed Method of Procedure.

The Method now to be proposed is, *in principle,* a modification of No. 5, viz. 'The Method of Marks,' since it assigns to each candidate a mark for every vote given to him, when taken in competition with any other candidate.

Suppose that, in the opinion of a certain elector, the candidates stand in the order *a, b, c, d:* then his votes may be represented by giving *a* the number 3, *b* 2, *c* 1, and *d* 0.

Hence all that is necessary is that each elector should make out a list of the candidates, arranging them in order of merit.

If 'no Election' is allowable, this phrase should be placed somewhere in the list.

If the elector cannot arrange all in succession, but places two or more in a bracket, a question arises as to how the bracketed names should be marked. The tendency of many electors being, as explained in Chap. I. § 5, to give to the favorite candidate the maximum mark, and bracket all the rest, in order to reduce their chances as much as possible, it is proposed, in order to counteract this tendency, to give to each bracketed candidate the same mark that the *highest* would have if the bracket were removed. This plan will furnish a strong inducement to avoid brackets as far as possible.

In order to illustrate this process, let us apply it to the various 'Cases' already considered.

	α	β	γ	δ	ε	ζ
a	25	27	23	24	21	37
b	12	18	15	15	21	33
c	20	11	14	14	20	16
d	9	10	14	13	10	5
o					38	19

It will be seen that in each case the candidate, whose election is obviously most to be desired, obtains the greatest number of marks.

CHAPTER IV.

Summary of Rules.

1. Let each elector make out a list of the candidates, (treating 'no Election' as if it were the name of a candidate), arranging

them as far as possible in the order of merit, and bracketing those whom he regards as equal.

2. Let the names on each list be marked with the numbers 0, 1, 2, &c., beginning at the last.

3. Whenever two or more names are bracketed, each must have the mark which would belong to the highest, if there were no bracket.

4. Add up the numbers assigned to each candidate.

The *first* Rule is all with which the electors need trouble themselves. Rules 2, 3, 4 can all be carried out by one person, as it is merely a matter of counting.

1a. Method of Nomination

[1873: LCH 96a: Princeton]

§ 6. *The Method of Nomination.*

In this Method, some one candidate is proposed, seconded, and the votes taken for and against. This Method is fair for those electors *only* who prefer that candidate to *any* other, or else *any* other to him. But any other elector might say 'I do not know whether to vote for or against *a* till I know *who* would come in if he failed. If I were sure *b* would come in, I would vote against *a:* otherwise, I vote *for a.*'

If this Method leads to a *majority* of votes being obtained for the proposed candidate, it is identical with 'the Method of an absolute Majority,' which was discussed in § 2. If a *minority* only is obtained, it may be thus represented:—

b	*b*	*c*	*c*	*d*	*d*	*a*	*a*	*a*	*a*	*a*
a	*a*	*a*	*a*	*a*	*a*	*b*	*b*	*c*	*c*	*d*
c	*c*	*b*	*b*	*b*	*b*	*c*	*c*	*b*	*b*	*b*
d	*d*	*d*	*d*	*c*	*c*	*d*	*d*	*d*	*d*	*c*

Here there seems no doubt that *a* ought to be elected; and yet, by the above Method, he would be rejected at once, and, *whichever* candidate came in, *nine* of the electors would say 'We would rather have had *a*.'

2. *Suggestions As to the Best Method of Taking Votes, Where More Than Two Issues Are to Be Voted On*

[1874: LCH 100, LCAT 372: Princeton]

This short pamphlet, the second of three on election procedures, is reprinted in Black, *Theory of Committees and Elections,* 222–24, and McLean and Urken, eds., *Classics of Social Choice,* 287–88.

❦

In the immediate prospect of a meeting of the Governing Body, where matters may be debated of very great importance, on which various and conflicting opinions are known to be held, I venture to offer a few suggestions as to the mode of taking votes. On this subject I printed a paper some little time ago, but have since seen reason to modify some of the views therein expressed. Especially, I do not now advocate the method, there proposed, as a good one to *begin* with. When other means have failed, it may prove useful, but that is not likely to happen often, and, when the difficulty does arise, the question what should next be done may fairly be debated on its own merits.

C. L. D.

Ch. Ch., June 13, 1874.

§ 1. *Votes to be taken in writing.*

The method here suggested is to divide a sheet of paper into as many columns as there are issues to be voted on, and place the name of each at the head of a column. The paper is then

Oxford, E. Pickard Hall and J. H. Stacy, 1874.

passed round, each voter placing his name in the column he prefers.

The only objection to this method, that I can think of, is that it takes rather more time than voting *vivâ voce;* and even *this* is not always the case, as it is by no means unusual for a doubt to arise as to the result of a *vivâ voce* vote, which makes it necessary to take the votes over again.

Its advantages are, that it enables the division-list to be put on record, which I think should always be done when an important matter is voted on, except in elections of Students, in which case there are obvious objections to the names of the voters being recorded.

At the end of a meeting, it should be settled which of the division-lists, if any, are to be entered on the minutes; and the other lists might then be destroyed.

§ 2. *A list to be made of all the issues to be voted on.*

This should be done before *any* vote is taken at all. The list should contain every issue which is proposed, and seconded, for entry on it. The *general negative* issue ('that there be no election,' or, 'that nothing be done') should, I think, find a place on this list (provided of course that it be proposed and seconded), and should not be voted on separately—a course sometimes adopted, but which I think I have shown, in a former paper on this subject, to be unsound.

§ 3. *The first vote to be taken on all the issues collectively.*

This course is suggested in the hope that it may give an absolute majority (or such a majority as may be previously declared to be binding), so as to settle the question at once.

§ 4. *Failing a settlement by this method, the issues to be then voted on two at a time.*

This course is suggested in the hope that by it some one issue may be discovered, which is preferred by a majority to every other taken separately. For this purpose, any two may be put up to begin with, then the winning issue along with some other, and so on. But no issue can be considered as the absolute winner, unless it has been put up along with *every* other.

§ 5. *Failing a settlement by this method also, further proceedings may be then debated on.*

If no settlement has been arrived at by § 3 or § 4, it will at least prove that the matter is one on which the meeting is *very evenly divided in opinion.* Such a state of things is of course very difficult to deal with, but the difficulty, though possibly not diminished, will certainly not have been increased by adopting the process I have here suggested.

3. A Method of Taking Votes on More Than Two Issues

[1876: LCH 113, LCAT 381: Lindseth]

This pamphlet was circulated privately, twice it seems: once in March 1876, and once in 1877. The second time it was accompanied by a cyclostyled sheet dated 7 December 1877, (item 3a, below). It appears that Dodgson meant to expand the material in this pamphlet into a book on elections that, in his diary entry of 3 July 1874, he claimed he would write. No known responses to his requests for remarks, criticisms, and additions were received, nor did he ever write the intended book.

The authors of the LCH describe the contents of this pamphlet as an improved anonymous form of the 1874 pamphlet, but more elaborate and less practical. In contrast, Duncan Black had this to say:

> Just eight days after the meeting of Convocation with its excitement and mixed feelings [in connection with the controversy over the Chair in Comparative Philology], Dodgson's third pamphlet was written—the one which entitles him to a position in the theory of elections and committees only a little lower than that of Condorcet.[1]

This pamphlet is reprinted in Black, *Theory of Committees and Elections,* 224–34, and McLean and Urken, eds., *Classics of Social Choice,* 288–97.

[*As I hope to investigate this subject further, and to publish a more complete pamphlet on the subject, I shall feel greatly obliged if you will enter in this copy any remarks that occur to you, and return it to me any time before*]

Probably Clarendon Press, Oxford, 7 March 1876.

1. Black, *Theory of Committees and Elections,* 212.

A METHOD OF TAKING VOTES.

§ 1. *Proposed Rules for Conducting an Election.*

I.

Each elector shall write down the issue he desires ('no Election' being reckoned as an issue) and hand in the paper folded, with his name written outside: and the Chairman, or some one appointed by him, having before him a list of the electors, shall enter these issues against their names.

II.

If the Chairman find any issue having an absolute majority of votes, he shall communicate the list to the meeting. This issue shall then be formally moved, and, if none object, the Chairman shall declare it carried.

III.

If the Chairman shall find no issue having an absolute majority of votes, he shall communicate to the meeting the list of issues only, without stating who vote for each, and shall return the papers, that each elector may add the other issues, arranged in his order of preference. The Chairman shall enter these on his list, and then communicate the whole to the meeting.

IV.

If an issue be found which has a majority over every other taken separately, it shall be formally moved as in Rule II: but if none be found, the majorities being 'cyclical', opportunity shall be given for further debate. In ascertaining which of any pair of issues is preferred to the other, any elector whose paper contains one only of the two shall be reckoned as preferring that one, and any whose paper contains neither shall be considered as not voting.

V.

If the issues cannot be all arranged in one cycle, but form a cycle and a set of issues each of which is separately beaten by each of the cycle, it shall be formally moved that this cycle be retained and all other issues struck out, and, if none object, this shall be done.

VI.

If, a formal motion having been made that a certain issue be adopted, or that a certain cycle be retained and all other issues struck out, any one object, he may move as an amendment that a division be taken between the issue he desires and the issue so to be adopted, or any one of the cycle so to be retained. If every such amendment be lost on a division, the Chairman shall declare the original motion carried: but, if any such amendment be carried, by some voting contrary to their written papers, they shall be required to amend their papers, and the process shall begin again.

VII.

When the issues to be further debated consist of, or have been reduced to, a single cycle, the Chairman shall inform the meeting how many alterations of votes each issue requires to give it a majority over every other separately.

VIII.

If, when the majorities are found to be cyclical, any elector wish to alter his paper, he may do so: and if the cyclical majorities be thereby done away with, the voting shall proceed by former Rules: but if, when none will make any further alteration, the majorities continue cyclical, there shall be no election.

§ 2. *The Legal Conditions.*

In any election, when there are only *two* issues to vote on—for instance (there being only one candidate), 'shall *A* be elected or not?' or again (there being only two candidates, and it being understood that there is to be an election) 'shall *A* or *B* be elected?'—and when the Chairman is able to give a casting vote, it is clear that there *must* be a majority for one or other issue, and in this case open voting is the obvious course.

But wherever there are three or more issues to vote on, any one of the following three cases may exist in the minds of the electors:—

(α) *There may be one issue desired by an absolute majority of the electors.*

(β) *There may be one issue which, when paired against every other issue separately, is preferred by a majority of electors.*

(γ) *The majorities may be 'cyclical,'* e.g. *there may be a majority for* A *over* B, *for* B *over* C, *and for* C *over* A.

The words of the Ordinance are **"That Candidate for whom the greatest number of votes shall have been given shall be deemed elected."**

It seems to me that this may be complied with by either of two modes of election:—

In case (α) *If a candidate be declared elected who, when all are voted on at once, has an absolute majority of votes.*

In case (β) *If a candidate be declared elected who, when paired with every other separately, is preferred by the majority of those voting.*

But that is *not* complied with by the following mode:—

In case (γ) *If a candidate be declared elected, though it is known that there is another who, when paired with him, is preferred by the majority of those voting.*

Mode (α) needs no discussion. Failing this, it seems clear that mode (β) would be a satisfactory result, as any one who preferred some other candidate might be allowed to take a division between the two.

If modes (α) and (β) both fail, it shows that the majorities on the separate pairs are 'cyclical,' and if, after all possible discussion, this continues to be so, any election that may be arrived at *must* introduce mode (γ). My own opinion is that, under these circumstances, there ought to be 'no Election': two other courses might be suggested, which I will now consider.

§ 3. *Courses that have been suggested for the case of 'Cyclical Majorities.'*

(1) *That all candidates should be voted on at once, and the one who has the greatest number of votes should be elected.*

This might be thought to fulfil the *letter* of the law, if after the words 'shall have been given' we supply the words 'in the final voting.'

Let us suppose that there are 11 electors, and 4 candidates, *a, b, c, d;* and that each elector has arranged in a column the names of the candidates in the order of his preference; and that the 11 columns stand thus:—

FIG. 1.

a	*a*	*a*	*a*	*b*	*b*	*b*	*c*	*c*	*c*	*d*
d	*d*	*b*	*b*	*c*	*c*	*d*	*b*	*b*	*b*	*c**
c	*c*	*d*	*d*	*a*	*a*	*c*	*d*	*d*	*d*	*b**
b	*b*	*c*	*c*	*d*	*d*	*a*	*a*	*a*	*a*	*a*

Here the majorities are cyclical, in the order *a d c b a,* each beating the one next following.

Moreover, if we make a table of majorities in the separate pairs, in which the numerator of each fraction represents the number voting for the issue which stands at the top of that column and the denominator the number voting for the issue which stands at the end of that row, and in which every division, where the issue at the top of the column is beaten, is distinguished by placing the fraction in a parenthesis, we have

FIG. 2.

	a	*b*	*c*	*d*
a		$\frac{7}{4}$	$\frac{7}{4}$	$(\frac{5}{6})$
b	$(\frac{4}{7})$		$\frac{6}{5}$	$(\frac{3}{8})$
c	$(\frac{4}{7})$	$(\frac{5}{6})$		$\frac{6}{5}$
d	$\frac{6}{5}$	$\frac{8}{3}$	$(\frac{5}{6})$	

Here *a* and *d* each need 4 changes of votes to win, but *b* and *c* each need one only: for instance, the interchange of the two issues which are marked * would make *b* win. It seems clear that *a* has much less claim to be elected than either *b* or *c* (observe that he is put *last* by nearly half the electors, and only needs *one* interchange of votes to cause him to be beaten by *every* other candidate separately), and yet by the above course he would win.

Again, let there be 13 electors and 4 candidates.

FIG. 3.

a	*a*	*a*	*a*	*b*	*b*	*b*	*c*	*c*	*c*	*d*	*d*	*d*
b	*b*	*b*	*b*	*d*	*d*	*d*	*d*	*a*	*a*	*b*	*b*	*b*
c	*c*	*c*	*c*	*c*	*c*	*c*	*a**	*b*	*b*	*c*	*c*	*c*
d	*d*	*d*	*d*	*a*	*a*	*a*	*b**	*d*	*d*	*a*	*a*	*a*

Here the majorities are cyclical, in the order *a b c d a;* the table of majorities being:—

FIG. 4.

	a	*b*	*c*	*d*
a		$(\frac{6}{7})$	$\frac{9}{4}$	$\frac{7}{6}$
b	$\frac{7}{6}$		$(\frac{3}{10})$	$(\frac{4}{9})$
c	$(\frac{4}{9})$	$\frac{10}{3}$		$(\frac{6}{7})$
d	$(\frac{6}{7})$	$\frac{9}{4}$	$\frac{7}{6}$	

Here *a, c, d* each need 4 changes of votes to win, while *b* needs only one, for instance, the interchange of the two issues marked *. Yet by the above course *a* would win—a candidate whom this single interchange would cause to be beaten by *every* other candidate separately.

(2) *That all candidates should be voted on at once, and the one who has the smallest number of votes should be struck out, and the process repeated till only two are left.*

FIG. 5.

a	*a*	*a*	*a*	*b*	*b*	*b*	*b*	*c*	*c*	*c*
b	*b*	*c*	*c*	*c*	*c*	*c*	*c*	*b*	*a*	*a*
c	*c*	*b*	*b*	*a*	*a*	*a*	*a*	*a*	*b*	*b*

Here the majorities are cyclical, in the order *a b c a*. Moreover, *a* beats *b* (6 to 5), *b* beats *c* (6 to 5), but *c* beats *a* (7 to 4).

If any one is to be elected, it would seem that *c* has the strongest claim; but by the above method *a* would win—a candidate who is put last by nearly half the electors.

Again, let there be 15 electors and 4 candidates:—

FIG. 6.

a	*a*	*a*	*a*	*b*	*b*	*b*	*b*	*c*	*c*	*c*	*c*	*d*	*d*	*d*
d	*d*	*d*	*d*	*c*	*c*	*c*	*c**	*d*	*d*	*d*	*d*	*a*	*a*	*b*
b	*b*	*b*	*b*	*d*	*d*	*d*	*d**	*a*	*a*	*b*	*b*	*c*	*c*	*c*
c	*c*	*c*	*c*	*a*	*a*	*a*	*a*	*b*	*b*	*a*	*a*	*b*	*b*	*a*

Here there is a cyclical majority, in the order *a b c d a;* therefore by above Rule *d* is excluded: we now have—

FIG. 7.

a	*a*	*a*	*a*	*b*	*b*	*b*	*b*	*c*	*c*	*c*	*c*	*a*	*a*	*b*
b	*b*	*b*	*b*	*c*	*c*	*c*	*c*	*a*	*a*	*b*	*b*	*c*	*c*	*c*
c	*c*	*c*	*c*	*a*	*a*	*a*	*a*	*b*	*b*	*a*	*a*	*b*	*b*	*a*

Here there is again a cyclical majority, in the order *a b c a;* therefore *c* is excluded.

The candidates are now reduced to *a* and *b,* and *a* wins by a majority of 8 to 7.

But if we tabulate the majorities thus—

FIG. 8.

	a	*b*	*c*	*d*
a		$(\frac{7}{8})$	$\frac{9}{6}$	$\frac{11}{4}$
b	$\frac{8}{7}$		$(\frac{6}{9})$	$\frac{11}{4}$
c	$(\frac{6}{9})$	$\frac{9}{6}$		$(\frac{7}{8})$
d	$(\frac{4}{11})$	$(\frac{4}{11})$	$\frac{8}{7}$	

we see that *a* needs 6 changes of votes to win, *b* 5, *c* 2, and *d* only 1. It seems clear that *d* ought to win; yet he is the very first to be excluded by the above course.

Lastly, let us take a case in which these two courses bring in different candidates, neither of them being the one that ought to win.

Let there be 23 electors and 4 candidates.

Fig. 9.

a	*a*	*a*	*a*	*a*	*a*	*a*	*b*	*b*	*b*	*b*	*b*	*b*	*c*	*c*	*c*	*c*	*c*	*c*	*d*	*d*	*d*	*d*
b	*b*	*c*	*c*	*c*	*c*	*d*	*d*	*d*	*d*	*d*	*d*	*d*	*b*	*b*	*b*	*b*	*b*	*b*	*b*	*b*	*c*	*c**
d	*d*	*b*	*b*	*b*	*b*	*b*	*a*	*a*	*a*	*a*	*a*	*a*	*a*	*a*	*a*	*a*	*a*	*d*	*a*	*a*	*b*	*b**
c	*c*	*d*	*d*	*d*	*d*	*c*	*c*	*c*	*c*	*c*	*c*	*c*	*d*	*d*	*d*	*d*	*d*	*a*	*c*	*c*	*a*	*a*

Here the majorities are cyclical in the order *a d c b a*. The table of majorities is:—

Fig. 10.

	a	*b*	*c*	*d*
a		$\frac{16}{7}$	$\left(\frac{8}{15}\right)$	$\left(\frac{11}{12}\right)$
b	$\left(\frac{7}{16}\right)$		$\frac{12}{11}$	$\left(\frac{5}{18}\right)$
c	$\frac{15}{8}$	$\left(\frac{11}{12}\right)$		$\frac{13}{10}$
d	$\frac{12}{11}$	$\frac{18}{5}$	$\left(\frac{10}{13}\right)$	

Now, by course (1) *a* wins.

By course (2) *d* is excluded; but we still have a cyclical majority *a c b a;* we then exclude *a,* and *c* wins.

But, if we reckon how many changes of votes each needs to win, we find that *a* needs 5, *c* needs 6, and *d* needs 8; whereas *b* needs only 1—a single interchange, such as the two marked *, would give him a clear victory.

Note also that this single interchange would cause *c* (who is brought in winner by course (2)) to be beaten by *every* other candidate separately.

The instances I have taken seem to show that neither of these courses can be relied on to give a satisfactory result. But there is a stronger, and as I think a fatal, objection to both; namely, that any elector, who had not consented to this course being adopted, would have a very strong ground of appeal against the election if he were able to say "*A* was declared elected, and yet he had not 'the greatest number of votes' given for him, since he was beaten when paired against *B*."

The conclusion I come to is that, in the case of persistent cyclical majorities, there ought to be 'no Election.'

I am quite prepared to be told, with regard to the cases I have here proposed, as I have already been told with regard to others, 'Oh, *that* is an extreme case: it could never really happen!' Now I have observed that this answer is always given instantly, with perfect confidence, and without any examination of the details of the proposed case. It must therefore rest on some general principle: the mental process being probably something like this—'I have formed a theory. This case contradicts my theory. *Therefore* this is an extreme case, and would never occur in practice.'

§ 4. *Reasons for beginning with a vote on all issues at once.*

One reason for this is that it *may* show an absolute majority for some one issue, and so save all further trouble. But another, and a stronger, reason is that, when a division is taken first of all between a certain pair of issues, there will very often be some of the electors who will not know which way to vote. I am not speaking of electors who are willing to vote contrary to their real opinion, but of electors generally.

An example or two will make this clear.

Suppose there are two vacancies, but that it is not necessary to fill both: and that a division is taken first of all on the question 'Shall both vacancies be filled, or only one?' An elector might reasonably say 'I wish to elect *A* alone. If I were sure he would come in, I would vote for electing *one* only: but if *B* is preferred, then, rather than lose *A*, I would vote for electing *two*.' And another might say '*I* wish to elect *A* and *B*, but I strongly object to *C*. If I were sure *A* and *B* would come in, I would vote for electing *two*: but if that would result in *A* and *C* coming in, then I vote for *one* only.' How much simpler to allow the one to write down '*A* alone,' and the other '*A* and *B*.'

Again, suppose it settled that two are to be elected, and a division to be taken between *B* and *D*. An elector might reasonably say 'I wish to elect *A* at any rate: the other to be *B* or *C*, I do not care which: but I object to *D*. I would vote for *B*, if I were sure that *A* would be elected as the other. But if I knew that *C* would beat *A* on a division, I should wish to get *C* and *A* elected, and this *might* be effected by voting for *D*. I happen to know that *C* and *A* can each beat *D*, so that he has no real chance. My voting for him would not mean that I wish to bring him *in*, but that I wish to keep *B* *out*, and so to get *C* and *A* elected, instead of *C* and *B*.' How much simpler to allow him to write '*A*, and then *B* or *C*.'

§ 5. *Reasons for allowing 'no Election' to be reckoned among the other issues.*

Evidently an elector who desires 'no Election' ought to have *some* opportunity of voting on the question. And if it be not reckoned as an issue, it must be voted on, as a separate question, at the beginning or the end of the proceedings.

(1) *The method of* beginning *with a vote on the question 'Election or no Election?'*

This Method has the strong recommendation that if 'no Election' be carried, it saves all further trouble, and it *might* be a just method to adopt, provided the electors were of two kinds only—one, which prefers 'no Election' to *any* candidate, even the best; the other, which prefers *any* candidate, even the worst, to 'no Election.' But it would seldom happen that *all* the electors could be so classed: and any elector who preferred certain candidates to 'no Election,' but preferred 'no Election' to certain other candidates, would not be fairly treated by such a procedure. He might say 'It is premature to ask me to vote on this question. If I knew that *A* or *B* would be elected, I would vote to *have* an election; but if neither *A* nor *B* can get in, I vote for having none.'

(2) *The method of* ending *with a vote on the question 'Shall* X *be elected, or shall there be no Election?'*

Here again a voter who preferred certain candidates to 'no Election,' but preferred 'no Election' to certain other candidates, would not be fairly treated. He might say 'If you had taken *A* or *B,* I would have been content, but as you have taken *C,* I vote for no Election,' and his vote might decide the point: while the other electors might say 'If we had only known how it would end, we would willingly have taken *A* instead of *C.*'

The conclusion I come to is that, where 'no Election' is allowable, the phrase should be treated exactly as if it were the name of a candidate.

§ 5. [*sic*] *Reasons for having a preliminary voting on paper and not open voting.*

Suppose *A* to be the candidate whom I wish to elect, and that a division is taken between *B* and *C;* am I bound in honour to vote for the one whom I should *really* prefer, if *A* were not in the field, or may I vote in whatever way I think most favourable to *A*'s chances? Some say 'the former,' some 'the latter.' I proceed to show that, whenever case α fails to occur, and there are among the electors a certain number who hold the latter course to be allowable, the result *must* be a case of cyclical majorities.

Let there be 3 candidates, *A, B, C,* each preferred by about one-third of the electors; and suppose that, when a division is taken between *A* and *B, A* wins. A division is now taken between *A* and *C,* which of course depends on the votes of the *B*-party; perhaps a majority of them *really* prefer *A,* and if they voted accordingly *A* would win under case β; it might need only two or three to vote contrary to their real opinion to turn the division in favour of *C.* We have now got '*A* beats *B, C* beats *A,*' and of course a division must be taken between *B* and *C;* this depends on the votes of the *A*-party, and, as before, it may only need two or three to vote contrary to their real opinion to prevent *C* winning the election. Thus we get '*A* beats *B, C* beats *A, B* beats *C.*'

This principle of voting makes an election more of a game of skill than a real test of the wishes of the electors, and as my own opinion is that it is better for elections to be decided according to the wish of the majority than of those who happen to have most skill in the game, I think it desirable that all should know the rule by which this game may be won. It is simply this:—'In any division taken on a pair of issues neither of which you desire, vote against the most popular. There *may* be some one issue which, if all voted according to their real opinion, would beat every other issue when paired against it separately: but, by following this rule, you *may* succeed in getting it beaten *once,* and so prevent its having a clear victory, by introducing a cyclical majority. And this will give, to the issue you desire, a chance it would not otherwise have had.'

Now, it is impossible to prevent such votes being given: and even if a preliminary voting on paper should seem to lead to case α or β, it is impossible, when it comes to the final formal vote, to prevent votes being given contradictory to previous votes.

The advantages of having the preliminary voting taken on paper and not openly are, first, that each elector, not knowing exactly how the others are voting, has less inducement to vote contrary to his real opinion, so that a more trustworthy estimate is arrived at of the real opinion of the body of electors, and cyclical majorities are less likely to occur, than with open voting; and secondly, that if cyclical majorities do *not* occur in this process, they cannot occur in the formal voting except by some one or more of the electors giving votes inconsistent with their written opinions, and I think it desirable that in such a case the body of electors should know who they are that have so voted—a result which this method would secure.

I do not suppose that any one would be so unwilling to have it known that he has so voted that this publicity would *prevent* an artificial cyclical majority—for I am sure that those who do so believe it to be an honourable course to take, and so have no motive for desiring concealment—but I think it would increase the sense of the responsibility incurred by those who thus exercise their right of voting, and so make its occurrence less likely.

These written lists will also be, in many cases, a great saving of time. An example will best show this. Suppose there are 2 vacancies to be filled, and 3 candidates, all recommended on various grounds by the examiners, and that the electors are divided among the following 6 issues, '*A B*', '*B A*', '*A C*', '*C A*', '*B C*', '*A* alone.' These, taken two and two, give 15 pairs: that is, it might require 15 divisions to be taken to get the information which the written lists furnish at once.

3a. Circular accompanying A Method of Taking Votes on More Than Two Issues

[1877: LCH 120c: Wakeling]

This sheet, written with an electric pen, accompanied the 1876 pamphlet (item 3, above) that Dodgson circulated for comments. The authors of the LCH omit the connection between this sheet and the 1876 pamphlet. The circular, with the asterisked note omitted, is reprinted in Black, *Theory of Committees and Elections,* 234.

Ch. Ch. Dec. 7/77

Would you kindly consider this pamphlet, & let me have it again, with any criticisms that it may suggest,* some time next term?

Also an account of any rules, written or unwritten, adopted in your College to settle difficulties arising in elections, will be very acceptable.

A really scientific method for arriving at the result which is, on the whole, most satisfactory to a body of electors, seems to be still a *desideratum.*

Truly yours,

C. L. DODGSON

*to yourself or others

Rationality in Sports

7, Lushington Road
Eastbourne
July 15/87

Dear Sir,

I thank you for your pamphlet on "Lawn Tennis", & having found a few copies of my own, I enclose one for your acceptance. One or two letters appeared in the "S. James's", when my pamphlet came out, by the well-known sporting authority "Cavendish", by which I learned that the existing method, though known to substitute "chance" for "skill" to a great extent, is deliberately preferred by most players. That fact seems to me to make the matter unworthy of any further investigation.

Faithfully yours
C. L. Dodgson.

Would you kindly let Mr. Robert Brodie have the other copy, for the "Miss Emma Brodie" who wrote to me, enquiring about it.

An 1887 letter from Dodgson to an unknown recipient, in which he comments on the players' preference for "chance" over "skill" to schedule lawn-tennis tournaments.

Introduction

Similar principles govern elections and sports tournaments, and Dodgson was intrigued by both. In the pair-comparison method, the basic unit is the comparison of the issues by one voter, who will choose one of them as his preference. Every voter will perform every possible pair comparison. This method corresponds to a round-robin tournament in sports, the role of the players in the tournament being that of the issues in the pair-comparison method.

Mathematically speaking, a tournament is a model of the pair-comparison method that Dodgson had introduced in *Suggestions As to the Best Methods of Taking Votes* (1874; item 2) and developed fully in *A Method of Taking Votes on More than One Issue* (1876; item 3), where he presented a round-robin tournament to rank all the proposals in a list.[1] But such a tournament, in which every player plays every other player exactly once, would be impractical for tennis matches because it would require 496 games for 32 players. Dodgson's solution requires 90 games of which 29 are "virtual"; their outcomes are determined without the matches actually being played.

Dodgson published the pamphlet, *Lawn Tennis Tournaments: The True Method of Assigning Prizes with a Proof of the Fallacy of the Present Method* (item 4) in August 1883, soon after he had participated in an exchange of letters on the topic in the *St. James's Gazette.* Dodgson wrote in his diary on 10 August 1883 that he received twenty copies of his pamphlet.

Lawn tennis, a variant of the game of tennis, was introduced in England in 1874. By 1876 the All-England Lawn Tennis and Croquet Club was established at Wimbledon, and the first tournament, men's singles, took place the following year. Women's singles and men's doubles were introduced in 1884.

Dodgson's interest in the game probably was sparked by a match he saw on 14 May 1880. He noted in his diary on that day, "In the afternoon we went to the Lawn Tennis ground in Norham Gardens, where their

1. Duncan Black was the first person to see that Dodgson used the logic of his theory of committees in his tennis tournament scheduling. See Black, *The Theory of Committees and Elections,* 213 and "Lewis Carroll and the Cambridge Mathematical School of P.R.: Arthur Cohen and Edith Denman," *Public Choice* 8 (1970), 4.

Frederick Greenwood (1830–1909), the editor of the Pall Mall Gazette *from 1865 to 1880 and the* St. James's Gazette *from 1880 to 1888, by Carlo Pellegrini, 1880.*

[Mr. & Mrs. Woodhouse's; George Girdlestone Woodhouse (1831–1897) was a close friend of Dodgson] cousin was playing in a match."[2]

In the first letter on lawn tennis tournaments, which appeared in the *St. James's Gazette* on 12 August 1882 (item 5), Dodgson laid out the injustices of the method currently used to award prizes and briefly described the elements of the method he developed in the pamphlet he published a year later. He referred to this letter in a diary entry of 11 July 1882: "Wrote off at last my letter to the *St. James's* on 'Lawn Tennis Tournaments.'"[3]

He also sent a copy to the publication, *Field.* As a diary entry of 17 September 1881 reveals, however, he had been working on the problem at least a year earlier: "Did the best experiment I have made in devising a new and better rule for Lawn Tennis (or any other) tournament."[4]

A year passed before the next letter appeared in the *St. James's Gazette,* on 1 August 1883 (item 6). It contained much of the content of the earlier letter; in addition, now Dodgson provided the details of his proposed method. He noted that his tournament would require less time than the knockout tournament currently in use but would have more contests being played at the same time, which would add to the spectators' enjoyment.

We can infer from the diary entries below of 13, 20, 23, and 30 July 1883 that Dodgson had completed the writing of the pamphlet when he wrote this letter because the two differ materially only in the length of the contests described: sixteen players in the letter, 32 in the pamphlet.

> *13 July:* Am hard at work . . . on the Lawn Tennis Tournament Question.[5]
>
> *20 July:* I only worked on that one day at the "Lawn Tennis" question. Tomorrow I hope to be able to attack it again.[6]
>
> *23 July:* I began (and finished in about six hours) my letter on 'Lawn Tennis' and sent Greenwood [Frederick Greenwood (1830–1909), editor of the *St. James's Gazette*] the first and only copy, as we are now so late in the season that it is better it should appear *soon* than be written *well.*[7]
>
> *30 July:* Am now printing at Baxters' my pamphlet on Lawn Tennis Tournaments.[8]

2. Unpublished manuscript diaries.
3. Green, *Diaries,* 408.
4. *Ibid.,* 399.
5. *Ibid.,* 418.
6. Unpublished manuscript diaries.
7. Green, 418.
8. *Ibid.,* 419.

Dodgson had twenty copies of the pamphlet printed, which, according to his diary, he received on 10 August.

On 2 August 1883, in a letter to the *St. James's Gazette* (item 7), a correspondent identified as "Cavendish" [Henry Jones (1831–1899), a retired London surgeon, an organizer of the first tournament at Wimbledon and a referee there, a well-known authority on whist and other card games, and the editor of the Card department of *Field*] dismissed Dodgson's concern for the fair awarding of prizes beyond the first. He advocated instead models of scoring that depend on luck rather than fairness, stating that the players preferred them. In a diary entry of 3 August 1883 Dodgson wrote, "Received from Greenwood the *'S.J.' Gazette* for the 2nd, with 'Cavendish' 's ans. [answer] to my letter—& a M.S. letter fm [from] 'Corrigenda.' I replied to both."[9]

In his answer to this letter, published 4 August 1883 (item 8), Dodgson defended his scheme as a way of making a lawn tennis tournament a game of pure skill, like chess. Addressing comments to Corrigenda, he pointed out that Corrigenda was mistaken in giving the odds of 21:1 against the occurrence of the extreme case of the players being paired in their order of merit in the random drawing of sixteen players. Dodgson stated that the odds against this event happening are greater, but did not give them.

More importantly, Dodgson turned Cavendish's own argument against him by establishing that a player winning six games, and therefore the set, who goes on to win three sets, and therefore the match, will defeat a player who has won twenty-seven games who, Dodgson believed, should be the tournament winner! How does this happen?

To establish the winner in the least number of games, that player, call him C, wins three sets of six games each for a total of eighteen games; his opponent wins no games at all. But when another player, B, wins three of five sets, where his opponent A loses three games, one in each of the three sets, B wins three sets by the score of 6 to 5; A wins two sets by the same score (winning a set by two games was not in the rules at this time). Although losing to B, A has won 27 games to C's 18 games.

In Dodgson's final public letter on this topic, published on 21 August 1883 (item 11), he took up the comments about his method given by two more critics, Phayllus, in a letter published on 16 August (item 9), and East Sheen L.T.C., in his letter published on the 18th (item 10). Actually, East Sheen's letter is directed more toward the content of Phayllus' letter, in which he advocates the adoption of a form of the "American tournament," also known as the Weybridge system, on which seeding, the

9. Unpublished manuscript diaries.

method currently used to schedule tennis tournaments, is based. Dodgson outlined two problems with this approach. First, too many games will be played because "virtual" decisions are not included. (In Dodgson's system, if A beats B and B beats C, no match between A and C is scheduled because it is assumed A will beat C.) Secondly, by dividing the set of players into separate divisions, where each division's players compete among themselves, the Weybridge method allows the seventeenth, ninth, and twenty-fifth best players to win the second, third, and fourth prizes, rather than the top four players winning them, as Dodgson's method guarantees. Dodgson mistakenly referred to his letter of 1 August 1883 as 4 August.

Dodgson's analysis in his pamphlet, that in a 32-member (knockout) tournament the second, third, and fourth prizes could be awarded to the seventeenth, ninth, and twenty-fifth best players, is a worst-case scenario that results from the random pairing of the players in the first round in order of merit. After beating player 2, player 1 beats player 3; then plays and beats player 5 (who previously has beaten player 7 after beating player 6) then beats player 9 and finally beats player 17 to win first prize. But the same pattern applied to players 9 to 16 gives the third prize to player 9. Similarly, player 17 wins second prize, and player 25 fourth prize.

Dodgson noted that the chance that the second-best player will get second prize is only $16/31$, while the chance the four best players will all get their prizes is only $1/13$. Actually, the player deserving second prize will win it only in the event that the initial random draw puts the best player into the second half of the draw. For 32 players, the chance of this placement occurring is $2^{31}/2^{32} - 1$, or about 50 percent. Dodgson's 52 percent is somewhat off the mark.[10]

Dodgson also wanted to improve the way in which the tournament is organized by having a match consist only of games, not sets of games. (At that time, to win a match a player had to win three sets, in each of which he had won six games. So a maximum of eleven games could be played in a set, and a maximum of five sets could be played in a match.) Dodgson proposed a maximum of twenty-eight games in a match, the winner being the player first winning eighteen games.

10. Two complete analyses of Dodgson's method have been published. In the context of sorting problems the reader should consult Donald E. Knuth, *The Art of Computer Programming, III: Sorting and Searching* (Reading, Mass.: Addison-Wesley, 1973), 209–17. In the context of tournament problems see Francine F. Abeles, "The Mathematical-Political Papers of C. L. Dodgson," in Guiliano, ed., *Lewis Carroll: A Celebration,* 195–210.

PARI-MUTUEL BETTING

In the late 1970s, several political scientists showed that majority preferences can be represented as a tournament. In seeking to identify the best proposal majority voting can produce, they examined triples of proposals. In doing so, the notion of a transitive relation called a *covering* emerged. The seeds of this relation can be found in Dodgson tennis tournament method.[11]

Until recently, *Lawn Tennis Tournaments* seemed to have no antecedents in Dodgson's work. However, the author has established links to an earlier letter to the editor that has received little attention, which was published in the *Pall Mall Gazette* on 19 November 1866 with the title, "The Science of Betting" (item 12). In this letter, Dodgson presented a version of pari-mutuel betting called "betting round."[12]

"The Science of Betting" in turn has its origins in an earlier unpublished letter to the editor of *Bell's Life in London and Sporting Chronicle,* written in 1857. In it Dodgson proposed a system prefiguring the pari-mutuel method of betting invented by Pierre Oller in 1865 in France. Pari-mutuel betting is based on the consensus of (subjective) probabilities of the group of bettors wagering on the competing horses which determines the payoff odds on each horse. Those odds are inversely proportional to the amount of money bet on the horse. The system ensures a fixed profit to the track operator independently of which horses win.

Dodgson had discovered the idea of pari-mutuel betting on 12 March 1856. He wrote in his diary,

> Discovered a principle (probably long known), of making a winning book on any race where *the sum of the chances* (according to market odds) *is not exactly one.* Reduce to a common denominator: put that back into odds, and make your bets in sums proportional to

11. The most relevant publication on the topic is Nicholas Miller, "A New Solution Set for Tournaments and Majority Voting: Further Graph Theoretical Approaches to the Theory of Voting," *American Journal of Political Science* 24 (1980), 68–96.

12. For a complete discussion the reader is referred to Francine Abeles, "Charles L. Dodgson's Version of Pari-Mutuel Betting," *The Carrollian* 3 (1999), 30–36. Footnote 8 in this article should read: "SUM can be expressed as the sum, for all the horses, of each winning probability multiplied by LCM. LCM provides a constant that yields integers for the entries in columns (5) and (6), the odds that determine the bets. Since SUM determines the total amount received by the track operator, and LCM determines the amount paid out, choosing a larger LCM does not change the ratio SUM/LCM, hence the profit remains the same."

> those numbers, *giving all* the odds if the sum of the chances *exceeds* one, and *vice versa.* [13]

A year later he wrote the first letter on betting and sent it to the editor of *Bell's Life* on 5 May 1857, "giving an instance (the Derby odds of the other day) of a certainly-winning book being made by taking the odds in the proper proportion."[14]

Except for the fact that the Derby, arguably the most famous horse race in the world, is held in late May or early June, what additionally may have motivated the discovery of this betting principle and the letter that he sent describing it is not known.

On 9 May 1857, Dodgson wrote in his diary that an answer to his letter appeared in the "Answers to Correspondents" section of *Bell's Life,* and he quotes from it.

> They say 'your theory looks well enough on paper; the difficulty would be to find backers to work it out.'. . . it is a fact known and recognized on the turf; it is called 'betting round,' and considered so ungentlemanly a practice, that they will not bet with any one known to do it, moreover the winnings are in any case so small, that few can find it repay the trouble and the risk of not negotiating all the bets.[15]

The above criticism is ironic given Dodgson's penchant for fair play, which is seen in the following incident. His diary entry of 15 November 1866 reads,

> Wrote to the *Pall Mall,* giving the same rule for making a winning rule in betting, that I once sent to *Bell's Life:* —this was in consequence of an announcement in last night's *Pall Mall* that a certain firm 'the Messrs. H. & J. Smith' were offering £500 for a secret of the kind.[16]

This firm, from Shrewsbury, Shropshire, had been distributing circulars advertising the secret of a new system of betting for sale, guaranteeing that everyone who bets will win. The firm had been recommended to the public by several sporting newspapers, and the firm used the recommendations in their circulars. Unknown to Dodgson, the newspapers had ac-

13. Edward Wakeling, *Lewis Carroll's Diaries,* vol. 2 (Luton, U.K.: Lewis Carroll Society, 1994), 50.

14. Wakeling, *Lewis Carroll's Diaries,* vol. 3 (1995), 55.

15. *Ibid.,* 56–57.

16. Green, *Diaries,* 247. Here Green mistakenly refers to the firm as that of H. & I. Smith.

tually recommended a different company, Messrs. James and Sydney Smith, turf agents located at 100 Jermyn Street, and members of Tattersall's, the well-regarded auctioneer of horses. These favorable representations were misappropriated by H. & J. Smith's firm. Dodgson responded to the Smiths' solicitation to deter some people from throwing their money away, and refused payment.

In diary entries several days later, on 19 and 20 November, Dodgson commented that he had made an error in an example he had provided that subsequently was discovered by his oldest friend and colleague at Christ Church, Thomas Vere Bayne. Dodgson wrote a corrective note both to the *Pall Mall Gazette* and to *The Times* (item 13), where the letter had also appeared.

Both *Lawn Tennis Tournaments* and "The Science of Betting" elaborate on a method for conducting two very popular sports. The former provides a scheme to schedule matches so that the best players will win the prizes. The latter establishes a betting scheme so that when the odds are unevenly adjusted (i.e., when the total of the associated probabilities is greater than one) the bookmaker will always have a profit. When the odds are evenly adjusted, the result will be, Dodgson wrote in the article, "'Gain = Loss – Nil'—a most desirable result."

The principles of fairness, rationality, and certainty underlie both *Lawn Tennis Tournaments* and "The Science of Betting." Implementing these principles requires only the use of simple mathematical techniques from algebra and concepts from probability theory applied in a logically meaningful way. Dodgson wrote in "The Science of Betting," "It may be mathematically demonstrated that, provided all the bets are paid, winning is a certainty." And in *Lawn Tennis Tournaments* he wrote, "If you play 2nd or 3rd best, you are certain of the proper prize."

4. Lawn Tennis Tournaments: The True Method of Assigning Prizes with a Proof of the Fallacy of the Present Method

[1883: LCH 157, LCAT 434: Princeton]

The authors of the LCH had this to say about *Lawn Tennis Tournaments:*

> But as usual with Dodgson's ideals of scoring or voting, the scheme proposed is too ingenious and elaborate for general use, though terribly near perfection. The results would be many fewer competitors, a shorter tournament, and less gate money![1]

Donald Knuth, the eminent computer scientist, has a different assessment:

> And it appears to be an excellent plan for a tennis tournament, because he built in some dramatic effects; for example he specified that the two finalists should sit out round 5, playing an extended match during rounds 6 and 7. . . . It would be nice to report that Lewis Carroll's tournament turns out to be optimal, but unfortunately that is not the case.[2]

In fairness to Dodgson, the optimality problem was first posed as a question in 1929. An algorithm for it was given in 1932, but only in 1964 was the algorithm proved to be optimal.[3]

London, Macmillan, 1883.

1. *The Lewis Carroll Handbook,* 120.

2. Donald Knuth, *The Art of Computer Programming, vol. III: Sorting and Searching* (Reading, Mass.: Addison-Wesley, 1973), 211, 209.

3. *Ibid.,* 211.

Palmam qui meruit ferat

CONTENTS.

§. 1. *Introductory.*

At a Lawn Tennis Tournament, where I chanced, some while ago, to be a spectator, the present method of assigning prizes was brought to my notice by the lamentations of one of the Players, who had been beaten (and had thus lost all chance of a prize) early in the contest, and who had had the mortification of seeing the 2nd prize carried off by a Player whom he knew to be quite inferior to himself. The results of the investigations, which I was led to make, I propose to lay before the reader under the following four headings:—

(a) A proof that the present method of assigning prizes is, except in the case of the first prize, entirely unmeaning.

(b) A proof that the present method of scoring in matches is constantly liable to lead to unjust results.

(c) A system of rules for conducting Tournaments, which, while requiring even less time than the present system, shall secure equitable results.

(d) An equitable system for scoring in matches.

§. 2. *A proof that the present method of assigning prizes is, except in the case of the first prize, entirely unmeaning.*

Let us take, as an example of the present method, a Tournament of 32 competitors with 4 prizes.

On the 1st day, these contend in 16 pairs: on the 2nd day, the 16 Winners contend in 8 pairs, the Losers being excluded from further competition: on the 3rd day, the 8 Winners contend in 4 pairs: on the 4th day, the 4 Winners (who are now known to be the 4 Prize-men) contend in 2 pairs: and on the 5th day, the 2 Winners contend together, to decide which is to take the 1st prize and which the 2nd—the 2 Losers having no further contest, as the 3rd and 4th prize are of equal value.

Now, if we divide the list of competitors, arranged in the order in which they are paired, into 4 sections, we may see that all that this method really does is to ascertain who is best in each section, then who is best in each half of the list, and then who is best of all. The best of all (and this is the only equitable result arrived at) wins the 1st prize: the best in the other half of the list wins the 2nd: and the best men in the two sections not yet represented by a champion win the other two prizes. If the Players had chanced to be paired in the order of merit, the 17th best Player would necessarily carry off the 2nd prize, and the 9th and 25th best the 3rd and 4th! This of course is an extreme case: but anything within these limits is possible: *e.g.* any competitor, from the 3rd best to the 17th best, may, by the mere accidental arrangement of pairs, and by no means as a result of his own skill, carry off the 2nd prize. As a mathematical fact, the chance that the 2nd best Player will get the prize he deserves is only 16-31ths; while the chance that the best 4 shall get their proper prizes is so small, that the odds are 12 to 1 against its happening!

If any one thinks that, after all, we are merely introducing another element of chance into the game, and that no one can fairly object to *that,* let him try the experiment in a rifle competition. Let him interpose when the man, who has made the 2nd best score, is going to receive his prize, and propose that he shall first draw a counter from a bag containing 16 white and 15 black, and only have his prize in case he draws a white one: and let him observe the expression of that rifleman's face.

§. 3. *A proof that the present method of scoring in matches is constantly liable to lead to unjust results.*

To prove this, let us suppose a "set" to mean "the best of 11 games," and a "match" "the best of 5 sets": i.e., "he, who first wins 6 games, wins a set; he, who first wins 3 sets, wins a match."

Suppose A and B to play the following 50 games ("A^2" means "A wins 2 games," and so on):—

$B^2A^5B^4 \mid A^6 \mid B^3A^5B^2A^* \mid B^*A^2B^4A^3B \mid B^2A^5B^3A$.

Here A wins 28 games to 22, and also wins the match. But, by simply transposing A*, B*, we get

$B^2A^5B^4 \mid A^6 \mid B^3A^5B^3 \mid A^3B^4A^3 \mid B^3A^5B^3$,

the last game of the original series not being played. Here A still wins 27 games to 22: yet he loses the match!

§. 4. *A system of rules for conducting Tournaments, which, while requiring even less time than the present system, shall secure equitable results.*

The method for conducting Tournaments, which I have to propose, involves two departures from the present method. First, I propose to make a "match" last only half a day (the necessary reduction in the number of games I will discuss in section 5): secondly, I propose to give only 3 prizes. The rules for a Tournament of 32 Players would be as follows:—

(a) The Tournament begins in the middle of the 1st day, so that there is only one contest that day—the 32 Players being arranged in 16 pairs.

(b) A list is kept, and against each name is entered, at the end of each contest, the name of any one who has been proved superior to him—whether by actually beating him, or by beating some one who has done so (thus, if A beats B, and B beats C, A and B are both "superiors" of C). So soon as any name has 3 "superiors" entered against it, it is struck out of the list.

(c) For the 2nd day (morning) the 16 unbeaten men are paired together, and similarly the 16 with 1 superior (the Losers in these last-named pairs will now have 3 superiors each, and will therefore be struck off the list). In all other contests they are paired in the same way; first pairing the unbeaten, then those with 1 supe-

rior, and so on, and avoiding, as far as possible, pairing two Players who have a common superior.

(d) By the middle of the 3rd day the unbeaten are reduced to two, one of whom is certainly "First-prize man." These two do not contend in the afternoon contest that day, but have a whole-day match on the 4th day—the other Players meanwhile continuing the usual half-day matches.

(e) By the end of the 4th day, the "First-prize man" is known (by the very same process of elimination used in the existing method): and the remaining Players are paired by the same rules as before, for the 2 contests on the 5th day. In some cases the 2nd and 3rd prizes will both be decided by the middle of the 5th day. If, in section *(a),* the Tournament were begun in the morning, the two men named in section *(d)* being still allowed a whole-day match, nothing would be gained in time, as the Tournament would still take 4½ days, while much would be lost in interest, as the first prize would be settled in 3 days.

To illustrate these rules, I will give the complete history of a Tournament of 32 competitors, with 3 prizes. If the reader will draw out the following Tables, in blank, and fill them up for himself, referring, if necessary, to the accompanying directions, he will easily understand the working of the system.

Let the Players be arranged alphabetically, and let the relative skill, with which they play in this Tournament, be:—

A	B	C	D	E	F	G	H	J	K	L	M	N	P	Q	R	S	T
19	22	14	32	16	25	15	28	3	10	8	1	29	4	12	2	17	23
		U	V	W	X	Y	Z	a	b	c	d	e	f	g	h		
		26	11	20	31	13	18	6	24	9	21	30	5	7	27		

These numbers ("1" meaning "best") will enable the reader to name the victor in any contest: but of course they are not supposed to be known to the Tournament-Committee, who have nothing to guide them but the results of actual contests. In the following Tables, "I (e)" means "first day, evening," and so on: also a Player, who is *virtually* proved superior to another, is entered thus "(A)." The victor in each contest is marked *: and ◉ means "struck out."

Directions for filling in the Tables:—

Tab. I. Day I (e). The names are written out alphabetically, and paired as they stand. The victors are marked with asterisks.

Tab. II. Day I (e). As B has been beaten by A, A is entered as his "superior"; C as D's superior; and so on.

Tab. I. Day II (m). We first pair together all the unbeaten, A, C, E, G, &c. Then those who have one superior, B, D, F, H, &c.

Tab. II. Day II (m). We first enter the *actual* superiors, C, G, &c. Then, since A has a superior C, and B has a superior A, we see that B has a *virtual* superior C; and so on. We then see that D has 3 superiors, and must be struck out; and so with H, &c.

Tab. I. Day II (e). We first pair together all the unbeaten, C, G, &c. Then all with one superior, A, E, &c.; but when we come to J, L, we find they have a common superior; so we pair J with P, and L with Q. This series ends with an odd one, g, who must therefore be paired with the first of those who have two superiors each, viz. B. Then we pair the rest of those who have two superiors each, F, T, &c.

Tab. II. Day II (e). We enter the actual, and then the virtual, superiors as usual. Note the curious result that d, though he has been actually beaten only once, has now 2 other virtual superiors, and must therefore be struck out of the list.

Tab. I. Day III (m). Here, in pairing those with one superior, we again end with an odd one, g, who must therefore be paired with the first of those with two superiors, viz. T. We end with an 'odd man,' c.

Tab. II. Day III (m). The unbeaten are now reduced to one pair, M, f, who therefore will do nothing this afternoon, but will have a whole-day contest to-morrow.

Tab. I. Day III (e). Those who have one superior are C, J, L, R, all with a common superior M; and then V, a, g, all with a common superior f. We therefore pair C with V, and so on, leaving an odd one R, who must be paired with the only one who has two superiors, viz. c.

Tab. II. Day III (e). Enter as usual.

Tab. I. Day IV (m). We pair the 2 unbeaten, M, f, for their whole-day contest. Then those with one superior.

Table I. (Pairs.)

I. (e)	II. (m)	(e)	III. (m)	(e)	IV. (m)	(e)	V. (m)	(e)
A B }*	A C }*	C G }*	C M }*	C V }*	M f }*	M f }*	R f }*	J f }*
C D }*	E G }*	M R }*	V f }*	J a }*	J V }*	J R }*	J	
E F }*	J M }*	V Y }*	A J }*	L g }*	R g }*			
G H }*	P R }*	a f }*	G L }*	R c }*				
J K }*	S V }*	A E }*	R S }*					
L M }*	W Y }*	J P }*	Y a }*					
N P }*	a c }*	L Q }*	g T }*					
Q R }*	f g }*	S W }*	c					
S T }*	B D }*	Z c }*						
U V }*	F H }*	g B }*						
W X }*	K L }*	F T }*						
Y Z }*	N Q }*	d h }*						
a b }*	T U }*							
c d }*	X Z }*							
e f }*	b d }*							
g h }*	e h }*							

Tab. II. Day IV (m). M and f are still contending. V and g are struck out.

Tab. I. Day IV (e). J and R must be paired together, though they have a common superior.

Tab. II. Day IV (e). M is First-prize man.

Tab. I. Day V (m). R and f must be paired together, though they have a common superior. J is 'odd man.'

Tab. II. Day V (m). R is now the only man with one superior, and is therefore Second-prize man.

Tab. I. Day V (e). J and f contend for the Third prize.

If this Tournament were fought by the present method, the 4 Prize-men would be C, M, V, f: f would get the 2nd prize, and C and V the 3rd and 4th: i.e. the 5th best man would get the 2nd prize, and the 14th and 11th best the other two.

§. 5. *An equitable system for scoring in matches.*

In order to make "matches" more equitable, I propose to abolish "sets," and make a "match" consist of "games." Thus, instead of "best of 11 games = set; best of 5 sets = match" (i.e. he who first wins 6 games wins a set; he who first wins 3 sets wins a match), where a player *may* win with as few as 18 games, and *must* win with 28, I would substitute "he who first wins 28 games, or who gets 18 games ahead, wins the match." I therefore propose as follows: "For a whole-day, he who first wins 28 games, or who gets 18 ahead, wins the match: for a half-day, he who first wins 14 games, or who gets 9 ahead, wins the match"

§. 6. *Concluding remarks.*

Let it not be supposed that, in thus proposing to make these Tournaments a game of pure skill (like chess) instead of a game of mixed skill and chance (like whist), I am altogether eliminating the element of luck, and making it possible to predict the prize-winners, so that no one else would care to enter. The 'chances of the board' would still exist in full force: it would not at all follow, because a Player was reputed best, that he was certain of the 1st prize: a thousand accidents might occur to prevent his playing best: the 4th best, 5th best, or even a worse Player, need not despair of winning even the 1st prize.

TABLE II. (Superiors.)

	I. (e)	II. (m)	(e)	III. (m)	(e)	IV. (m)	(e)	V. (m)	(e)
A	. . .	C	. . .	J (M) ◉					
B	A	(C)	g ◉						
C	. . .	. . .	. . .	M	V (f) ◉				
D	C	B (A) ◉							
E	. . .	G	A (C) ◉						
F	E	(G)	T ◉						
G	. . .	. . .	C	L (M) ◉					
H	G	F (E) ◉							
J	. . .	M	. . .	. . .	. . .	. . .	R	. . .	Pr. III.
K	J	L (M) ◉							
L	M	. . .	. . .	. . .	g (f) ◉				
M	. . .	. . .	. . .	. . .	. . .	. . .	Pr. I.		
N	P	Q (R) ◉							
P	. . .	R	J (M) ◉						
Q	R	. . .	L (M) ◉						
R	. . .	. . .	M	. . .	. . .	. . .	. . .	Pr. II.	
S	. . .	V	. . .	R (f) ◉					
T	S	(V)	. . .	g ◉					
U	V	T (S) ◉							
V	. . .	. . .	. . .	f	. . .	J (M) ◉			
W	. . .	Y	S (V) ◉						
X	W	Z (Y) ◉							
Y	. . .	. . .	V	a (f) ◉					
Z	Y	. . .	c (V) ◉						
a	. . .	. . .	f	. . .	J (M) ◉				
b	a	d (c) ◉							
c	. . .	a	(f)	. . .	R ◉				
d	c	(a)	(f) ◉						
e	f	h (g) ◉							
f	. . .	. . .	. . .	. . .	. . .	. . .	M	R	J ◉
g	. . .	f	. . .	. . .	. . .	R (M) ◉			
h	g	(f)	d ◉						

Nor, again, let it be supposed that the present system, which allows an inferior player a chance of the 2nd prize, even though he fails to play above his reputation, is more attractive than one which, in such a case, gives him no hope. Let us compare the two systems, as to the attractions they hold out to (say) the 5th best Player in a Tournament of 32, with 3 prizes. The present system says 'if you play up to your reputation, your chance of a prize is about 1-4th; and even if, by great luck and painstaking, you play 2nd or 3rd best, it never rises above a half': my system says 'it is admitted that, if you only play up to your reputation, you will get nothing; but, if you play 2nd or 3rd best, you are certain of the proper prize.' Thus, the one system offers a chance of 1-4th, where the other offers nothing; and a chance of a half, where the other offers certainty. I am inclined to think the second the more attractive of the two.

If, however, it be thought that, under the proposed system, the very inferior Players would feel so hopeless of a prize that they would not enter a Tournament, this can easily be remedied by the process of handicapping, as is usual in races, &c. This would give every one a reasonable hope of a prize, and therefore a sufficient motive for entering.

The proposed form of Tournament, though lasting a shorter time than the present one, has a great many more contests going on at once, and consequently furnishes the spectacle-loving public with a great deal more to look at.

THE END.

5. *Lawn Tennis Tournaments*

[1882: LCH 145: Colindale]

❦

To the Editor *of the* St. James's Gazette.

Sir,—Players of Lawn Tennis, and those interested in other kinds of sport in which Tournaments occur, have no doubt often realized the very unsatisfactory way in which the prizes are at present adjudged. I propose to deal with the subject mathematically, and to point out, first, the extraordinary injustice of the existing laws; and secondly, a method of adjudging the prizes which would, as I hope, really carry out the principle of *detur digniori.*

Suppose there are 32 competitors. These are arranged as 16 pairs for the contests of the first day: on the second day, the 16 winners are arranged as 8 pairs, the losers being excluded from further competition: similarly, on the third day, there are 4 pairs, and the 4 winners (supposing 4 prizes to be given) are now known to be the prize-winners. In order to settle their claims, 2 pairs contend on the fourth day, and the 2 winners have a final contest on the fifth day, to decide which is to take the first prize and which the second: the two losers have no further contest, since the third and fourth prizes are of equal value.

The injustice of this system needs few words to prove it. Any one of your readers, who will write down 32 numbers, and bracket them in 16 couples, and then, after marking the supposed winner in each couple, will bracket these winners in 8 couples, and so on, will easily convince himself that the result is really as follows: if the original list be divided into 4 quarters, the best man in each quarter is a winner of one of the 4 prizes—the best in each half wins one of the first 2 prizes—and the best in the whole list (it would indeed be a strange system which failed

St. James's Gazette, 12 August 1882, 5–6.

to secure *this!*) wins the first prize. Now suppose the original list chanced to be arranged in the order of merit: in this case it will be found that the 17th best player gets the second prize, while the 9th and 25th best get the third and fourth!

This, or course, is an extreme case: but, in every case, the 2nd best player has only 16-31ths of a chance of getting the prize he deserves, and the chance, that the best 4 players shall get their prizes, is almost exactly 19-250ths: *i.e.* the odds are more than 12 to 1 against it!

Now, if any Lawn-Tennis-player is content that the element of pure chance should so largely enter into a contest of skill, I have nothing to say against it: every one to his taste: but to those who think, with me, that a Tournament would give more general satisfaction if the prizes were always given to those who played best, the following suggestions may prove interesting.

It is quite unimportant how the names are bracketed for the first set of contests; but, after that, the contests should be arranged thus:—the 16 winners (I am taking, as before, 32 competitors) and 4 prizes should be bracketed together, and the 16 losers should also be bracketed together. A list should be kept of the players, and against each man's name should be entered the names of those who have been proved superior to him, either by actually beating him or by beating those who have done so (*e.g.* if A beats B, and B beats C, both A and B are "superiors" of C). The contests should all be arranged on the principle of bracketing together, as far as possible, those who have the same number of superiors but have no common superiors (*e.g.* if A has been beaten by K and L, B by K and R, C by L and S, D by S and T, we should bracket A with D, and B with C). It would not be at all necessary to have only one set of contests each day: as soon as any court was finished with, the committee would assign it to any two disengaged players, who could be properly bracketed together.

The 4 prizes would be assigned thus:—so soon as any player had 4 superiors entered against his name, he would be struck out of the list: so soon as all, but one, had at least one superior, that one would be marked as "first prize:" of the remainder, so soon as all, but one, had at least 2 superiors, that one would be marked as "second prize:" and, of those then remaining, so soon as all, but two, had at least 4 superiors, those two would receive the remaining prizes.

This system would require many more contests than the present one does, so that there would be much more spectacle for the public to see: but, since the courts would usually be filled up as fast as vacated, I do not think that the whole Tournament would be likely to occupy more time than under the present most unsatisfactory system, which may often result in the 2nd, 3rd, and 4th best players all returning home empty-handed, while their prizes are carried off by players known to be far inferior to them.—I am, Sir, your obedient servant,

CHARLES L. DODGSON.

Late Mathematical Lecturer of Ch. Ch. Oxford, August 10.

6. The Fallacies of Lawn Tennis Tournaments

[1883: LCH 145: Colindale]

❧

To the Editor *of the* St. James's Gazette.

Sir,—In treating this subject I propose to myself four things:—

(1.) To prove that the existing method of assigning prizes in lawn tennis tournaments is, except in the case of the first prize, entirely absurd;

(2.) To prove that the existing method of scoring in matches leads, in many cases, to an unjust result;

(3.) To suggest a method for conducting tournaments which, while requiring less time than the present, shall give more equitable results;

(4.) To suggest a better method of scoring in matches.

(1.) To prove the absurdity of the present method of assigning prizes in lawn tennis tournaments will not need many words. Suppose there are 32 competitors and 4 prizes. On the 1st day, these contend in 16 pairs: on the 2nd day, the 16 winners contend in 8 pairs, the losers being excluded from further competition: on the 3rd day, the 8 winners contend in 4 pairs: on the 4th day, the 4 winners (who are now known to be the 4 prize-men) contend in 2 pairs: and on the 5th day, the 2 winners contend together, to decide which is to take the first prize and which the second—the 2 losers having no further contest, as the 3rd and 4th prize are of equal value.

St. James's Gazette, 1 August 1883, 5–7.

Now, if we divide the original list of competitors into 4 sections, we may see that all, that this method really does, is to ascertain who is the best man in each section, then who is the best in each half of the list, and then who is the best of all. The best of all (and this is the only equitable result arrived at) wins the first prize: the best in the other half of the list wins the second: and the best men in the 2 sections not yet represented by a champion win the other two prizes. If the original list had chanced to be arranged in the order of merit, the 17th best player would necessarily carry off the 2nd prize, and the 9th and 25th best the 3rd and 4th! This of course is an extreme case: but anything within these limits is possible: *e.g.* any competitor, from the 3rd best to the 17th best, may, by the mere accidental arrangement of names, and by no means as a result of his own skill, carry off the 2nd prize. As a mathematical fact, the chance that the 2nd best player will get the prize he deserves is only 16-31ths: while the chance that the best 4 shall get their proper prizes is so small that the odds are 12 to 1 against its happening!

(2.) To prove that the existing method of scoring in matches leads, in many cases, to an unjust result, let us suppose a "set" to mean "the best of 5 games," and a "match" "the best of 5 sets."

Suppose A and B to play the following 23 games:—B A A B B | A A A | B A A B A* | B* A B A B | B A A B A. Here A wins 13 games to 10, and also wins the match. But, by simply transposing A*, B*, we get B A A B B | A A A | B A A B B | A A B A | B B A A B | , the last game of the original series not being played. Here A still wins 12 games to 10: yet he loses the match!

(3.) The method for conducting tournaments, which I have to propose, involves two departures from the present method. First, I propose to make a "match" last only half a day (the necessary reduction in the number of games I will discuss in section 4): secondly, I propose to give only 3 prizes. The rules for a tournament of 32 players would be as follows:—

(a.) The tournament begins in the middle of the 1st day, so that there is only one contest that day—the 32 players being arranged in 16 pairs.

(b.) A list is kept, and against each name is entered, at the end of each contest, the name of any one who has been proved superi-

or to him—whether by actually beating him, or by beating some one who has done so (thus, if A beats B, and B beats C, A and B are both "superiors" of C). So soon as any name has 3 "superiors" entered against it, it is struck out of the list.

(c.) For the 2nd day (morning) the 16 unbeaten men are paired together, and similarly the 16 with 1 superior (the losers in these last-named pairs will now have 3 superiors each, and will therefore be struck off the list). In all other contests they are paired in the same way; first pairing the unbeaten, then those with 1 superior, and so on, and avoiding, as far as possible, pairing two players who have a common superior.

(d.) By the middle of the 3rd day the unbeaten are reduced to two, one of whom is certainly "first-prize man." These two do not contend in the afternoon contest that day, but have a whole-day match on the 4th day—the other players meanwhile continuing the usual half-day matches.

(e.) By the end of the 4th day, the "first-prize man" is known (by the very same process of elimination used in the existing method): and the remaining players are paired by the same rules as before, for the 2 contests on the 5th day. In some cases the 2nd and 3rd prizes will both be decided by the middle of the 5th day. If, in section *(a),* the tournament were begun in the morning, the two men named in section *(d)* being still allowed a whole-day match, nothing would be gained in time, as the tournament would still take 4½ days, while much would be lost in interest, as the first prize would be settled in 3 days.

These rules will, I think, be sufficiently illustrated by going through a tournament of 16; and if the reader will draw up for himself these Tables, in blank, and fill them up, column by column, according to the following directions, he will easily understand the working of the system.

Let the players be arranged alphabetically, and call them A, B, C, etc., and let their relative skill be represented by the following numbers:—

A	B	C	D	E	F	G	H	J	K	L	M	N	P	Q	R
6	10	13	5	15	9	7	12	1	14	3	2	8	16	11	4

These numbers will enable the reader to decide which will be the victor in any contest: but of course they are not supposed to be known to the Tournament Committee, who have nothing to guide them but the results of actual contests. In the following tables, "I. (e)" means "first day, evening," and so on: also a player, who is *virtually* proved superior to another, is entered thus "(A)." The victor in each contest is marked *.

In contest I. (e), we see that A beats B, and so on: hence we enter A as a "superior" to B, D to C, and so on. For contest II. (m), we pair the winners A, D, and so on; and then the losers, B, C, and so on. After it, we enter the *actual* superiors, D, G, etc.: we then find that, A having a superior D, and B a superior A, B has a *virtual* superior D; and so on. Having done this, we see that C, E, K, P, have three superiors each, and must be struck out. For contest II. (e) we should avoid pairing F and H, because they have a common superior; and the same may be said of N, Q. After it, we strike out B, F, H, Q. On the 3rd day, as there are only 2 unbeaten left, they contend during the whole day, the others having half-day contests: L and N have to be paired, even though they have a common superior. After the morning contest, we strike out A, G, N. For the evening, D and J are still contending; so that M and R must be paired, though they have a common superior; and L is "odd man." After the evening contest, J is seen to be "first-prize-man." After contest IV. (m), we strike out R; and we see that M is "second-prize-man." After contest IV. (e), we strike out D, and give L the 3rd prize.

If this tournament were fought by the present method, the 4 prize-men would be D, G, J, R: D would get the 2nd prize, and G and R the 3rd and 4th: *i.e.* the 5th best man would get the 2nd prize, and the 7th and 4th best the other two.

(4.) To make "matches" more equitable, I propose to abolish "sets," and make a "match" consist of "games." Thus instead of "best of five games = set; best of 5 sets = match" (*i.e.* he who first wins 3 games wins a set; he who first wins 3 sets wins a match), where a player *may* win with as few as 9 games, and *must* win with 13, I would substitute "he who first wins 13 games, or who gets 9 games ahead, wins the match." This, however, is a short match. The London Athletic Club say "he who first wins 6 games wins a set; he who first wins 3 sets wins a match." Here a

Table i. (Pairs.)

I. (e)	II. (m)	(e)	III. (m)	(e)	IV. (m)	(e)
A }* B	A } D*	D }* G	D } J	D } J*	D } M*	D } L
C } D*	F } G*	J }* R	A } M*	M }* R	L }* R	
E } F*	J }* M	A }* F	G } R*	L		
G }* H	N } R*	H } N*	L }* N			
J }* K	B }* C	M }* Q				
L } M*	E } H*	B } L*				
N }* P	K } L*	. . . . . .				
Q } R*	P } Q*	. . . . . .				

Table ii. (Superiors.)

	I. (e)	II. (m)	(e)	III. (m)	(e)	IV. (m)	(e)
A	. . .	D	. . .	M (J) out			
B	A	(D)	L out				
C	D	B (A) out					
D	. . .	. . .	. . .	. . .	J	M	L out
E	F	H (G) out					
F	. . .	G	A (D) out				
G	. . .	. . .	D	R (J) out			
H	G	. . .	N (D) out				
J	. . .	. . .	. . .	. . .	First		
K	J	L (M) out					
L	M	(J)	. . .	. . .	. . .	. . .	Third
M	. . .	J	. . .	. . .	. . .	Second	
N	. . .	R	(J)	L out			
P	N	Q (R) out					
Q	R	. . .	M (J) out				
R	. . .	. . .	J	. . .	M	L out	

player *may* win with 18 games, and *must* win with 28: so that it might need as many as 55 games to decide a match. This again seems needlessly large. I am inclined for a compromise, and propose as follows: "For a whole-day, he who first wins 24 games, or who gets 16 ahead, wins the match: for a half-day, he who first wins 12 games, or who gets 8 games ahead, wins the match." The proposed form of tournament, though lasting a shorter time than the existing one has a great many more contests going on at once, and consequently furnishes the spectacle-loving public with a great deal more to look at.—I am, Sir your obedient servant,

CHARLES L. DODGSON.

Student and late Mathematical Lecturer of Christ Church, Oxford, July 30.

7. "Cavendish" on Lawn-Tennis Rules

[1883: Colindale]

❦

To the Editor *of the* St. James's Gazette.

Sir,—Your correspondent Mr. Charles L. Dodgson has taken a great deal of trouble to tell match-players and the draftsmen of the laws and regulations which settle "the existing method of assigning prizes in lawn-tennis" what they knew before he wrote. Mr. Dodgson further proposes a method of assigning prizes which is only a variation of similar methods that have already been considered and rejected.

In matches open to all comers on equal terms the primary object is to give the first prize to the best man. This is the "equitable result" it is desired to arrive at. Whether the second-best man, or the best man in the other half of the list, wins the second prize or not is a matter of comparatively small concern. In the interest of sport, however, it is better that the second prize should not be a certainty for the second-best man. If it were, the entries would be confined to two or three first-class players, with perhaps one or two more who are willing to throw away their entrance-money for the fun of the thing. The championship entries, for instance, would include the Renshaws, Lawford, Richardson, and possibly one or two more. The prize-winners could easily be predicted before the draw, and the interest of the whole meeting would suffer accordingly. One object is to entice second-class players to enter. They know they have no chance of first prize; but they hope that a lucky draw may enable them to win a second or third prize. These prizes are not even supposed to be given to the second and third best men. They are of the nature of consolation prizes; and they make the second flight (whose form is more

St. James's Gazette, 2 August 1883, 5–6.

variable than that of the first flight) strive their utmost to get a "place." To call this method "unjust" and "entirely absurd" is to beg the question. Nearly all, if not all, the players who enter for the championship, and for other open meetings, know how it works as well as Mr. Dodgson: the great majority are not merely satisfied with it, but prefer it to other methods.

All popular games have, and must have, an element of luck. The proposition of Mr. Dodgson is equivalent to a proposition to abolish honours at whist or flukes at billiards. To make a game popular there must be some hope even in the breast of a second-class player: a hope of success through fortune, if not through skill. An answer on similar lines may be given to the proposal to make matches consist of games instead of sets. If this idea were carried to its logical conclusion, matches should consist of strokes and not of games; for the winner of the majority of games may be (and sometimes is) the loser of the majority of strokes.

The method which makes the result a certainty for the winner of the greatest number of strokes (or of games, if preferred) would lead to an uninteresting fight, in which, as between two even players, the one who got a little ahead at first would have too much the best of the match: and for this reason, that luck is too nearly eliminated. By the existing method a lucky game (or game won by a lucky stroke) on one side is often balanced by a lucky game on the other side; and so the excitement is constantly kept up. Mr. Dodgson's proposal is equivalent to a proposal to make the game of whist, say, fifteen up, instead of making a rubber the best of three games of five up. At whist, as at present constituted, A may score 5 + 4 + 4 = 13, and Y (A's adversary) may score 5 + 5 = 10, and yet Y wins the rubber. Nobody says this is "unjust" or "entirely absurd." Even admitting that it is, the great majority of players like this method of scoring and of assigning the stakes; for if they did not, the method would long ago have been altered. I could readily give similar illustrations taken from other popular games.

It is true that in handicapping, a player's public performances are taken into account, and a second or third class man who has won a second or third prize in an open meeting would very likely for a time be handicapped out of handicap meetings. But this is just as it should be. He has had his slice of luck. It is only right that some one else, who has been unfortunate in his draw, should have his turn.

The real argument is not a mathematical one. It is this: What do the players like, and what is it that induces them to enter for matches? I unhesitatingly answer, The element of luck.

Consequently, I advocate modes of scoring which favour luck to some extent, though they may be "unjust" and "entirely absurd" from a mathematical point of view. The only difficulty is to avoid the error of introducing too much luck. What is the amount of luck calculated to promote the greatest amount of interest is a problem which can only be solved by repeated trials, and by reference to the number of persons who voluntarily enter for the various contests. At chess, for example, the entrance of luck is too small for a perfect game; at beggar-my-neighbour, the entrance of luck is too great.—I am, Sir, your obedient servant,

CAVENDISH.

August 1.

8. Lawn Tennis: Reply to "Cavendish"

[1883: LCH 145: Colindale]

❦

To the Editor *of the* St. James's Gazette.

Sir,—I am honoured by the attention such an authority as "Cavendish" has given to my letter on Lawn Tennis Tournaments, and hope you will afford me space for a brief reply.

He says "the primary object is to give the 1st prize to the best man," but that it is "a matter of comparatively small concern" to give the 2nd to the 2nd best. Why so wide a distinction between them? Is it fair that the one should be certain of his prize, while the other has only an even chance of his?

Again, he says that, under my system, "the prize-winners could easily be predicted, and the interest of the whole meeting would suffer." Is he not ignoring the "chances of the board," where the element of luck enters largely, even under my system? The man reputed best is by no means certain of the 1st prize: many things may prevent his playing best. Also, does he find that the interest of a rifle-match suffers, because he who makes 2nd score is certain of getting 2nd prize?

Again, he thinks the present system "entices" 2nd-class players to enter more than mine would. Let us see what he and I, representing the two systems, would say to players before a tournament of 32 with three prizes. (We may assume that every one hopes to play at least up to his reputation.)

To the man reputed 2nd best, he would say, "If you play up to your reputation, your chances are—of the 2nd prize, one half; of the 3rd, 1-4th; of getting nothing, 1-4th:" whereas I should say, "If you do so, you will get the 2nd prize." Here undoubtedly I make the best bid.

St. James's Gazette, 4 August 1883, 5–6.

To the man reputed 5th best, he would say, "If you play up to your reputation, your chance of a prize is about 1-4th; and even if, by great luck and pains-taking, you play 2nd or 3rd best, it never rises above a half:" whereas I should say, "I admit that, if you only play up to your reputation, you will get nothing; but, if you play 2nd or 3rd best, you are certain of the proper prize." Thus he offers a chance of 1-4th, where I offer nothing; and of a half, where I offer certainty. I am inclined to think that here also I make the best bid.

I agree with him that "all popular games have, and must have, an element of luck." This is true of all games—whether of pure chance, *e.g.* pitch-farthing; or of pure skill, *e.g.* chess; or mixed, *e.g.* whist. My proposal is to make Lawn-Tennis Tournaments a game of pure skill, instead of being mixed: but this would not destroy, what he thinks necessary, "some hope, even in the breast of a second-class player, of success through fortune, if not through skill."

He says the logical conclusion of my proposal, to make a match consist of games, is to make it consist of strokes. I admit it, but think that would be going too far.

He thinks a match consisting of games would be uninteresting, so soon as one of two even players got a little ahead, while under the present system "a lucky game on one side is often balanced by a lucky game on the other side." And why should not the being a little ahead on one side be balanced by a lucky game on the other side? *Suo sibi gladio hunc jugulo.*

I believe that a system of handicapping, such as is usual in races, would be a much more satisfactory way of equalizing players, and thus giving all a reasonable hope of winning a prize, than the present lottery-system. But in any case I protest against the present absurdity of excluding a man, who has been beaten only once, from all further competition in a tournament with more than one prize.

May I add a few words in reply to "Corrigenda," whose letter, in MS., you have kindly sent me? He thinks I am estimating too highly the chance of its happening that the players should be paired "in order of merit," because I have not allowed for the rule "that the players draw for their oponents *(sic)* every time:"

and he calculates that, with 16 players, the odds against this event are 21 to 1. Let me remind "Corrigenda" that I spoke of it as "an extreme case:" the odds against it, I do not mind admitting, are more than 21 to 1: how much more, I do not feel bound to say.

He also says that the absurdity I pointed out in scoring matches, where A wins twelve games to ten and yet loses the match, could never happen, because one must "always" win six games, not three, to win a "set." I think that for "always" we should read "always in Corrigenda's experience;" but I gladly accept a correction which strengthens my case so much. If he, who wins six games, wins a set; and he, who wins three sets, wins a match; then a player may actually win 27 games to 18, and yet lose the match!—I am, Sir, your obedient servant,

CHARLES L. DODGSON.

August 3.

9. *Lawn Tennis (by Phayllus)*

[1883: Colindale]

❦

To the Editor *of the* St. James's Gazette.

Sir,—During the present month a large number of clubs in the country, especially at watering-places, hold "one-day tournaments" for visitors, some of whom come from a distance. The day is usually spent in double-handed matches for "scratch" pairs, and several prizes are given. The *desiderata* for these tournaments are not only that the best couples shall take the three or four prizes presented, but that all the players shall be occupied during the greater part of the day and not be forced to look on idly if they have lost their match in the first round. To effect these objects, I venture to suggest that some form or modification of the "American tournament" system of competition should be adopted. The so-called American system consists in each combatant playing every one of his opponents: the winner of the greatest number of matches taking the first prize, the winner of the next greatest number the second prize, and so on. The same principles apply if the contestants are single individuals or pairs. Now for a large number of contestants—say eighteen or thereabouts—to play every opponent in a day is of course impossible. The method suggested, therefore, is to modify this by dividing the players into divisions of four, five, or six apiece, and then making every player in each separate division meet all his opponents. The winners of the respective divisions then compete for the prizes upon either the American system or the English system of "rounds." To give an example. Let us suppose there are eighteen players: Divide these by lot into three divisions of six each. In each division there will be the following rounds:—

St. James's Gazette, 16 August 1883, 6.

1st round.	A plays B:	C plays D:	E plays F.
2nd round.	A " C:	B " E:	D " F.
3rd round.	A " D:	B " F:	C " E.
4th round.	A " E:	B " D:	C " F.
5th round.	A " F:	B " C:	D " E.

The three who score the greatest number of wins in the three divisions will then do battle for the prizes. Let us call them X, Y, and Z.

X plays Y: X plays Z: Y plays Z.

And the prizes can be awarded according to their wins. By using this arrangement every one who enters for the tournament is certain of having five matches at least, and of getting a good day's sport; and although, of course, fortune may possibly place the best competitors or pairs in the same division, those who are next but one to the winners will not find themselves idle after their first round through having met and succumbed to the ultimate victors. If necessary a "consolation prize" can be given, to be competed for by the second best in each division.

It may be urged that the system is too complicated to work successfully. I do not think the difficulty is a real one. Upon the notice-board or upon a large sheet of paper can be placed first a plan like that given above, and then a key like the following:—

First Division.	Second Division.	Third Division.
A. Mr. Smith	A. Mr. ———	A. Mr. ———
B. Mr Jones	B. Mr. ———	B. Mr. ———
C. Mr. Robinson	C. Mr. ———	C. Mr. ———
D. Mr. Brown	D. Mr. ———	D. Mr. ———
E. Mr. White	E. Mr. ———	E. Mr. ———
F. Mr. Black	F. Mr. ———	F. Mr. ———

If the tournament is a double-handed one the names of the pairs can be filled in similarly. The competitors can then play off their own rounds without any further drawings of ties and without consulting the badgered secretary. I may add that the system has been tried and found to work successfully in practice.—I am, Sir, your obedient servant,

PHAYLLUS.

10. Lawn Tennis (by East Sheen L.T.C.)

[1883: Colindale]

❦

To the Editor *of the* St. James's Gazette.

Sir,—I was much interested in reading a letter which appeared in your issue of yesterday signed "Phayllus." Your correspondent gave an accurate description of a method of playing tournaments which has been tried in several clubs with success to my knowledge; but I do not think he carried his letter quite far enough. The difficulty which has beset secretaries in trying to work tournaments of this class (which, by the way, are generally known among lawn-tennis players in our neighborhood as tournaments on the Weybridge principle) has been to apply the principle to tournaments where the entries are not received, or the pairs drawn, till the players come on to the ground on the day of the tournament. The problem can be successfully solved by an extended application of the algebraic signs on which the system is based. If the secretary works out on the day preceding the tournament the order in which the pairs ought to meet in the different rounds, utilizing symbols such as the A B C, etc., suggested by "Phayllus" and then makes a neat copy of it, it becomes a very simple matter to draw the pairs at haphazard, to divide them into batches of not more than six pairs, and to place the reference symbol before the names of the pairs even on the morning of the tournament. At our last tournament this plan was found to work admirably, though none of the players had had any experience of it.

Another point not alluded to by "Phayllus" is as to the mode in which the scores of the different pairs in each division should be kept. I have found that by making three or four copies of the

St. James's Gazette, 18 August 1883, 5–6.

sketch-plan, and giving one to some player in each division who knew the game, an accurate score could be kept, though the names of the couples did not appear. Thus A beat B by 64–63 in the first division, though unintelligible to persons who did not know what A and B meant, is a simple means of making a note of the fact that Mr. Jones and Miss Smith in the first division beat Mr. Brown and Miss Robinson by six games to four and six to three.

One last word as to the number of sets each pair should play with the other. In deciding this, the secretaries should remember that most people prefer to play the best of three sets, even though the sets are short ones. My own experience is that where a large number of couples are entered three sets of seven games each suit most players; but allowance should in all cases be made for the length of time the tournament is expected to occupy, the weather, etc.—I am, Sir, your obedient servant,

EAST SHEEN L.T.C.

August 17.

11. Lawn Tennis

[1883: LCH 145: Colindale]

❧

To the Editor *of the* St. James's Gazette.

Sir,—I am glad to see, in the letters of "Phayllus" and "East Sheen L. T. C.," which appeared in your columns on August 16 and 18, signs that opinion is changing as to the best form of tournament, and that two *desiderata,* which the present form fails to supply, are beginning to be recognized, namely (almost in the words of "Phayllus"), "that the best players shall take the prizes, and that all the players shall be occupied the greater part of the time, and not be forced to look on idly if they have lost their match in the first round." The "American," or "Weybridge," form, which they advocate, though a great improvement on the existing one, yet labours under two defects. One is, the pairing together of players whose rival claims have been already *virtually* decided. When A has been beaten by B, and B by C, a match between A and C is surely a foregone conclusion, since we may fairly assume that their relative skill is the same to-day as it was yesterday. If not—if it be held that one night may make such a difference that A may now beat C—why not apply the same principle to A and B, and thus prolong the tournament *in sæcula sæculorum?* The other defect is the breaking up the whole set of players into several independent tournaments, and letting the winners in the respective divisions contend among themselves for the prizes—thus making it possible (as I showed in my letter of August 4) for the four prizes, in a tournament of thirty-two, to be won by the 1st, 17th, 9th, and 25th best players.

If these superfluous contests were omitted, there would then be plenty of time for all to play in one grand tournament; and the

St. James's Gazette, 21 August 1883, 5–6.

American system, minus these two defects, will be found to be identical with the system I advocated in your columns on the 4th of August, in a letter since published by Messrs. Macmillan as a pamphlet, enlarged and with a full account of a tournament of thirty-two players.

It will not be long, I hope, before the "American" system, with these necessary modifications, supplants the present one, under which, though a first prize may fairly be placed among those won by rowing or running, yet a second prize has very little more right to such a position than if it had been won in a raffle.—I am, Sir, your obedient servant,

CHARLES L. DODGSON.

August 19.

12. The Science of Betting

[1866: LCH 55: Colindale]

The letter was reprinted in *The Times* on 20 November 1866.

❦

To the Editor *of the* Pall Mall Gazette.

Sir,—The magical system of betting, the secret of which Messrs. H. and J. Smith offer to the world on such reasonable terms, has probably been known, and practised, ever since betting has been in existence. It is applicable to almost every event on which bets are made, and it may be mathematically demonstrated that, provided all the bets are paid, winning is a certainty. I chanced upon the principle myself some years ago, and, in the hope that it may serve to deter some from throwing away their money, I now beg to offer it to your readers gratis.

The rule may be stated thus:—"Write all the possible events in a column, placing opposite to each the odds offered against it: this will give two columns of figures. For the third column add together the odds in each case, and find the least common multiple of all the numbers in this column. For the fourth column divide this least common multiple by the several numbers in the third column. For the fifth and sixth columns multiply the original odds by the several numbers in the fourth column. These odds are to be given, or taken, according as the sum total of the sixth column is greater or less than the least common multiple." The last two columns give the *relative amounts* to be invested in each bet.

An example will make this clear. Suppose that in a race about

Pall Mall Gazette, 19 November 1866, 3.

	1		2	3	4	5		6
A.	2	to	3	5	12	24	to	36
B.	4	to	1	5	12	48	to	12
C.	5	to	1	6	10	50	to	10
D.	9	to	1	10	6	54	to	6
The Field. .	14	to	1	15	4	56	to	4

to be run there are four horses in the betting, the odds being 3 to 2 *on* the favourite, which is equivalent to 2 to 3 *against.* The least common multiple of the third column is 60, and the sum total of the last 68, and as this is *greater* than 60, the odds in this case are all to be *given* in the *relative* amounts given in the fifth and sixth columns. Suppose, for example, that I multiply these columns by 10, and make the bets in pounds; that is, I *take* £360 to £240 on A., I *give* £480 to £120 against B., and so on. Now suppose C. to win the race; in this case I lose £500, and win £(360 + 120 + 60 + 40) = £580. It will be found on trial that I win the same sum, £80, in each of the five events.

If all betting men tried to work this system, they would either be all offering odds or all taking odds on each event, and so no bets could be made. But the fact that this system of winning is *ever* possible arises from the odds being unevenly adjusted, so that they do not represent the real chances of the several events. Supposing this system to be applied only in cases where the odds were evenly adjusted, the sum total of the sixth column would always be equal to the least common multiple, and thus, whether the odds were given or taken, the concluding entry in every betting-book would be "Gain = Loss – Nil"—a most desirable result.—I am, Sir, your obedient servant,

CHARLES L. DODGSON.

Mathematical Lecturer, Christ Church, Oxford, Nov. 15, 1866.

13. The Science of Betting

[1866: LCH 159a: Colindale]

This item addresses a computational error in the original letter. A similar corrective note also appeared in the *Pall Mall Gazette* on 20 November 1866.

❦

TO THE EDITOR OF THE TIMES.

Sir,—As you have thought my communication to the *Pall-mall Gazette* on the above subject worth republishing in your columns, will you allow me to correct a mistake in the arithmetical example? It should stand thus:—

	1.	2.	3.	4.	5.	6.
A	2 to 3		5	6	12 to 18	
B	4 to 1		5	6	24 to 6	
C	5 to 1		6	5	25 to 5	
D	9 to 1		10	3	27 to 3	
The Field	14 to 1		15	2	28 to 2	

The least common multiple of the third column is 30, not 60. The truth of the rule is not affected by this, as any common multiple would serve the purpose.

I am, Sir, your obedient servant,

CHARLES L. DODGSON.

Christ Church, Oxford, Nov. 20.

The Times, 21 November 1866, 10.

Proportional Representation

20, ARLINGTON STREET.
S.W.

May 21. 81.

Dear Mr. Dodgson

Many thanks for your letter & its enclosure. I have never seen your proposal before. It has been suggested, in order to attain the same end that all elections should be on one day. But that proposal would have the inconvenience of partially disfranchising those who have votes in more than one constituency. Your idea would be free from that objection.

Yours very truly

Salisbury

Letter from Lord Salisbury to Dodgson, 21 May 1881, acknowledging the receipt of Dodgson's letter on "Purity of Election" (item 14), published in the St. James's Gazette, *and praising it as superior to another approach to the same problem.*

Introduction

Beginning in 1881, Dodgson turned his interest in voting theory away from the local Oxford scene to the wider stage of general elections in Britain. Between 1881 and 1885 he wrote eleven letters and articles (items 14, 15, 17, 20, 21, 22, 24, 26, 27, 29, and 33) to the *St. James's Gazette* on aspects of this subject, particularly proportional representation and redistribution, provoking and responding to letters by others with equally strong views (items 16, 18, 19, 23, 25, and 28).[1] His research on the topic culminated in the pamphlet *The Principles of Parliamentary Representation* (1884) and the *Supplement* and *Postscript to Supplement* (1885) that followed it (items 30, 31, and 32).

Dodgson's interest in proportional representation can be linked directly to his work on the Governing Body of Christ Church, particularly to the problem of electing four members to a newly created Electoral Board that would be responsible for appointing students. On 17 May 1882 he wrote in his diary,

> The question came on in the Governing Body Meeting as to a mode of taking votes for the 'Electoral Board' of four, which, by the new Ordinance, we have to elect. I proposed a scheme, devised while lying awake last night, the principal object of which was to enable a minority to get *one* member in. It was, in essence, to let everyone give *four* votes, all to one candidate or separately, and consider anyone elected who gets more than one fifth the total number of votes. My scheme was not even seconded.[2] . . . My belief is that the rejected method would be more just, in the interest of *minorities*.[3]

1. *The Lewis Carroll Handbook* and Green, "Lewis Carroll and the *St. James's Gazette*," 134–35, are the two bibliographic references for these letters, but both are incomplete. Green omitted the letters of 23 May 1882 (on cloture), 5 July 1884 (on proportional representation), and 7 August 1884 (on redistribution), leading Duncan Black to report an incorrect number for these letters in his *The Theory of Committees and Elections* (p. 190). The letter of 22 October 1884 (on redistribution) is not listed in *The Lewis Carroll Handbook*.

In his article, Green claims that a letter of 30 December 1881, "Traitors in the Camp," is on the same topic, general elections, as the letter of 4 May 1881, "Purity of Election." Black correctly notes that this is not the case, and that the former should not be listed among the letters on political topics since it concerns church matters.

2. Green, *Diaries*, 405–6.

3. Unpublished manuscript diaries.

Later in the month, Dodgson began to work on a theoretical framework to accomplish his purpose. In a long diary entry on 31 May 1882, he presented some of the possible difficulties that could arise.

> G.B. meeting. Election of Electoral Board. I suggested 2 difficulties that *might* arise, but they wd [would] not consider them—(1) If more than 4 get an absolute majority, it may easily happen that the 5th is really preferred to one of the first 4, e.g. if (mental) orders of 11 lists were
>
> | a | a | a | a | a | a | a | a | b | b | b |
> |---|---|---|---|---|---|---|---|---|---|---|
> | b | b | b | b | b | c | c | c | c | c | c |
> | c | d | d | d | d | d | d | f | f | f | f |
> | e | e | e | e | e | e | e | e | g | g | g |
>
> a gets 8 votes, b 8, e 8, c 7; and d gets 6, f 4, g 3. Here it is possible that all but 1st and 8th prefer d to e. (2) If most of voters want *one* but not *both,* of a certain two, & wd [would] vote for either rather than have neither, yet *both* may fail, unless alternative voting be
>
> | x | x | x | x | x | x | y | y | y | y | y |
> |---|---|---|---|---|---|---|---|---|---|---|
> | a | a | a | a | a | a | a | a | a | b | b |
> | b | b | b | b | b | b | c | c | c | c | c |
> | c | c | c | d | d | d | d | d | d | a | d |
>
> allowed, e.g. if all want x or y here a, b, c, d, get in with alternative voting. $\{\frac{x}{y}$ or $\{\frac{y}{x}$, we get 2 results, one if all alternatives are counted for x, the other for y—In each case a, b, c get in, & a new voting is wanted betw [between]—x & y—Neither of my difficulties occurred in voting. . . .[4]

On 10 June a special meeting of the Governing Body was held for the election of Studentships and University Readers. Dodgson commented on the mode of taking votes at this meeting in his diary that day.

Back on 4 May 1881, writing as Lewis Carroll, Dodgson had published his first letter relating to voting theory, titled "Purity of Election" (item 14). In it, writing in a humorous vein at the outset, he commented that the

4. Unpublished manuscript diaries. In alternative voting, if no candidate obtains a majority, then the successive elimination of the candidates with the fewest first place votes will produce a majority winner.

Ballot Act of 1872, which required secret voting in conducting general elections, had been successful in reducing the bribery that had been rampant before. He then took up the issue of individual voters wishing to cast votes for the winning side once it has become clear which side is going to win, calling it evil and describing the harm it could cause. To ensure that the late votes of constituencies are as independent as those cast on the first day, Dodgson advocated keeping the results of the election secret until all the voting ends. Ultimately, Parliament did act on this proposal and passed it, but not until 1917.

This letter was solicited by Frederick Greenwood, the editor of the *St. James's Gazette.* Dodgson wrote in his diary on 16 April 1881, "Mr. Greenwood approves my theory about General Elections (that the *results* should all be announced at once), and wants me to write on it in *The St. James's Gazette.*"[5] Dodgson wrote the letter on 28 April: "Spent the afternoon in composing the letter Mr. Greenwood wants me to write, advocating my theory about General Elections."[6] On the 29th, he finished the letter and sent it off. On 5 May he remarked in his diary that it had appeared in the newspaper, and on the 19th he wrote, "Received from Mr. Greenwood fifty copies of my letter on 'Purity of Election' and sent off a number of copies—to Gladstone, Lord Salisbury, etc."[7]

On the same day that he wrote to Lord Salisbury, enclosing this letter, he expressed his view that the subject of sealed votes "appears to me to be a matter of really national importance: and I feel that, in urging a change, I am writing neither in Conservative nor Liberal, but in British interests."[8] Although Dodgson's political beliefs strongly favored the Conservative party, his purpose in writing this letter and indeed all of his pamphlets on elections, was not influenced by any political bias.

Lord Salisbury acknowledged receiving the enclosure two days later, remarking that he had never seen his proposal (sealed votes) before, and that it was a better one than another that had been suggested—to have elections held on just one day, which would partially disenfranchise those who vote in more than one constituency.[9]

The next letter (item 15) appeared almost a year later, on 23 March 1882, and addresses a very different issue, *cloture,* or closure, which gave

5. Green, *Diaries,* 395.

6. Unpublished manuscript diaries.

7. Green, *Diaries,* 396.

8. Cohen, *Letters,* 429.

9. Salisbury to Dodgson, 21 May 1881, Berol Collection, item 262, Section VII, p. 224. Plural voting, as voting in more than one constituency was known, applied to estate owners who could not be registered in the borough (urban constituency) where their property was located. They were able to vote both in the borough as well as in the county of the borough. See Charles Seymour, *Electoral Reform in England and Wales* [*1915*]: *The Development and Operation of the Parliamentary Franchise 1832–1855* (Hamden, Conn.: Archon Books, 1970), 272–73.

the House of Commons the right to close debate on an issue and then to vote on it immediately afterward. The bill allowing cloture was enacted in February 1882. Dodgson explained his concern in a diary entry on the same date: "My letter—raising the question whether the Resolution to have 'Cloture' voted by a bare majority can be carried legitimately by the same bare majority—appeared in the *St. James's Gazette.*"[10] Pointedly and somewhat humorously, Dodgson attacks both the propriety and the logic of cloture. The issue Dodgson questions is whether the majority of the House of Commons can legally close debate when the minority wishes to keep debate open, first by passing a regulation giving itself that right, and then executing the right.

LETTERS ON PROPORTIONAL REPRESENTATION

Two years passed before Dodgson actively addressed the vexing proportional representation problem. The event that brought him back to this issue may have been the campaign by the Proportional Representation Society, founded on 16 January 1884 by Sir John Lubbock (1834–1913), M.P., to establish proportional representation in Britain. The idea of proportional representation, first proposed in the eighteenth century, did not take hold in England until the second half of the nineteeth century. In 1883 it became involved with the redistribution issue. Redistribution forced a choice between "equal" (redrawn) electoral districts and proportional representation as the mechanisms to achieve the goal of fair representation.

Dodgson participated in a lively exchange of views in the *St. James's Gazette,* publishing five letters from 15 May 1884. The letters and the debate itself are shadowed by many entries in his diary. On 2 May Dodgson wrote in his diary that he spent the previous afternoon doing calculations with Robert Edward Baynes (1849–1921), Student and Tutor at Christ Church, in connection with proportionate representation. And on the 15th he wrote, "My letter on 'Proportionate Representation' appeared in the *S. James' Gazette*—An article by Sir J. Lubbock was in the *Daily News* this morning, in which he talks of the chance of the wrong man coming in on their system as 'microscopical' & 'infinitesimal.' In my instance it exceeds ½!"[11]

Sir Lubbock's letter (item 16) appeared in the *Daily News* (London) on 15 May 1884. In it Lubbock argued the merits of the single transferable vote and explained the scheme for employing it in detail. The principle of proportional representation using the single transferable vote, first sug-

10. Green, *Diaries,* 405.

11. Unpublished manuscript diaries.

Sir John Lubbock (1834–1913).

gested by Thomas W. Hill in 1821, was put forward by Thomas Hare (1806–1891) after the general election in 1857. In this system a voter can indicate his first, second, and subsequent preferences. When a candidate receives the necessary quota of votes, he is declared elected, and any surplus votes he obtained will be transferred, in the voters' orders of preference, to the candidates who have failed to achieve the quota. Lubbock denied there is any significant element of chance in the method and gave an example showing the chances that the "wrong" candidate would be elected is 2000 to 1.

Thomas Hare (1806–1891), by Lowes Cato Dickinson, 1867.

The quota originally proposed by Hare to ensure that each of two parties will obtain its proportion of seats in relation to the number of votes it receives in an election, $\frac{\text{total votes}}{\text{total seats}}$, appears to be better than the quota ultimately adopted, the Droop quota, the next integer above $\frac{\text{total votes}}{\text{total seats} + 1}$, because it uses every vote cast to fill a seat. But the Droop quota produces a smaller quota to win a seat, enabling more seats to be allotted to the parties at the first distribution of votes. An example will make this point clear.

Suppose there are 1,400 votes distributed between two parties in the ratio 18⁄17, the district has seven seats, and each of the two parties puts up four candidates to fill these seats. Assume the results for the candidates $a_1 - a_4$; $b_1 - b_4$ are:

	Party A		*Party B*
a_1	230	b_1	180
a_2	210	b_2	170
a_3	200	b_3	168
a_4	80	b_4	162
	720		680

Using the Hare quota, 1400⁄7 = 200, party *A* has 40 votes to transfer to other candidates who need them: 30 from a_1 and 10 from a_2. However, these are not sufficient to prevent a_4 from being eliminated. So party *A*, the one with greater support, can win only three of the seven seats.

Using the Droop quota, (1400⁄8) + 1 = 176, party *A* has 112 votes to transfer: 54 from a_1, 34 from a_2, and 24 from a_3, enough to elect a_4.

In this example, party *B*'s overrepresentation when the Hare quota is used happens because the distribution of the votes among its four candidates is more uniform. The general implication is that the single transferable vote used with the Hare quota can give the party having less support more seats than the party with more support if the former is able to exercise sufficient control over its supporters so that they will divide their votes evenly among the party's candidates, and the latter allows its supporters more freedom to decide which candidates to vote for. It is precisely this issue that Dodgson will confront in *The Principles of Parliamentary Representation* (item 30) later that year.

The system based on the single transferable vote enjoyed wide support among advocates of proportional representation. How the method worked, however, was not so clear to the voter. In a letter to the *St. James's Gazette,* dated 19 December 1884, a correspondent signing himself as "J.K.S." asked,

> How do you prevent the element of chance from playing an important part in the elections of members? . . . Each elector votes first for the candidate he wants most; next for the candidate he wants second most . . . and so on. Any candidate who gets a certain quota of votes is elected . . . no candidate is to have more than the quota of votes. If an elector's first, first two, first three, or other votes is or are of no use, either because the candidate to whom it is given has his quota without it or because he cannot attain his quota even with it, then the second, third, fourth, or later vote of such elector becomes his efficient and registered vote, and goes to the credit of the candidate to whom it is given. . . . How are you to determine whether candidate A, to whom you and I give our first votes, shall utilize my vote, which sets free a vote for candidate B, or your vote, which sets free a vote for candidate C? By chance?[12]

In the first letter titled "Proportionate Representation" (item 17), published on 15 May 1884, Dodgson criticized the system of voting advocated by the Proportional Representation Society on two grounds: it is vulnerable to cheating by the teller, and it is flawed in that an unsuccessful candidate (among three candidates, two of whom are to be elected) can gain a majority of votes over a successful candidate. In the example he provided, Dodgson showed that the transfer of votes contains an arbitrary element that can bring in the wrong candidate.

Dodgson claims correctly that in the transfer of surplus votes, the voters' preference orders are handled in different ways. For example, if a voter's preferred list of candidates is *a, b, c,* and *a* is elected without surplus votes, then the votes for his next preferred candidate, *b,* do not count. On the other hand, if *a* is eliminated, then his votes for *b* will count. Should *a* be elected with a surplus of votes, these transferred votes will count but have a lower value.

A published response to his letter, duly noted by Dodgson in his diary on 16 May, came from Arthur Cohen (1829–1914), M.P., a high honors graduate in mathematics of Magdalene College, Cambridge University, and one of Britain's distinguished members of the Inner Temple (item 18). Cohen took Dodgson's example and by assuming that a voter indeed wishes his surplus votes to be transferred to his second preferred candidate in the same ratio given by the voter's initial preference order, vindicated the single transferable vote method.

William Carr Sidgwick (1834–?), an acquaintance of Dodgson's from their student days, a member of Lincoln's Inn, and a former lecturer in political economy at Oriel College, Oxford, also wrote a response pub-

12. *St. James's Gazette,* 19 December 1884, p. 6.

lished on 17 May to Dodgson's criticism of the method of transferring votes (item 19). Titled "Sir John Lubbock's Scheme," Sidgwick's letter correctly gave the view that Dodgson's argument in his example produces an outcome that is not in the interests of proportional representation. Alluding to Lubbock's letter, Sidgwick claimed that Dodgson's method will indeed elect a candidate whom the majority of electors do not desire, but he stated that is the intent of the scheme supported by the Proportional Representation Society.

Dodgson wrote in his diary on 17 May that he replied to Mr. Cohen's letter. His answer to the criticisms of both Cohen and Sidgwick appeared in a letter published on 19 May, titled "Proportionate Representation" (item 20). He quickly dismissed Sidgwick's argument but would return to it in his next letter. To counter Cohen's reasoning he developed further the example he gave in his first letter; he made the point that 6,400 voters want A and B to be returned, while only 5,599 voters want to have A and C elected. Dodgson's reasoning includes the *second-place* preferences in the lists headed by A, i.e., B is preferred to C by 5,000 of the 8,000 electors, and C is preferred to B by 3,000 of the 8,000 electors. Cohen's reasoning includes only the first-place preferences which accounts for his totals of 3,900 votes for B and 4099 votes for C, while Dodgson's totals are 6,400 for B and 5,599 for C.

In this next letter of the same title published on 27 May (item 21), Dodgson presented his method of voting, the one he gave in the examples in his letters of 15 and 19 May, in the same degree of detail that Lubbock had in laying out the scheme supported by the Proportional Representation Society and their allies. In contrast to the methodology of the single transferable vote, Dodgson's scheme can be executed as an algorithm, thereby removing the element of chance he found objectionable in the single transferable vote. Moreover, Dodgson claimed that his method (in a two-party system) allows the minority of voters to elect a fair share of candidates, while at the same time, in the case of electing one of two candidates, the majority of voters is guaranteed to return their preferred candidate. It seems that Sidgwick's criticism, which Dodgson considered to be a misunderstanding of his method, motivated this letter.

A few days later, on 29 May, Dodgson reported in his diary that he had made a discovery that would make representation more fair in the case of members of the House of Commons representing widely different constituency sizes. He also built in a factor reflecting the size of the vote given to the member by the electorate by subtracting the votes against him.

> A new plan for 'Proportionate Representation' occurred to me yesterday, and I have now worked it into a very hopeful shape. It is to have *one* Member only for each constituency, & to give him voting-

> power in the House, as follows—if he has 'a' supporters, & 'b' vote for next man (or, if he is sole candidate, agst [against] him), his power = $^{(2a-b)}/_{1000}$, taking integer nearest to this, unless it be $<\frac{1}{2}$, when power must be '1'.[13]

Several days later, on 2 June 1884, Dodgson concluded that his new plan will not work.

> I have come to the conclusion that varied voting-power will not do—It would require (if we give all Libs [Liberals] equal power, & D°, [ditto] for all Cons. [Conservatives]) that each man's power shd [should] vary *inversely* as the no. of members of his party, wh [which] wd [would] never be endured. And it wd [would] not mend matters to divide the total voting-power of the party in other proportions amongst its members—The best plan seems to be to give each district one member for every m electors in it, & to use the Society plan, modified as I have suggested. (m = No. of electors in Kingdom divided by No. of members in House).[14]

The next day he reported another new plan.

> Concocted a new 'Proportional Representation' scheme, far the best I have yet devised, & sent the M.S. to Mr. Greenwood, to add to a letter now in print. The chief novelty in it is the giving to each candidate the power of transferring to any other candidate, the votes given for him.[15]

A day later Dodgson had the idea to incorporate his new scheme in an article. "Wrote a new version of above scheme, wh [which] I hope Mr. Greenwood will print as an *article:* it is too long for a letter—4th letter appeared."[16]

Dodgson's fourth letter actually appeared on 5 June. He was still not satisfied with his arguments against the single transferable vote presented in his three previous letters. In this letter, also titled "Proportionate Representation" (item 22), he now wanted to show just how wrong-headed that method was by providing an example illustrating that in a contest involving five candidates—three to be returned, where four of the five belong to one party—the single transferable vote elects the single candidate of the Conservative party over the third preferred candidate of the Liberal party, even though this candidate is in a preference list receiving 10,160 votes compared to 7,999 votes for the Conservative candidate. This example became the core of chapter III, section 3 on the method for preventing

13. Unpublished manuscript diaries. 14. *Ibid.*
15. *Ibid.* An abbreviated entry is in Green, *Diaries,* 426.
16. *Ibid.*

John Bright (1811–1889), by Walter William Ouless, 1879.

the waste of votes in his pamphlet, *The Principles of Parliamentary Representation* (item 30), that appeared in October.

Sidgwick was not put off by Dodgson's latest gambit. In a letter dated 6 June (item 23), he reaffirmed the superiority of the single transferable vote in protecting minorities, reiterating its advantage in permitting smaller minorities to win, as it does in Dodgson's example. The reference Sidgwick makes is to John Bright (1811–1889), M.P., a member of Gladstone's cabinet, one of the country's elder statesmen, and a frequent speaker on electoral reform. The last line of this letter contains an inversion error, and it should read, "try to get three out of four."

On 9 June 1884 Dodgson reported in his diary that Greenwood had agreed to print his scheme for parliamentary elections as an article, but wanted him to abridge it; the next day Dodgson sent a condensed version of the piece to Greenwood.

THE REFORM BILL: REPRESENTATION AND REDISTRIBUTION

The Reform Bill, introduced by the Liberal Prime Minister Gladstone in 1884, would, like the previous bills of 1832 and 1867, extend the franchise, in this instance to agricultural workers and miners. It would thereby increase the electorate from 2,618,453 to 4,380,540, a 67 percent increase. In addition to the effect the extension of the franchise would have on the balance of voting between the Liberal and Conservative parties in England, proportional representation and redistribution were important for another reason. The franchise extension would apply to Ireland and Scotland as well, and there was concern over an increase in the number of seats that might be given to those who favored home rule in Ireland.

The Reform Bill had passed the House of Commons late in June only to be stalled in the House of Lords early in July over an amendment requiring an accompanying redistribution of the seats in the House of Commons. The complications caused by debating the two issues in tandem delayed resolution until December, and redistribution did indeed become separated from the extension of the franchise. The latter became law on 6 December 1884; the former was not enacted until 25 June 1885, with the next general election taking place the following November.

In his diary entry of 5 July Dodgson announced that his article (item 24) on "Parliamentary Elections," which addressed issues of representation in the House of Commons that were raised by the Reform Bill, had appeared in the *St. James's Gazette* that day. Five days later, Dodgson wrote that Arthur Cohen, who earlier had misunderstood his objection to the single transferable vote, approved his article.

Dodgson presented five principles that he believed would ensure that the two political parties, the Liberals and the Conservatives, would be properly represented in the House of Commons. Of these, the first three are the most significant for proportional representation. The first is that each member should represent the same number of voters, which would be the case if each district had several members and their number was proportional to the number of voters in the district. In the second, the minority of the two parties in each district should be represented properly, which would happen if each voter had just one vote to cast and each district had the same Droop quota. In the third principle Dodgson took up the issue of surplus votes that he and the proportional representation advocates had debated in the earlier letters. He alluded to his letter of 27 May that refuted the single transferable vote where the voter determines how the surplus will be used. He did not suggest the use of his algorithmic method from that letter, but instead offered the novel idea of "clubbing"—that the candidate who has been returned should decide which of the other candidate(s) will have his surplus votes. It appears that Dodgson found his algorithmic approach wanting, because in principle 3.b he stated that he knew of no fixed rule for handling surplus votes in all cases.

In the fourth and fifth principles, Dodgson addressed the need to simplify the election process because the proposed extension of the franchise will bring in "voters of the very narrowest mental calibre" (p. 159). In all likelihood, this is the reason Dodgson abandoned the preferential voting schemes of the pamphlets he published in the 1870s. He now favored the mechanism of the single vote, followed by clubbing, to handle the surplus votes, a process he had described in principle 3.c.

On 6 July, the Conservatives in the House of Lords introduced an amendment to the Reform Bill requiring a complete redistribution of the seats in the House of Commons. On 8 July Dodgson wrote to Lord Salisbury, "How I wish the enclosed [Parliamentary Elections article] could have appeared as *your* scheme! . . . That *some* such scheme is needed, and much more needed than *any* scheme for mere redistribution of electoral districts, I feel sure."[17]

On the 9th, Lord Salisbury replied to Dodgson's letter of the previous day stating, "[S]ome such scheme having this object in view [proportional representation] is much needed I am fully convinced. . . . Anything which is absolutely new, & not a mere patch, has a poor chance—however Conservative its object & tendency may be."[18]

Dodgson responded immediately, first congratulating Lord Salisbury

17. Cohen, *Letters,* 544n.

18. Salisbury to Dodgson, 9 July 1884, Berol Collection, item 265, Section VII, p. 224.

on his speech and successful handling of the debate attaching a redistribution requirement to the Reform Bill. But then he added forcefully, "[*P*]*lease* don't call my scheme for Proportionate Representation a 'Conservative' one! . . . *all* I aim at is to secure that, *whatever* be the proportions of opinions among the Electors, the *same* shall exist among the Members. Such a scheme may at one time favour one party, at one time another: just as it happens. But really it has *no* political bias of its own."[19] The letters that follow reflect this new concern with redistribution in the parliamentary representation problem.

On 9 July 1884, a writer using the initials "F.R.C." published a letter, "Justice to London" (item 25), referring to the article that had appeared on 14 March 1884 titled "Justice to England," which examined the proportionate number of members in Parliament for England and for Wales, Scotland, and Ireland. Using the same criteria of population and property values, F.R.C. took a closer look at the distribution of seats for metropolitan boroughs, great towns, smaller towns, and urban and rural districts; he then claimed that the province of London, at this time holding 5 percent of the voting power in the House of Commons, should have in any new distribution of seats more than twice that percentage.

Lord Salisbury, as leader of the Conservative opposition to Gladstone's government, was insistent that redistribution should accompany the extension of the voting franchise. Joseph Chamberlain (1836–1914), M.P., at this time president of the Board of Trade under Gladstone, used the humorous metaphor of a shower of new voters, requiring an umbrella for protection, to deride Salisbury for his stand.

In a letter published on 7 August 1884, signing himself as the correspondent "Dynamite" (item 26), Dodgson borrowed Chamberlain's metaphor and turned it around to show that it actually supported Salisbury and the Conservative party. Dodgson referred to Bright, who was one of the main speakers at a large meeting of Liberals held in support of the Reform Bill in Manchester on 26 July. Dodgson reported the publication of this letter in a diary entry of 7 August 1884:

> My letter (signed "Dynamite") on Mr. Chamberlain's metaphor of the shower-bath, appeared in the *St. James's* [in the column 'Notes']. It was the first time, that I can remember, when I have written a letter straight off for print, and not even corrected it.[20]

On 11 October 1884, Dodgson published an article titled "Redistribution" in the *St. James's Gazette* (item 27). He had referred to the writing of this article and its publication four times in his diary, on 23 and 24 September and on 6 and 11 October.[21]

19. Cohen, *Letters,* 544–45.

20. Green, *Diaries,* 428.

21. *Ibid.,* 429.

Joseph Chamberlain (1836–1914).

Referring to his earlier article on proportional representation, which sets out the principles for assigning to the two parties the proper number of members in each district, he now took up the other half of the issue, redistribution: how to determine how many members each district should have. He hoped that his apportionment scheme would be the core of the anticipated redistribution. First he addressed the issue of deciding how the number of electors in a district would be determined, opting for some formulas that can assign relative weights to the district's voters, value of property, and town vs. country location. Once this was done (he does not supply the formulas), the number of electors would be determined.

Using three tables, Dodgson argued that in deciding the next question, how many members to assign to each district, the best outcome occurs if there are fewer districts, with the result that more members are assigned to each district, and each elector has a smaller number of votes. Referring to Table III, in a district with ten members, each voter having one vote, just 9 percent of the voters are unrepresented (because their votes would not count in the outcome). Dodgson used this percentage to measure the degree of representation achieved; the lower the percentage of unrepresented voters, the higher the degree of representation.

Next, Dodgson presented a formula based on a uniform quota (a constant) to determine the number of members assigned to each district. This quota is a generalization of the quota he used in his earlier proportional representation letters, a variant of the Droop quota. Dodgson's form of the Droop quota, applied in small districts with a relatively large number of members, permits a political party to fill seats with a smaller number of votes than the regular Droop quota allows.

The uniform quota is $Q = E/(M + D)$, where E is the total number of electors, M the total number of members of the House of Commons, and D the number of districts. Q becomes the key element in establishing proportional representation among the districts: each member should represent the *same* number of electors.

In a letter published on 17 October 1884 titled "Redistribution by Rule of Three" (item 28), G. A. Simcox commented extensively on Dodgson's "Redistribution" article and its attractive feature of having just 9 percent of the electorate unrepresented in districts returning ten members, where each elector has one vote. One of Simcox's chief concerns with Dodgson's scheme was the weight given to the political parties rather than to the individual candidates. Simcox hoped that there might be a way to fix Dodgson's method, perhaps by applying the single transferable vote differently. He then went on to propose a scheme of his own. Why he used the term "rule of three" in the title of his method is not immediately apparent; the usual meaning of this term is that in the proportion $a/b = c/d$ any one of the four elements a, b, c, d can be found in terms of the other three, e.g., $a = bc/d$.

Dodgson responded quickly to Simcox's letter. In a short letter titled

"Redistribution" published on 22 October (item 29), he referred him to his letter of 5 July on parliamentary elections, adding that Simcox's concerns were those of proportional representation, not redistribution, and that he had already addressed these concerns in that letter. Dodgson mentioned, for the first time, that he was in the process of incorporating the letters of 5 July and 11 October in a pamphlet about to be published, and he would send Simcox a copy. (*The Principles of Parliamentary Representation* was published the next day for private distribution.)

The first publicly distributed edition of *The Principles of Parliamentary Representation* appeared on 5 November 1884. Dodgson hoped it would be in time to influence the outcome of the Reform Bill.

Dodgson made several entries in his diary relating to the publication of this pamphlet. The first was on 28 October. On 1 November he wrote, "Copies are to sent to all M.Ps. I sent one, made up of proof-sheets, a few days ago to Sir Stafford Northcote [(1818–1887), Conservative leader of the Opposition in the House of Commons]."[22]

On the next day, as he noted in his diary, he wrote to Lord Salisbury enclosing a copy of the pamphlet, adding that he had also sent one to Northcote. Dodgson expressed the hope that "the Lords will not a second time give Mr. Gladstone a chance of going into the highways with the cry—untrue though it be—'the Lords have rejected the Franchise Bill!' but will pass the Bill, *with the proviso* that it shall not come into operation while incomplete, and then 'come weal come woe' will *stand to their amendment* [Redistribution]."[23] Lord Salisbury wrote Dodgson the next day, 3 November, promising to study the pamphlet without delay.[24]

On 5 November Dodgson wrote, "At last received 50 finished copies of the pamphlet. I hope that during today & tomorrow, copies will go to all M.P's'."[25] On 17 November 1884, the day before the scheduled second reading of the Reform Bill in the House of Lords, Dodgson wrote to Lord Salisbury suggesting the right form for the redistribution amendment: "'provided that, in case a General Election should take place before a Redistribution of the Seats has been effected, it shall be conducted on the existing Franchise.'"[26] Lord Salisbury responded the next day, saying that Dodgson's form was a very good solution, and expressed his own dismay that the government chose not to adopt it.[27]

Although Dodgson had sent *The Principles of Parliamentary Representa-*

22. Green, *Diaries,* 430.

23. Cohen, *Letters,* 554.

24. Salisbury to Dodgson, 3 November 1884, Berol Collection, item 266, Section VII, p. 224.

25. Unpublished manuscript diaries. An abbreviated entry is in Green, *Diaries,* 430.

26. Cohen, *Letters,* 555.

27. Salisbury to Dodgson, 18 November 1884, Berol Collection, item 264, Section VII, p. 224. This letter is incorrectly dated 1887 in the Checklist.

tion to Salisbury, Northcote, and the members of Parliament, it had no impact because the three leaders who engineered the details of the redistribution—Salisbury in particular, Gladstone, and Sir Charles Dilke, who represented the Radical wing of the Liberal party—were not receptive to such a sea change. Salisbury thought fair representation could be achieved by having suitably drawn single-member districts so that in an election each major component of the population would be represented proportionately in the Commons. Proportional representation, which would achieve fair representation by giving the two parties seats in the Commons in proportion to the votes they received in the election, did not have support. By 18 November Salisbury was testing the waters for the adoption of the single-member principle, and on 26 November he proposed all single-member districts, with the exception of London.

The main provisions of the Redistribution Bill they put together using the 1881 census data were as follows: boroughs with a population under 15,000 and agricultural boroughs were merged with their respective counties; boroughs and counties with a population between 15,000 and 50,000 lost one seat each; and London lost two of its seats in the House of Commons. These newly available seats were to be assigned by application of a uniform rule to the new or now larger industrial and manufacturing areas in England, Wales, Scotland, and Ireland. Ireland would retain, but not increase its 101 members, and Scotland alone would gain twelve members, thereby increasing the House total to 670 seats. Except for London, twenty-three boroughs, and the universities of Oxford, Cambridge, and Trinity College (Dublin) , which retained two members, all other districts would be represented by one member. In creating these single-member districts, the Boundary Commissioners were instructed to "take note of variety [of separate interests] and in a rough manner keep like with like."[28]

This bill, emerging as it did from the negotiations of the parties' leaders, was presented to Parliament on 1 December, before the Boundary Commissioners began their work and without any information about which of its provisions benefited which party. With scanty information, members of the House were forced to either reject their leadership or unite behind the bill. Just thirty-one members supported proportional representation. The Redistribution bill was passed by the Commons on 11 May without any change in its main points and became law on 25 June 1885.

Soon after the general election in November 1885, which was the first election following the redistribution of seats in the House of Commons,

28. Andrew Jones, *The Politics of Reform 1884* (London: Cambridge University Press, 1972), 9.

Sir Stafford Henry Northcote (1818–1887), first Earl of Iddesleigh, by Edwin Long, 1882.

Dodgson wrote a letter using his pseudonym Lewis Carroll titled "Election Gains and Losses" (item 33). In it he illustrated how one can calculate the relative gain or loss experienced by the political parties in a given district resulting from the redistribution of seats.

THE SOURCES FOR "PRINCIPLES OF PARLIAMENTARY REPRESENTATION"

In the context of Dodgson's work on election theory, *The Principles of Parliamentary Representation* (item 30) is a watershed publication, bringing together ideas and theories he had explored over many years. The pamphlet is an elaboration of the points Dodgson wrote about in his two articles, "Parliamentary Elections" and "Redistribution," in the *St. James's Gazette.* Sections 2 and 3 of the second chapter and section 1 of the third chapter have their roots in the Redistribution article, while most of chapter I and sections 2, 3, and 5 of chapter III find their source in the "Parliamentary Elections" article. Material from some of the other letters is also included. The example from the letter of 5 June 1884 on proportional representation, illustrating a flaw Dodgson perceived in the single transferable vote, is found in section 3 of the third chapter; elements from his "Purity of Election" letter (4 May 1881) appear in the fourth section of this chapter. Tables I, II, and III in the article on redistribution carry over as Tables IV, V, and VI in abbreviated form, and with many entries corrected in the first section of chapter III. The origins of the theory in this pamphlet go back to the early pamphlets of the 1870s, particularly the 1873 pamphlet where Dodgson indicated that the cumulative vote (method of marks) and the method of a simple majority are equivalent, and the 1876 pamphlet where the voter preference lists give rise to consensus based on inversion to elect a Condorcet winner, one who beats every other candidate in all pairwise comparisons. Here we see the roots of the clubbing mechanism described in section 5 of chapter III. In the committee setting, elector preference schedules can be used in negotiations designed to achieve consensus.[29]

Several months after the publication of the pamphlet on parliamentary representation, Dodgson issued a *Supplement* (item 31) and a *Postscript to Supplement* (item 32). In the second of these he used a positional method

29. If we use the number of inversions required by a candidate to become a Condorcet winner to define a measure of the "closeness" of that candidate being a Condorcet winner, we can then formalize a measure of the "power" of a voting bloc to achieve this goal. A complete development of these ideas is included in Francine F. Abeles, "Power in Decisions among Multiple Alternatives," *Journal of Information and Optimization Sciences* 5 (1984), 43–48.

somewhat like the modified method of marks, the scheme he had championed in his 1873 pamphlet.

Dodgson's goals in his 1884 pamphlet are clearly stated in the principles listed in the first chapter. The proportional representation goal is fulfilled by the condition that the proportions of the political parties in the House of Commons be practically the same as in the total electorate. The goal of equitable apportionment is met by the condition that each elector should be represented by an equal fraction of a member, and that each member of the House should represent the same number of electors. Dodgson goes on to state the main principle of his method to reach the apportionment goal: to return a member to the House of Commons the number of electors in the quota should be uniform.

Dodgson was the first to show that proportional representation (assigning seats to political parties) and apportionment (allocating seats to districts) are mathematically one and the same problem. Dodgson's belief that he could reach both goals appealed to his sense of logic and to the apparent symmetry of the two problems. His apportionment method is an extraordinary one because it gives the same results as one of the six methods recognized as modern workable apportionment methods by E. V. Huntington in 1928. This method, first proposed by Thomas Jefferson (1743–1826) and independently rediscovered by Victor d'Hondt (1841–1901), a Belgian mathematician working at the University of Ghent in 1882, is the strictest of the proportional methods for a preference list system because if any list wins a seat for a given quota of votes, all other lists will win at least the number of seats as the multiple of that quota contained in its vote. Dodgson was not familiar with the work of either Jefferson or d'Hondt.

An example will make these points clear. Consider an apportionment of five members m to four districts, with the number of electors e being 110,000, 83,000, 66,000, and 41,000, respectively. Members are allocated in the numerical order (in bold) in the table below. D'Hondt's quota is the last quota for which a member is assigned, here 41,500. The second row of the table is obtained by dividing the entry in the first row by 2; the third row by dividing by 3, etc.

District 1		*District 2*		*District 3*		*District 4*
110,000	**1**	83,000	**2**	66,000	**3**	41,000
55,000	**4**	41,500	**5**	33,000		20,500
36,668		27,668				

Two seats are allotted to District 1, two to District 2, and one to District 3. District 4 is unrepresented since its number of electors, 41,000, is less than the quota, 41,500.

With Dodgson's uniform quota method in chapter II, section 3, where $E = 300{,}000$, $M = 5$, $D = 4$, and $Q = E/(M + D)$ = about 33,400 (rounded up to the next hundred), we obtain the number of members for each district using $m = (e/Q) - 1$:

2 members for District 1 (2.29);
2 members for District 2 (1.49);
1 member for District 3 (0.98);
0 members for District 4 (0.23).

For example, District 1 is allotted two members because $\frac{110{,}000}{33{,}400} - 1 = 2.29$.

As an apportionment method for proportional representation, both d'Hondt's method and Dodgson's tend to overrepresent large districts and underrepresent small ones. D'Hondt's method, and by association Dodgson's, encourages coalitions to form, thereby influencing small political parties to merge before elections, which promotes political stability. With either of these two methods, each political party is always assigned the whole number of members contained in its quota, and any changes in an apportionment will always reflect proportionately the changes in the size of the electorate. It is remarkable that of all the established methods of assigning members to districts, the only one that promotes coalition formation, allocates to each political party the integer number of members in its quota, and is robust is d'Hondt's method.[30]

These strikingly original ideas are the result of Dodgson's use of game theory to analyze elections. Informal game theoretic ideas in connection with politics circulated in Britain from the mid-1850s, but it was not until the mathematicians Ernst Zermelo (1871–1953) and John von Neumann (1903–1957) systematized them beginning in 1912 and 1928, respectively, that game theory was officially born.

Tables IV and V give the percentages of voters represented by "red" and "blue" members of the House of Commons, $6/11$ and $5/11$, respectively,

30. There are six principal apportionment methods: smallest divisors, greatest divisors (d'Hondt's method), harmonic mean, geometric mean, major fractions, and greatest remainders. For a complete analysis of Dodgson's method, see Francine Abeles, "C. L. Dodgson and Apportionment for Proportional Representation," *Ganita-Bhāratī* 3 (1981), 71–82. For a complete discussion of d'Hondt's method in the context of modern methods, see Michel Balinski and H. Peyton Young, *Fair Representation* (New Haven, Conn.: Yale University Press, 1982), ch. 12.

assuming that in any district all proportions between "red" and "blue" voters are equally probable. Why did Dodgson choose these percentages? Possibly because they were the percentages Salisbury hoped to achieve in the next general election (1885) using his proposed electoral reform of single-member districts, suitably redrawn.

Table III gives the percentage of voters necessary and sufficient to obtain the election of 1, 2, 3, etc. candidates, assuming any percentage of support for each of the two parties, with each using a minimax strategy. The actual entries are calculated from the equations on the page before. What Table III shows is that voter representation is maximized if each voter has one vote to cast in multimember districts, with districts being as large as possible. From a practical standpoint, Dodgson suggests 4- or 5-member districts, with as few 1- or 2-member districts as possible.

If we compare Tables IV and V with Table III, by first summing the entries in Tables IV and V appropriately, we see changes in about half the entries in the last columns of Table III, but no changes in the percentages of voters represented for the least number and most number of votes a voter can give, reinforcing Dodgson's conclusions.

An added benefit from this analysis is Table VI, the percentage of unrepresented voters, i.e., those voters whose votes were not used to elect the candidates, and hence were wasted. This is a useful and completely original way to judge the fairness of an electoral system.

Dodgson published a second edition of his pamphlet early in 1885. On 23 December 1884, he wrote in his diary, "I am preparing a second edition of the 'Representation' pamphlet, as I need about 150 more, to give to members of the Proportional Representation Society who are not M.P.'s."[31] In this second edition he placed the mathematical arguments in an appendix. Except for some rewriting and rearranging material, the second edition does not substantially add to the contents of the first; even the number of pages in the two is the same. There are some refinements, however, as in the first paragraph of the Preface which reads, "A System of Parliamentary Representation, and of the conduct of Elections, which shall secure, for the majority and for the minority, a due share in the government of the country, is the great *desideratum* of the day."[32]

New to the second edition is Table 1 in chapter II, giving the number of members to be assigned to a district by population. One member would be assigned to any district whose population falls between 64,000 and 107,000; ten members to a district with a population between 451,000 and 494,000. The table is an abbreviation of Table II in chapter II of the first edition (p. 184). However, in the final summary of both editions, which is

31. Green, *Diaries,* 430.

32. Charlie Lovett supplied me with a copy of this second edition.

the same, the cutoffs in the Population/Members table are different. There is also some confusion in the Index of the second edition where Table I is listed as being the same as Table VII, whereas it is only an abbreviation.

Dodgson issued the *Supplement to the Principles of Parliamentary Representation* early in February 1885, which he distributed to the members of the House of Commons and to the membership of the Proportional Representation Society. Dodgson had been considering the publication of a supplement in mid January. He wrote in his diary on the 16th, "After two days of experiments, I have at last constructed a clear crucial case of failure for the Proportional Representation Society method, which I think of circulating as a supplement to my pamphlet."[33] He referred again to the supplement in an entry on 22/23 January, and on 2 February he wrote that he had "Ordered of Baxter 1,000 copies of the supplement to *Parliamentary Representation,* to be posted to all M.P.'s, and members of the 'Prop. Rep. Soc.'"[34]

The motivation for this short piece was the publication of an article by Lord Salisbury, "The Value of Redistribution: A Note on Electoral Statistics" that appeared in October 1884 in the *National Review* (see Appendix). Here Salisbury presented his argument for the necessity of redistribution. Using statistics from the general election of 1880 to which he added assumptions based on the proposed extension of the franchise, he showed that the Conservative party, the minority of the two parties in this election, not only was underrepresented in the House of Commons by 35 to 89 Members, but that this result was due to the votes of only 2,000 electors. If redistribution were not to occur, the Conservative party would lose another 47 seats. Salisbury claimed, "The argument I have followed proceeds on the assumption that no system of distribution is completely just which does not, formally or virtually, give to the minority a representation corresponding to its actual weight."[35] However, there is no mention of proportional representation as the mechanism for redistribution. Salisbury preferred the balancing of regions dominated by one of the parties with regions dominated by the other party, in effect suggesting the plurality rule and the single-member district as the method to achieve redistribution.

In the *Supplement,* Dodgson wanted to reaffirm proportional representation and the multimember district, rather than the plurality rule and the single-member district, as the model for redistribution. So he gave his qualified support to the Society—in all aspects except the handling of sur-

33. Green, *Diaries,* 431.

34. *Ibid.*

35. Lord Salisbury, "The Value of Redistribution: A Note on Electoral Statistics," *National Review,* October 1884, 160.

plus votes. For this he provided an example showing that the clubbing method in his pamphlet is superior to the transfer of votes the Society advocated.

Leonard H. Courtney (1832–1918), M.P., a high honors graduate in mathematics from St. John's College, Cambridge University, Financial Secretary to the Treasury, and a leader of the proportional representation movement, objected to the third candidate Dodgson's method selected in the example he provided in the *Supplement* showing that of five candidates, three of whom are to be elected, the Proportional Representation Society's method elects the wrong candidate. Courtney disagreed with Dodgson's conclusion.

To justify his choice, achieved through the clubbing of votes, Dodgson issued later in February the *Postscript to Supplement,* returning to the method he used in his letters on proportionate representation of 15, 19, and 27 May and 5 June 1884 (items 17, 20, 21, and 22) to "prove" the correctness of the results of clubbing. He wrote in a diary entry of 11 February 1885 that he "Sent to Baxter the MS. of a Postscript to the Supplement to meet an objection of Mr. Courtney's."[36]

Essentially, in the *Postscript* Dodgson is using a pairwise approach in which he claims that the candidate receiving the highest number of preference votes should be returned, or elected. Using a new example, he first shows that the Society's method fails to return any candidate because with one seat left to assign, no candidate achieves the quota even after votes are transferred. Next he applies a pairwise comparison test and shows that using the Society's method (the single transferable vote) to select the third candidate results in a cyclical majority, where there can be no election.

Next in the *Postscript,* Dodgson returns to the example in the *Supplement* and applies the algorithm from his letters of 27 May and 5 June 1884. Step 2 of the algorithm selects the first preferred candidate; step 3 the second preferred candidate. Applying the algorithm to the example, (using just the first letter or two of the named candidates) where the quota to return a member is 3000 votes, *GL* is the first choice of 3,030 + 2,020 = 5,050 electors, so *GL* is returned; the pair *GL, H* is the first and second choice, in that order, of 3,030 electors; *H, GL* is the first and second choice, in that order, of 2,980 electors, a sum of 6,010 electors, so both *GL* and *H* should be returned because they have more than two quotas. Now applying step 3 of the algorithm again, this time to the second preferred candidate after *GL* on the lists that do not have *H* as the second preferred candidate, we obtain 2,020 electors who prefer *GL, C,* in that order, and 1,100 who prefer *C, GL* in that order, a total of 3,120 votes which meets the quota requirement to return *C.*

36. Green, *Diaries,* 432.

Leonard H. Courtney (1832–1918), by George Coates, 1912.

The pairing of candidates that Dodgson uses preserves the preference orders of the lists in the sense that in the two preference orders of four candidates, *BADC* and *BDAC,* the votes for *A* are valued higher in the first list, being second-place votes, whereas in the second list they are third-place votes. Clearly, this positional voting method does not necessarily return a Condorcet winner when more than one member must be returned.[37] As the table below shows (reading downward, e.g., *G* is preferred to *C* by 6,800 votes) *GL* as the first member returned is the Condorcet winner, and once he is removed from contention, *H* is the next Condorcet winner. But in the contest between *C* and *G, G* is the Condorcet winner, which probably accounts for the objection that was raised to Dodgson's choice *C* in the *Supplement.*

	C	*GL*	*G*	*H*
C		8,820	6,800	6,800
GL	1,100		790	2,980
G	3,120	9,130		9,130
H	3,120	6,940	790	

CONCLUSION

On 29 March 1885, in a list of fifteen literary projects he had on hand, Dodgson included a new edition of his pamphlet that would embody the *Supplement* (and most likely the *Postscript to Supplement* as well).[38] In November of that year, the results of the first general election held after the redistribution bill became law proved that Salisbury's method not only failed to increase the representation of the Conservative party, but gave the Liberal party almost a majority in the House of Commons—334 of 670 seats.

Perhaps the failure of the proportional representation movement in England can be attributed largely to the failure of the Proportional Representation Society to clear up the public's ignorance and confusion over the expected outcomes and the methods to achieve them. Proportional representation was thought by many to favor independent candidates and possibly threaten the two-party system. The first and second extensions of the franchise, in 1832 and 1867, had not disturbed the central features of the British government. But the 1884 extension caused uncertainty over whether the greatly enlarged electorate would transform the two major political parties. The leaders of the Proportional Representation Society

37. In any scheme using a quota less than a simple majority for selection, the Condorcet principle can apply when a candidate achieves a multiple of the quota greater than a simple majority of the electors. Positional methods are Borda's method of marks (Dodgson's modified method of marks), and the plurality method, among others.

38. Green, *Diaries,* 434. Dodgson did not produce this edition.

seemed unable to bring their message of the benefits that would accrue through proportional representation to the general population. Certainly, Gladstone's and Salisbury's need to quickly settle the redistribution question in the only way that would avoid the "'curious results' which might be expected from a matter upon which 'local preferences and partialities' dwarfed any 'well-defined principle'"[39] (i.e., going behind the backs of the members of the House of Commons) was the overriding reason for the failure of the movement.

39. Jones, *The Politics of Reform 1884*, 199.

14. Purity of Election

[1881: LCH 145]

❧

To the Editor *of the* St. James's Gazette.

Sir,—Utopia is a pleasant and a well-ordered country, and enjoys many blessings to which our little island is a stranger. Some of these must, no doubt, be by us eternally despaired of (for example, no one is ever bored at a Utopian dinner-party, or overcharged by a Utopian cab-driver). Others we may hope with fitting effort to make our own; and among these attainable prizes none seems more precious than "purity of election." Utopian electors (pardon me for mentioning so trite a fact, but we need some definite basis to begin from) are all sufficiently educated to be able to form independent opinions on the political questions of the day; and in accordance with these opinions they vote, without fear or favour. Who dares deny that this is a state of things to be wished for and striven for; and that, even though the jealous Parcæ may withhold its full fruition, still the more nearly we can attain to it the better and happier we shall be? This, then, being our goal, what are the main obstacles that beset our path—the primary well-springs of corrupt voting?

Bribery, I suppose, comes first—that subtle poison which, ever since the fatal day when Jacob sold pottage and Esau sold his birthright, has rankled in the veins of society. But every corrupt influence, which makes an elector vote on any other ground than his own unfettered judgment as to what is best for the nation, is the same in kind, if not in degree, with bribery. I say "corrupt," for I will not assert that the uneducated elector, who is simply incompetent to form an opinion of his own, is necessarily voting corruptly. It may not be, and in my opinion it is not, for the good of the nation that such a man should vote at all; still, his motives

St. James's Gazette, 4 May 1881, 4–6.

in voting may be pure. For instance, one of the candidates may be personally known to him as an exemplary private character, and though the maxim—that a statesman "can't be wrong whose life is in the right"—may be (logically) weak, it is not (morally) corrupt. Again, he may act under the advice of some wiser friend. These are not exalted motives, and they are distinctly extra-political; but they do not produce the great evil I am now considering—corrupt voting. But there is a bribery that is not to be expressed in terms of *£ s. d.;* and many a man to whom gold might be offered in vain will strain his political convictions in order to go with the stream, and will lend his voice to swell the shout of victory rather than own his allegiance to the vanquished few.

Both forms of bribery were rampant in the days of open elections. The introduction of vote by ballot has, we may hope, largely diminished both: the rogue has less chance of getting a high price for his vote now that he cannot prove that he has earned his money; nor can he certainly, however he may wish it, be on the winning side, since in many elections no one knows till all is over where the victory lies. But, though lessened for the individual voters, this evil influence—the passion for being on the winning side—still flourishes in unabated vigour as regards constituencies; and it is to this form of it that I desire to draw attention.

No thoughtful observer of the general elections of 1874 and 1880 can have failed to be struck by the way in which, when once the stream had taken a definite direction, it rolled on in ever-gathering volume, and seemed to carry with it, like straws tossed upon a flooded river, the elections of the later days. During the first day or two each little constituency felt itself an independent factor in the general result—it could do something real to swell or stem the stream; but long before the general election was over, the battle was virtually lost and won: the beaten Government was striking its camp; the late Opposition was exulting over the huge majority with which it would take office; and the unfortunate constituencies who returned their members in the last few days found they had a much humbler function to fulfil. The question no longer was "Which policy is best for the nation?" but "Which position is best for us—to swell the tide of victory, or to efface ourselves by adding a unit to a hopelessly beaten minority?"

But this is not all. The evil extends further than to the single constituency thus washed away in the high tide of popular passion: nay, it extends further than to a single general election; it constitutes a feature in our national history; it is darkly ominous for the future of England. So long as general elections are conducted as at present we shall be liable to oscillations of political power like those of 1874 and 1880, but of ever-increasing violence—one Parliament wholly at the mercy of one political party, the next wholly at the mercy of the other—while the Government of the hour, joyfully hastening to undo all that its predecessors have done, will wield a majority so immense that the fate of every question will be foredoomed, and debate will be a farce; in one word, we shall be a nation living from hand to mouth, and with no settled principle—an army whose only marching orders will be "Right about face!"

To those who recognise the existence of this evil, and who admit that it is desirable that every constituency should be as free in its choice of a member as those who elect on the first day of the general election, let me suggest a simple practical remedy. It is that the result of each single election should be kept secret till the general election is over. It surely would involve no real practical difficulty to provide that the boxes of voting-papers should be sealed up by a Government official and placed in such custody as would make it impossible to tamper with them; and that, when the last election had been held, they should be opened, the votes counted, and the results announced? It may be worth while to point out that, as regards the particular evil I am considering—the mischief done by announcing results before all is over—there is an exact parallelism between the single election, as it was before the Ballot Act, and the general election as it still is; "voters" in the one answering to "constituencies" in the other. My proposal is, in fact, that the benefits derived from secret voting, already conferred on single elections, shall be extended to their aggregate.

Let me, in conclusion, say one word to the possible objector to this new application of an accepted principle—who is saying, so far as audible speech goes, "This is indeed a Utopian scheme! These fine sentiments will not stand the rough wear of a practical age!" but whose secret soul is saying "I prefer the high-tide theory of a general election, because I fancy my pet party has more chance than the other party of being washed into power on the top of that tide!" "What I have here written," I would say to such a man, "is not meant for you. You and I have no common premisses to argue from. Between us all discussion is impossible. I have written for that insignificant and unenlightened section of society who still cling to the antiquated notion that the world we live in is the work of a Personal Being, not of a Blind Force; that from that Being each of us has received all he has of what men call power, and that to that Being each of us is finally accountable for the use he makes of the power entrusted to him."—I am, Sir, your obedient servant,

LEWIS CARROLL.

April 30.

15. Untitled Letter to the Editor

[1882: LCH 145]

This letter on cloture begins, "May I (writes Lewis Carroll). . . ." It has been partially reprinted in Green, *Diaries,* 405.

❦

May I (writes "Lewis Carroll") presume to anticipate the *Daily News* in making an announcement which will shake to its centre the whole scientific world? The *Perpetuum Mobile* is discovered! We may confidently expect that a clock will shortly be exhibited which, as often as it runs down, is able to wind itself up again. The discoverer of this marvellous principle—the mere details of construction being trifles that any watchmaker can arrange—is no less a person than Mr. Gladstone, on whose great mind it has dawned, for the first time in the world's history, that a body of men *can confer on themselves* rights, over another body of men which they do not already possess. What he says is, in effect, this:—"We, the Majority of the House of Commons, admit that we have not at present any constitutional right to close a debate against the wish of you, the Minority. We can, however, effect our object by a twofold process. First, we will propose and carry against your wish, a Resolution conferring upon us this right: secondly, we will transfer ourselves from the position of donors to that of recipients, and will proceed to exercise the right we have thus received." That is to say, Mr. Pyke will first introduce Mr. Pluck, and then Mr. Pluck, being regularly introduced, will be qualified to introduce Mr. Pyke. It will not, I hope, be deemed impertinent, while the fate of the First Resolution is yet hidden in the future, to raise the question whether the operation proposed by Mr. Gladstone is either ethically or logically possible.

St. James's Gazette, 23 March 1882, 4.

16. Proportional Representation (by Sir John Lubbock)

[1884: Colindale]

❦

You lately did me the honour of inserting an article in which I endeavoured to prove that the *scrutin de liste* system of voting is uncertain in its operation, leads to violent fluctuations in political power, and fails to secure in Parliament a true representation of the people; and that under Proportional Representation, on the contrary, the House of Commons would be a true mirror of the country, our leading statesmen would be certain of re-election, the minority in the country would be sure of a hearing in the House, and last, but not least, the majority would rule. I ended by challenging contradiction on any one of these statements; and it is perhaps not too much to say that no refutation has yet been attempted.

Surely then a system which would secure such results, which would give us a really representative Government, is worth serious study. But if no refutation of our main position has been attempted there have been expressions of opinion that our system is open to objection, mainly, I think, on three grounds, as to each of which I should be glad to say a few words, and I will take the letter signed "An Official Liberal" as a type of many others.

The objections are—1st, that it would put more power into the hands of agents and caucuses; 2ndly, that the electors would not understand it; 3rdly, that it is impracticable. As regards the first point, I will merely observe that so far from placing more power in the hands of caucuses and agents, the very reverse is the case. In fact one of the advantages of the system is just that it would free the elector from dictation, and that is, I believe, the

Daily News, 15 May 1884, 5.

true reason why our proposals have met with such bitter opposition in certain quarters. The second objection is that the electors would never be brought to understand the system. Those who write and say that they cannot understand the proposal shelter themselves (and very naturally) under the veil of anonymous signatures. It would indeed be humiliating openly to confess such extreme obtuseness. Moreover, those who bring forward this argument seem to forget that we have already two forms of proportional representation actually in operation in this country—namely, the limited vote in the three-cornered constituencies, and the cumulative vote in School Board elections. No one ever alleged that the electors had any difficulty in understanding either of these, and we might, of course, adopt one or the other of them, but many of us think that there is a better system, namely, the single transferable vote. Now, in considering the simplicity or complexity of any proposed system we must draw a broad line between that which the elector has to do, and that which devolves on the returning officer. The first cannot be too simple. But as regards the latter we are dealing with skilled and trained officials. I shall, however, hope to show that the duty imposed even on them would be simple enough, and such as even an average school boy would have no difficulty in carrying out. First then let us deal with the elector only. It is proposed that he should have one vote, but that he should be able to indicate the order of preference. Let us suppose for instance an election at Liverpool for three members, and that two Liberals and two Conservatives were in the field, each party endeavouring to secure two out of the three seats. The elector would receive his ballot paper, say, as follows:

Brown	. . . .
Jones	. . . .
Robinson	. . . .
Smith	. . . .

All he would have to do would be to place 1 and 2 in the vacant spaces opposite the names of the candidates in the order of his preference. To say that this is beyond the comprehension of the average elector is really trifling. An "Official Liberal" is presumably in favour of the Franchise Bill, and surely any "capable citizen" who is fit to express a voice on the affairs of the nation can be trusted to perform so simple an operation.

I now come to the third objection, namely, that the system is impracticable. To that objection I oppose the conclusive answer that it has been done over and over again without hitch or difficulty. The instructions to the returning officer would be somewhat as follows:

1. The returning officer shall first ascertain the total number of votes given. By a sum in simple division he can then ascertain how many votes are required to secure the election of a candidate, and this number is called the quota.

2. The returning officer shall declare all candidates who have obtained the quota elected, and shall distribute the votes given for such candidate in excess of the quota to the other candidates who have not been declared elected in the order indicated by the voters.

3. This shall be repeated till there are no candidates having more than the quota.

So far as proportional representation is concerned we might stop here. There is, however, one other evil under the present mode of voting which our system enables us, if thought desirable, to neutralise—that, namely, which arises when too many candidates of one party insist on coming forward. All that would be necessary would be the following additional clause, which, however, is, I repeat, no necessary part of our system.

4. If the number of candidates still exceed by more than one the number of vacancies, the returning officer shall declare the candidate then having the least number of votes not elected, and shall distribute the votes given for him to the other candidates not already declared elected, according to the directions, if any, given by the voter, commencing with the voting paper having the lowest registered number. The returning officer shall declare elected any candidate whose votes during such distribution reach the quota. 5. This shall be repeated until the number of candidates exceeds by one only the number of vacancies. The return-

ing officer shall then declare the candidates having the largest number of votes elected.

This will not seem complex to any one who will compare it with the duties imposed on corresponding officials under other Acts of Parliament.

One point still remains to be dealt with. It is alleged that under this system the selection of the votes to be distributed introduces an element of chance. But in the first place I must observe that there need be no elements of chance in the actual votes transferred. I believe, indeed, that in so large a number of votes as we shall have to deal with it would be practically fair to take simply the votes last counted. As a matter of fact, however, the voting papers being numbered, in our experimental election we took the voting papers bearing the highest numbers, *i.e.,* those last filled up. I should myself prefer in a real election to take those bearing the lowest numbers. In either case nothing would be left to the returning officer. But what is the extent of the chance? It has been calculated out by Mr. Andrae, and again independently by Mr. Parker Smith. Suppose a candidate A has a surplus to be distributed, and that the second votes were given equally between B and C. If the surplus is 4,000 the average difference between B and C, supposing the papers to be taken at random, would not exceed 11 votes. The chances are 2,000 to 1 that neither would gain nor lose more than 60 votes. For all practical purposes therefore this can hardly be urged as a serious objection to the system.

We do not, however, allege that the system is perfect. On the contrary, we frankly admit that there is an element of chance, though to an infinitesimal extent, not indeed in the counting but in the result. But does not chance enter to some extent into all the events of life? Are there no chances in the present system of voting? Even in this respect we maintain that our system need fear no comparison. Moreover, it must be remembered that the element of chance, microscopical as it is, lies not between candidates of different parties, but between two almost equally acceptable candidates belonging to the same party. For instance, in the case I have taken above, a vast majority of the surplus votes taken from the first Liberal candidate would be given to the second. In all ordinary elections the votes split between a Liberal and a Conservative are a very small minority of the whole. But if between two candidates there is very little to choose, and the electors are all but evenly divided, then, from a national point of view, it cannot much matter which comes in; and, indeed, under any system of voting, the result would be very much a matter of chance. Without, then, denying the existence of an infinitesimal element of chance in the system, as in all other affairs of life, I must say that *de minimis non curet lex.*

Moreover, I must once more repeat that proportional representation does not stand or fall by the single transferable vote system. Many of us think it the best, but the Limited vote and the Cumulative vote are already in operation. They have some inconveniences which might, I think, be remedied; but at any rate they do give us, though somewhat roughly, a fair representation. For my own part, however, I think it has been already shown that there is not only no insuperable, but no substantial, difficulty in the matter; and I trust that Great Britain, the mother of Parliaments, may once more take the lead among the great nations of the world by securing for herself a House of Commons which shall really represent the nation.

17. Proportionate Representation

[1884: LCH 145: Colindale]

❦

To the Editor *of the* St. James's Gazette.

Sir,—The system of taking votes advocated by "The Proportionate Representation Society" labours under a very serious defect in its application, to which the attention of all interested in the question should be directed. An instance will make this clear.

The system proposed is that each voter shall have one vote; that he shall hand in a list of candidates numbered 1, 2, 3, etc.; and that it shall be counted as a vote for his No. 1, unless that candidate has already received enough votes to secure his return, in which case it shall be counted for his No. 2. The difficulty is that it will often depend on *which* lists are thus transferred whether the one or the other of two candidates shall be returned. If the lists in which A stands as No. 1 are of two kinds, some having B as No. 2 and some C, and if there are more than enough to return A, it may easily happen that, if the transferred lists are of the first kind, B will be returned, but if of the second kind, C.

Take a town containing 11,999 voters, and returning two members: so that 4,000 votes are enough to return a member. Let there be three candidates, A, B, and C.; and let A have 8,000 supporters, 5,000 of whom take B as their No. 2, and the other 3,000 take C. Let B have 1,400 supporters and C 2,599. It does not signify whom these voters put as their No. 2, since A's return is obvious, so that the only transferred lists are those on which he is No. 1.

Now A is returned with 4,000 votes to spare. Hence, if any teller has the opportunity of seeing the lists, he can easily arrange for the 4,000 transferred lists to contain 2,600 favourable to B,

St. James's Gazette, 15 May 1884, 5.

thus securing B's return; or else to contain 1,401 favourable to C, thus securing C's return.

But let us suppose all such cheating provided against, and that it is a matter of pure chance which 4,000, of the 8,000 lists headed "A," are transferred. It is mathematically certain that the most probable event is that they will be divided between A and B in the same proportion—5 to 3—as the whole 8,000; *i.e.,* that they will contain 2,500 lists headed "A B," and 1,500 headed "A C." Hence B will get 3,900 votes, and C 4,099; and C will be elected by a majority of nearly 200 over B. But there are 6,400 voters who prefer B to C, and only 5,599 who prefer C to B: so that, as a matter of fact, the unsuccessful candidate B has a majority of 801 over the successful candidate C!—I am, Sir, your obedient servant,

CHARLES L. DODGSON.

Ch. Ch, Oxford, May 12.

18. Proportionate Representation (by Arthur Cohen)

[1884: Colindale]

❦

To the Editor *of the* St. James's Gazette.

Sir,—Mr. Charles L. Dodgson, in the very able and lucid letter inserted in your paper of yesterday, has established the following proposition:—"Take a town containing 11,999 voters and returning two members, so that 4,000 votes are enough to return a member. Let there be three candidates—A, B, and C—and let A have 8,000 supporters, 5,000 of whom take B as their No. 2 and the other 3,000 take C. Let B have 1,400 supporters and C 2,599. Let it be supposed that it is a matter of pure chance which 4,000 of the surplus votes headed A are transferred. Then the probability is that 2,500 will be transferred to B and 1,500 to C; so that B will get 3,900 votes and C 4,099, and C will be consequently elected by a majority of nearly 200 over B."

Mr. Dodgson, having established this proposition, seems to think that he has proved that a system which leads to such a result must be unfair and absurd, because, he says, there are 6,400 voters who prefer B to C and only 5,599 who prefer C to B. But is this view correct? It is not the fact that there are 6,400 voters who *simply* prefer B to C and 5,599 who *simply* prefer C to B. The truth is this: there are 8,000 voters who prefer A to B and C; and of these 5,000 desire, if their votes are not required for A, that they should be transferred to B, and 3,000 desire that under similar circumstances their votes should be transferred to C. What, then, is the fair and proper way of giving effect to the desire of the 5,000 and 3,000 voters, when there is a surplus of 4,000 votes not required for A? Surely it is by distributing the 4,000 votes

St. James's Gazette, 16 May 1884, 5.

amongst B and C in the proportion of 5,000 to 3,000. And this is, as Mr. Dodgson admits and indeed proves, what will be generally effected by the system which he has criticised. I think Mr. Dodgson has not weakened but has materially strengthened the argument in favour of the system advocated by the Proportionate Representation Society.—I am, Sir, your obedient servant,

ARTHUR COHEN.

Temple, May 15.

19. Sir John Lubbock's Scheme (by W. C. Sidgwick)

[1884: Colindale]

❦

To the Editor *of the* St. James's Gazette.

Sir,—Mr. Dodgson's ingenious argument about proportional representation is unanswerable. He demonstrates that this method will cause candidates to be elected who are not desired by the majority of the electors. He does not, however, seem to have observed that this is precisely the object with which the scheme is put forward. Those who wish the majority in each constituency to return all the members will no doubt sympathize with Mr. Dodgson's objection to a method which gives the minority their share; but I imagine Sir John Lubbock will not regard his scheme as hopelessly damaged by a neat mathematical proof that it will secure the ends at which it aims.—I am, Sir, your obedient servant,

W. C. SIDGWICK.

Reform Club, May 16.

St. James's Gazette, 17 May 1884, 6.

20. Proportionate Representation

[1884: LCH 145: Colindale]

Dodgson added a humorous postscript to this letter, including four lines of verse.

❦

To the Editor *of the* St. James's Gazette.

Sir,—Mr. Cohen may rest assured that I should never think of applying the term "absurd" to any method of voting which had his support; though I do think that its practical application may prove in some cases "unfair." The principle of the society is, in my belief, entirely right. Where the voters are divided into two parties, and where several members are to be returned, I hold that these should be divided, as nearly as possible, in the same proportion as the voters—*e.g.,* if, in a town returning four members, rather more than five-eighths of the voters were Liberals and the rest Conservatives, the Liberals ought to return *three* of the members; if rather less than five-eighths, *two.* But this principle is not applicable where only *two* issues are possible; for then one party or the other must carry the day, and a compromise is no longer possible. And the case I proposed may easily be reduced to one of this sort.

Permit me to re-state the data, adding a new but not inconsistent hypothesis. A town containing 11,999 voters is to return two members, so that 4,000 votes are enough to return a member. There are three candidates—A, B, and C: 5,000 voters say "A B," 3,000 "A C," 1,400 "B A," and 2,599 "C A." The most probable result, if the Society's method be adopted, is (as Mr. Cohen admits) to elect "A C."

St. James's Gazette, 19 May 1884, 5–6.

But this is a case where, as it appears to me, the society's method is not fairly applicable; for there are, in fact, only *two* possible issues: the 6,400 voters, though differing as to the order in which they name the candidates, agree in wishing that A and B should be the two members returned; while the other 5,599 similarly wish to return A and C. Surely in this case, where no compromise is possible, the majority ought to have their wish, rather than the minority.

That the theory "A C ought to be elected" should commend itself with exceptional force to Mr. Arthur Cohen is not to be wondered at; but when he proposes to tell the unfortunate 6,400 voters that the reason the minority are allowed to carry all before them, and to return *both* their nominees, is that this is "the fair and proper way of giving effect to the desire of the voters," and when Mr. Sidgwick adds his assurance that this method only claims "to give the minority their share (!)," I think the disappointed majority may be excused if they show some little coyness in accepting such doubtful consolation.—I am, Sir, your obedient servant,

CHARLES L. DODGSON.

Ch. Ch, Oxford, May 17.

P.S.—Mr. Sidgwick must surely have been reading the American Naturalist? "The snakes in this country may be divided into one species—the venemous." Or else he is inspired by the poet who sang:

I give thee all, I can no more,
Though small thy share may be:
Two halves, three thirds, and quarters four,
Is all I bring to thee!

21. Proportionate Representation

[1884: LCH 145: Colindale]

❦

To the Editor *of the* St. James's Gazette.

Sir,—Having put before your readers, on the 15th and 19th of May, an instance where Sir John Lubbock's method of taking votes fails to do justice, I propose now to state the additional rules needed to guard against such a result. Mr. Sidgwick has misunderstood me when he thinks it is my wish that the majority of a constituency shall return all the members, and that I object to giving the minority their share; and I think your readers are likely to misunderstand *him* when he says of me, "he demonstrates that this method will cause candidates to be elected who are not desired by the majority of the electors": what I had demonstrated was something very different, namely, that it might cause one of two issues to triumph over the other, where (no compromise being possible) it had fewer supporters than the other issue; and *that* result I am sure neither Mr. Sidgwick, nor any other supporter of the method, would desire.

It may sound a paradox to say that this method enables the *minority* to return a fair share of members, and yet always gives the preference, when the question is whether one of two members shall be returned, or one of two issues (no compromise being possible) shall be adopted, to that side which has a *majority* of votes. Yet so it is. An instance will, I hope, make this clear. Take a town containing 29,999 voters, and returning five members. And let the voters be divided into two parties (call them "red" and "blue"). According to the method, 5,000 votes are enough to return a member. The reason is that each voter has only *one* vote, and that the five candidates who get the greatest numbers of votes are returned. Hence, a "red" candidate with 5,000 votes must be among the first five, for there cannot be more than four "blue" candidates who have as many votes as he: five such would

St. James's Gazette, 27 May 1884, 5–6.

require 25,000 votes, and there are only 24,999 to be had. Again, if the "reds" can muster 10,000 votes, they can return two members, by giving them 5,000 each; for there cannot be more than three "blue" candidates who have as many: four such would require 20,000 votes and there are only 19,999 to be had. Observe that, though the "reds," being the *minority,* return two members, yet each of these has a *majority* of votes, compared with any rejected "blue" candidate.

The rules, required to complete the method, are as follows:—

(1). Divide the number of voters by the number of members to be returned, increased by one: and let *n* be the lowest whole number greater than the quotient.

(2). If there are *n* lists in favour of A, A is returned: and so for B, or any other candidate.

(3). If there are *n* lists which suffice to return A, and which, erasing A, are in favour of no other than B; and other *n* lists which, erasing A, are in favour of B; B is returned: and so for A and C, or any other 2 candidates.

(4). If there are 2 *n* lists, which suffice to return A and B and which, erasing A and B, are in favour of no other than C; and other *n* lists which, erasing A and B, are in favour of C; C is returned: and so for A, B, and D, or any other 3 candidates. Similarly for 3 *n* lists, 4 *n* lists, etc.

The words "no other than" are used in Rule 3, in order to meet the case of lists being handed in which contain A only. And there can be no doubt that, in thus disposing of the surplus lists, headed A, no such injustice can be done as I showed to be possible—and indeed probable—in the case examined in my former letters: for the lists, used to return A, could not, by being transferred, help any one but B; consequently the surplus lists may fairly be used in his interests.

Each rule must be applied as far as possible before taking the next. When all are exhausted, if there are still members to be returned, some other principle must be introduced. In the example, given in my former letters, these rules serve to return A, and then cease to be applicable.—I am, Sir, your obedient servant,

CHARLES L. DODGSON.

Ch. Ch, Oxford, May 23.

22. *Proportionate Representation*

[1884: LCH 145: Colindale]

❦

To the Editor *of the* St. James's Gazette.

Sir,—In reply to the charge which I brought (on the 15th of May) against the method of voting proposed by the "Society for Proportionate Representation," that it is liable to bring in the wrong man, two pleas have been put forward: one, that the most probable result is also the most equitable; the other, that it can never be a matter of chance which of two candidates shall get in, unless they are *of the same party.*

The following instance will, I think, give the *coup de grâce* to both these pleas.

Take a town of 39,999 electors, returning three members, so that 10,000 votes will suffice to return a member; let there be four Liberal candidates, A, B, C, D, and one Conservative, Z; and let there be 21,840 lists "A B D," 10,160 "A C B," and 7,999 "Z." There can be no shadow of doubt that, as a matter of justice, A, B, C, ought to be returned. Let us see what, under the society's present rules, would be the most probable result.

The 32,000 lists headed "A" are of two kinds, bearing to each other the ratios of the numbers 273, 127. Hence the most probable event is that the 10,000 lists, used in returning A, will contain 6,825 "A B D" and 3,175 "A C B." Erasing "A" from the remaining lists, we have now in hand 15,015 "B D," 6,985 "C B," and 7,999 "Z"; so that B is returned. Erasing "B" from the remaining lists, we now have 5,015 "D," 6,985 "C," and 7,999 "Z"; so that Z is returned with a majority of more than 1,000 over C. And the Liberals must derive what consolation they can from the reflection that their rejected candidate really had 2,161 more supporters than the successful Conservative!—I am, Sir, your obedient servant,

CHARLES L. DODGSON.

Ch. Ch., Oxford, June 4.

St. James's Gazette, 5 June 1884, 6.

23. *Untitled Letter to the Editor (by W. C. Sidgwick)*

[1884: Colindale]

This untitled, unsigned, undated letter begins, "In reference to Mr. Dodgson's recent letter in our columns, Mr. W. C. Sidgwick writes: . . ."

❦

In reference to Mr. Dodgson's recent letter in our columns, Mr. W. C. Sidgwick writes:—Mr. Dodgson's ingenious problems in proportional representation have an added charm in the fact that they always admit of an answer. His last hard case supposes a Liberal majority to run four candidates for three seats and so let in a Conservative—a result not unknown under any system of voting, for a majority divided against itself is naturally less effective. It is true that smaller minorities will win in this way under a system designed to protect minorities—as his instance very well illustrates. But Mr. Dodgson insists that in this case a candidate is rejected whom the majority of the constituency prefer. No doubt he is—and this is precisely what must happen and is intended to happen in all schemes for representing minorities. The majority desire to get all three seats for their own party; if every member of the majority can score an equally effective vote for all three seats, they will get them all, and the minority get none. Mr. Bright says that is only justice to the majority. To me and to Mr. Dodgson it seems inexpedient to silence the minority; but any measure for giving a share of the representation to the minority must necessarily frustrate the desire of the majority, which is, of course, to keep it all to themselves. I do not think to practical politicians that it will seem a great grievance that it should be possible for a minority of one-fifth to return one member out of three when the majority are so foolish as to try to get four out of three.

St. James's Gazette, 6 June 1884, 6.

24. *Parliamentary Elections*

[1884: LCH 145]

This letter was partially reprinted in Collingwood, *Life and Letters of Lewis Carroll,* 234–36.

❧

The question, how to arrange our Constituencies and conduct our Parliamentary Elections, so as to make the House of Commons, as far as possible, a true index of the state of opinion in the nation it professes to represent, is surely equal in importance to any that the present generation has had to settle. And the leap in the dark, which we seem about to take, in a sudden and vast extension of the Franchise, would be robbed of half its terrors could we feel assured that each political party will be duly represented in the next Parliament, so that every side of a question will get a fair hearing.

The method which, after much thought, I venture to propose, will best be explained by showing how it carries out those general principles which ought to guide us in this matter.

(1) That each Member of Parliament should represent, approximately, the *same* number of Electors is almost an axiom. The monstrous injustice of letting a Member who speaks for a few hundreds cancel the vote of one who speaks for thousands needs no proof. Equal electoral districts, each returning one Member, would seem at first sight to secure this. But they do not really do so, since the Member only represents the *majority* of the district. Suppose the Electors to consist of 5 millions of one party and 3 millions of the other (call them "blue" and "red"). Now, if these 8 millions were scattered broadcast over the land, the *most*

St. James's Gazette, 5 July 1884, 5–6.

probable proportion (*i.e.* the one more probable than any other one), in which they would fall in any district, would be 5 to 3. Such a district would return a "blue" member, as indeed any district would, even with less than 5-8ths "blue," so long as they were more than one-half. Hence a possible result of an election would be a House—not containing, as it ought to do, 3 "red" for every 5 "blue," but wholly "blue." This extreme case is of course unlikely: but it is mathematically certain that the House would contain much too large a proportion of "blue" to fairly represent the Electors. It seems clear that each district should return several Members, so that Minorities may have a chance of returning some. But, if this be so, there is no reason why the districts should be *equal,* provided only that the number of Members returned be proportioned to the number of Electors in the district.

(2) That the Minority of the two parties into which, broadly speaking, each district may be divided, should be adequately represented, is another axiom. The common plan for electing several persons at once is to give each voter as many votes as there are vacancies to fill—and this fallacy still holds its ground, in spite of the obvious absurdity that it enables a bare majority of the Electors to fill *all* the vacancies. The plan, of giving each voter several votes, but *fewer* than there are vacancies to fill, is only a partial remedy of this injustice: *e.g.,* with 3 Members to return, and each Elector having 2 votes, it is possible for just over 3-5ths of the Electors to fill *all* the vacancies. The plan, of letting a voter give 2 or more votes to one man, simply increases the "specific gravity"—so to speak—of a vote. Give each voter 6 votes, with permission to lump them if he pleases—and in the end you will find most of the votes given in lumps of 6, and the result much the same as if each had had one vote only. So we are brought to the plan advocated by the "Proportionate Representation" Society—quite the best, I believe, that has yet been suggested—to give each Elector *one* vote only, and to fix, for each district, the "quota" which shall suffice to return a Member. (The rule is easily seen to be to divide the total number of votes by the number of Members to be returned, increased by one, and to take the whole number next greater than the quotient.)

(3) That the waste of votes, caused by accidentally giving one

candidate more than he needs, and leaving another of the same party with less than he needs, should be if possible avoided, is much more easily seen than is any practicable method for effecting this. The *packing* of votes—needing the constant supervision of a "caucus," and also a very docile body of Electors, each willing to vote for *any* man on the "right" side—is a way, but a very clumsy one, for doing this. A much better way would be to let each man vote as he likes, and find some means of utilising surplus-votes, in order to bring in other Members of the same party. But how is this to be done? It is quite the most difficult question we have yet had to face. The P. R. Society says, "let each voter hand in an arranged list, and let his vote, if not required by his No. 1, be transferred to his No. 2, and so on." But this involves a great difficulty, often pointed out, and never yet successfully grappled with. *Which* of the surplus-votes are we to transfer? The first thing to settle is, *where* the answer is to come from. Are we to leave it to chance? Or is some fixed rule to be made, which shall meet all such cases? Or is it to be settled arbitrarily? I must ask your readers' patience while I discuss these three questions separately.

(3. a.) Shall we leave it to chance? "Yes," says the P. R. Society: "and you will find that the surplus lists, headed 'A,' will be divided among B, C, &c., in the same proportions as the entire set of such lists; and this is surely what the voters wish, and will give an equitable result." But this is precisely what I have shown, in my letter of June 5, will in many cases *not* give an equitable result.

(3. b.) Shall we have a fixed rule for transferring the surplus-lists? Yes, if you can find one that will, in *all* cases, work satisfactorily. None such has yet been suggested.

(3. c.) To this course we seem inevitably driven; namely, that *somebody* shall decide how to use the surplus votes. But who? The voter? That is what the P. R. Society wants: and it necessitates the arranged lists, which we have already seen cause to abandon. This power *cannot* be given to the voter: it is impracticable: the only practicable plan seems to be to let him name his one favourite, and leave to other hands the further disposal of his vote, in case it is not used for that candidate. But, what hands? The next idea that suggests itself is, the committee of the candi-

date. But surely the Electors would not have so much confidence in the committee as in *the man himself.* And to *him* I would refer the question, who is to have the surplus-votes. The Elector should be made to understand that, in giving his vote to A, he gives it him as his absolute property to treat as he will—either by using it to secure his own return, or to help another candidate of whom he approves, or (if there be none such in the field) by leaving it unused. If he cannot trust the man, for whom he votes, so far as to believe that he will use the vote for the best, how comes it that he can trust him so far as to wish to return him as Member? Your readers may, no doubt, find objections to this scheme: but let them remember that what we are in search of is not a scheme *free* from objections (the quest would be hopeless) but the scheme which has the *fewest.*

(4) That the process of marking a ballot-paper should be reduced to the utmost possible simplicity, to meet the case of voters of the very narrowest mental calibre, I should have put as an axiom, but that the above-named Society appears to ignore it. No doubt they have found many school-children able to tick off, with great readiness, lists of kings and conquerors in a supposed descending scale of merit—but try it on Hodge, fresh from the plough! Give *him* a list of half-a-dozen of the neighbouring farmers, to be arranged in their order of merit, and see if he will ever be able to make up his mind! "I knows who's best of *two,*" he might tell you, "but blessed if I can say who's first, and second, and third, and fourth!" This simplicity of process is secured by my method.

(5) That the process of counting votes should be as simple as possible will be admitted by all who agree (as who does not?) that the sooner the result can be announced, and the less liable it is to be set aside owing to errors of calculation, the better. This also is secured by my method.

I proceed to give a summary of rules for the method I propose. Form districts which shall return 3, 4, or more Members, in proportion to their size. Let each Elector vote for one candidate only. When the poll is closed, divide the total number of votes by the number of Members to be returned *plus* one, and take the next greater integer as "quota." Let the returning-officer publish the list of candidates, with the votes given for each, and declare as "returned" each that has obtained the quota. If there are still Members to return, let him name a time when all the candidates shall appear before him: and each returned Member may then formally assign his surplus-votes to whomsoever of the other candidates he will; while the other candidates may in like manner assign their votes. If, by this process, any fresh candidate obtains the quota, let him be declared "returned."

This method would enable each of the two parties in a district to return as many Members as it could muster "quotas," no matter how the votes were distributed. If, for example, 10,000 were the quota, and the "reds" mustered 30,000 votes, they could return 3 Members: for suppose they had 4 candidates, and that A had 22,000 votes, B 4,000, C 3,000, D 1,000: A would simply have to assign 6,000 votes to B, and 6,000 to C, while D, being hopeless of success, would naturally let C have his 1,000 also. There would be no risk of a seat being left vacant through two candidates of the same party sharing a quota between them: an unwritten law would soon come to be recognised—that the one with fewest votes should give place to the other. And, with candidates of two opposite parties, this difficulty could not arise at all: one or the other could always be returned by the surplus-votes of his party.

C. L. DODGSON.

Ch. Ch. Oxford, July 4, 1884.

25. *Justice to London (Signed by F. R. C.)*

[1884: Colindale]

❦

To the Editor *of the* St. James's Gazette.

Sir,—As the question of distribution of seats has now entered on the phase of practical politics, it may be of use to point out some of the facts which must have a material importance in the formation of any impartial scheme to that effect.

It was shown in the *St. James's Gazette* of the 14th of March last that the proportionate numbers of English, Scottish, and Irish members of Parliament ought to be—if determined by numbers of population alone—486, 70, and 96; and if determined partly by numbers and partly by taxation, 522, 65, and 65, respectively. Taking, in the first place, the actual number of 489 English members, it may be of service now to show what the same principles of distribution would effect if similarly applied in England.

If we take, first, the basis of numbers alone, the ten metropolitan boroughs, with a population of 3,500,000 souls, are entitled to sixty-five members.

Six great towns, containing upwards of 200,000 inhabitants apiece and an aggregate of 2,800,000 inhabitants, are entitled on the same basis to fifty-two members.

Thirteen towns of the second magnitude (being all that remain containing above 105,000 inhabitants apiece) have 1,400,000 inhabitants, and would claim twenty-six members among them.

The remaining 771 urban districts, with a population of 9,600,000, and the whole of the rural districts of the country, with 8,700,000 inhabitants, would have to divide among them the remaining 346 members.

If we inquire how far the members thus elected would repre-

St. James's Gazette, 9 July 1884, 5–6.

sent the rateable value of England, we shall find that each metropolitan member (of the sixty-five) would represent a rateable value of £420,000. Each member for the towns of first magnitude would represent £200,000; for those of the second magnitude, £220,000; and for the minor urban and rural districts £270,000 of rateable property.

Comparing these figures with those for Ireland, each of the actual 103 members represents 50,000 instead of 53,333 souls, and £134,000 instead of the English mean of £285,000 of rateable property.

There are not the same returns as to the rateable property of Scotland as exist with regard to England and Ireland; but if we assume the same proportion that prevails as to the net revenue, each Scottish member represents 62,000 souls and £255,000 of rateable property.

Adopting the proportionate representation of one member to 53,333 souls, we should have 65 metropolitan members, each representing £420,000 of rateable property; 460 other English members, each representing £256,000 of rateable property; 65 Scottish members, each representing £236,000 of rateable property; and 65 Irish members, each representing £213,000 of rateable property.

It is only on the pretext, new in politics, that representation should be in the inverse proportion to intelligence or stake in the country, that the claims of London can be overlooked in any new distribution of seats. If we take the whole area now watered by the eight metropolitan water companies, it contains 19 per cent. of the population of England and Wales and 25 per cent. of the aggregate rateable value of the kingdom. This vast and important province at present has only 5 per cent. of the English voting-power in the House of Commons. Are not 5,130,000 Londoners, rated at £7.21 each, entitled to as much consideration as 5,159,000 Irish folk, rated at £2.68 each? And is it not more constitutional to give London her proper weight in our ancient Parliamentary Council than to attempt to "repeal the Union" between her and the rest of the country, by giving her a rival Parliament of her own, with no Senate, no administration, no laws, and no historic tradition?—I am, Sir, your obedient servant,

F. R. C.

July 4.

26. *Untitled Letter to the Editor*

[1884: LCH 145: Colindale]

Dodgson's entry in his diary for 7 August 1884, begins, "My letter (signed 'Dynamite')," clearly identifying him as the author of this letter.[1]

❧

A correspondent signing himself "Dynamite" sends us the following:—"Those who take the Constitutional side in this great Franchise Agitation are from time to time indebted to their opponents for some energetic expression of the truth, or some happy illustration of the fallacy of the Radical position. Mr. Bright's emphatic denunciation of all Franchise bills which did not also deal with Redistribution deserves, and will I trust obtain, the widest publicity: the Hyde Park banners emblazoned with 'The Bill, the whole Bill, and nothing but the Bill!' was a capital thought; they ought to be brought up and used at all Conservative meetings: and the Franchise-medal, used at the Birmingham meeting on Monday, inscribed "Our Queen, our country, and our rights; the Constitution in all its fulness for the people of the United Kingdom," is exactly what Conservatives should delight to wear. And now Mr. Chamberlain presents us with a most appropriate metaphor. I quote his exact words as spoken at Birmingham:—

> I have read somewhere of a patient who was ordered a shower-bath by his physician. He had never seen one before, and when he was introduced to the startling invention he stoutly declared, "I will not enter that machine without an umbrella." (Laughter and cheers.) Now Lord Salisbury insists on an umbrella (laughter): he will not submit the Con-

St. James's Gazette, 7 August 1884, 4–5.

1. Green, *Diaries,* 428.

> stitution to a bracing shower of new voters unless he can preserve it from the shock by a carefully manipulated scheme of redistribution.

We ought to be extremely obliged to Mr. Chamberlain for having hunted up a metaphor so exactly suited to the Conservative orators. He has not got the details quite right, but the correction is easily made. The patient discovered that there was only one hole at the top of the shower-bath, through which the whole of the water would have fallen *en masse* upon one shoulder only; and prudently declared 'I will not enter that machine until a proper system of holes are made, so that the water may be fairly distributed.' Every one knows that the bracing effect of a shower-bath wholly depends on this distribution. Let us return thanks to Mr. Chamberlain for so admirably illustrating a great truth."

27. Redistribution

[1884: LCH 145: Colindale]

❦

Now that the Government scheme for Redistribution has been made public, it seems a fitting time for calling attention to the general principles on which Redistribution ought to be conducted.

In the article on "Parliamentary Elections," which you did me the honour to publish on July 5, I explained a method for conducting Elections which (given that the various Districts had had Members assigned to them in proper proportions) would give the most equitable result possible: in the present article I propose to explain a method of Redistribution, by which Members would be equitably assigned to the various Districts. If both parties could agree to accept some such general principles for Redistribution and the conduct of Elections, each would feel secure that, whether it comprised a majority or a minority of the Electors, it would be fairly represented in the House, and there would be no objection, on either side, to passing the Franchise Bill, with the proviso that it should not come into operation till the Redistribution Bill had also been passed.

Assuming for a moment, for the sake of simplicity, that all Electors, whatever the value of their rateable property, and whether they be in town or country, are to have equal political weight, it is plain that an ideally perfect House would be one where each Member represented the same number of Electors, where the proportion between parties in the House was exactly the same as in the whole body of Electors, and where every Elector was represented by the same fraction of a Member. Such a result is however unattainable. The nearest possible approach to it would be to make the whole Kingdom into one gigantic District,

St. James's Gazette, 11 October 1884, 3–5.

and let each Elector give one vote only: in this case, if the House consisted of 600 Members, and if means were used to prevent votes being wasted, each Member would represent 1-601th of the whole body of Electors, the proportion of parties in the House would be almost exactly the same as in the Kingdom, and only 1-601th of the whole body of Electors would be unrepresented: but it would be impossible to conduct an Election on so gigantic a scale. The other extreme would be the scheme of "equal electoral Districts, each returning one Member," which would leave nearly half of the whole body of Electors unrepresented.

Before settling a formula by which, given the number of Electors in a District, it could be calculated how many Members should be assigned to it, it would be necessary to agree what weight, if any, should be given to value of rateable property, and whether any difference should be made between town and country voters. The simplest way of giving effect to whatever were agreed on would be to have formulæ for multiplying the actual number of Electors in a District, and to use the number so obtained, instead of the actual number, in assigning Members to it: *e.g.* suppose it were agreed that the unit of rateable property should be £5 a year, and that the multiplier employed should be the square-root of the average value, then, in a District where the average value was £20 (4 times the unit), the multiplier would be '2'; and, if it were further agreed that town Electors should have 10 p. c. more weight than country Electors, then, in a District containing 20,000 town Electors and 30,000 country Electors, with an average value of £20 a year of rateable property, we should first add 2,000 to the number of town Electors, and then multiply the whole 52,000 by 2: that is, we should consider the District to contain, for the purpose of assigning Members, 104,000 Electors.

The question, how many Districts to make, which is the same thing as to ask how many Members to assign (on an average) to each District, and the question how many votes to allow each Elector to give, will be best considered in connection with the following Tables, which are calculated on the assumption that 6-11ths of the House are 'red' and 5-11ths 'blue.' Table I. gives the percentage, of the whole body of Electors, represented by the

TABLE I.

Number of Members assigned to each District.	Number of votes each Elector can give.									
	10	9	8	7	6	5	4	3	2	1
1. . .	. . .	. . .	. . .	. . .	. . .	. . .	. . .	. . .	. . .	28
2. . .	. . .	. . .	. . .	. . .	. . .	. . .	. . .	. . .	28	37
3. . .	. . .	. . .	. . .	. . .	. . .	. . .	. . .	28	33	41
4. . .	. . .	. . .	. . .	. . .	. . .	. . .	28	31	37	44
5. . .	. . .	. . .	. . .	. . .	. . .	28	31	34	39	46
6. . .	. . .	. . .	. . .	. . .	28	30	33	37	41	47
7. . .	. . .	. . .	. . .	28	30	32	35	38	43	48
8. . .	. . .	. . .	28	29	31	34	37	40	44	49
9. . .	. . .	28	29	31	33	35	38	41	45	49
10. . .	28	29	30	32	34	37	39	42	46	50

TABLE II.

Number of Members assigned to each District.	Number of votes each Elector can give.									
	10	9	8	7	6	5	4	3	2	1
1. . .	. . .	. . .	. . .	. . .	. . .	. . .	. . .	. . .	. . .	23
2. . .	. . .	. . .	. . .	. . .	. . .	. . .	. . .	. . .	23	31
3. . .	. . .	. . .	. . .	. . .	. . .	. . .	. . .	23	28	34
4. . .	. . .	. . .	. . .	. . .	. . .	. . .	23	26	31	37
5. . .	. . .	. . .	. . .	. . .	. . .	23	26	29	33	38
6. . .	. . .	. . .	. . .	. . .	23	25	28	31	34	39
7. . .	. . .	. . .	. . .	23	25	27	29	32	36	40
8. . .	. . .	. . .	23	24	26	28	31	33	37	41
9. . .	. . .	23	24	26	28	29	32	34	38	41
10. . .	23	24	25	27	28	31	33	35	38	41

TABLE III.

Number of Members assigned to each District.	Number of votes each Elector can give.									
	10	9	8	7	6	5	4	3	2	1
1...	...	...	...	...	...	...	...	...	...	49
2...	...	...	...	...	...	...	...	...	49	32
3...	...	...	...	...	...	...	...	49	39	25
4...	...	...	...	...	...	...	49	43	32	19
5...	...	...	...	...	...	49	43	37	28	16
6...	...	...	...	...	49	45	39	32	25	14
7...	...	...	...	49	45	41	36	30	21	12
8...	...	...	49	47	43	38	32	27	19	10
9...	...	49	47	43	39	36	30	25	17	10
10...	49	47	45	41	38	32	28	22	16	9

'red' Members, Table II. the percentage represented by the 'blue,' and Table III. the percentage unrepresented:—

By inspecting these Tables we see that, the fewer the Districts (*i.e.* the greater the number of Members assigned to each District) and the smaller the number of votes each Elector can give, the more equitable is the result. With less than 10 Members to a District, or with more than one vote to an Elector, it is always possible that the majority of the Electors should be 'blue,' although 6-11ths of the House are 'red.' For example, if 3 Members be assigned to each District, and each Elector have 2 votes, the 'reds' in the House represent 33 p. c. of the Electors, and the 'blues' 28 p. c., while 39 p. c. are unrepresented. It might easily happen that 25 of these 39 were 'blue' and 14 'red': in which case 53 p. c. of the Electors would be 'blue,' and only 47 p. c. 'red,' and yet the 'reds' would have a large majority in the House!

These Tables have been calculated for equal Districts, but probably the results would be much the same for unequal Districts, so long as very small Districts were as far as possible avoided.

We have now to determine a formula by which, given the number of Electors in a district (that is the *nominal* number, making due allowance for rateable property & c.) it may be calculated how many Members ought to be assigned to it. This formula should be such as to make the "quota," necessary to return a Member, as nearly as possible the same for every District. Now, if 'Q' be this uniform quota, and if 'e' be the (nominal) number of Electors in a District, and 'm' the number of Members assigned to it, and if it be agreed that each Elector is to have one vote only, we know that Q must be just greater than $\frac{e}{m+1}$. Hence we get $\frac{e}{Q} - 1$, as the formula required. For example, if the quota were 5,000, a District containing (nominally) 30,000 Electors would have 5 Members assigned to it.

It remains to be seen how to find an equitable value for Q. Let e_1 be the (nominal) number of Electors in District No. 1, and m_1 the number of Members assigned to it, and so on: also let E be the total (nominal) number of Electors, M the total number of Members, and D the number of Districts: then we have

$$(m_1 + 1).\ Q = e_1$$

$$(m_2 + 1).\ Q = e_2$$

&c.

$$\therefore\ (M + D).\ Q = E;\ \text{i.e. } Q = \frac{E}{M + D}.$$

Let me say in conclusion that the object aimed at, in the methods I have proposed for Redistribution and the conduct of Elections, is fully as much to secure that the *Majority* of the Electors shall be duly represented as that the *Minority* shall be so. The same is true of the method (a less perfect one, as I believe) proposed by "the Proportional Representation Society." In speaking to friends about this Society, I have had such answers as this:—"I have no interest in their proposal. All I care for is that the Majority of the Electors shall be fully represented in the House: it matters little whether the Minority are represented or not." Such people seem to think that the existing system secures what they desire. In this they are utterly mistaken: there is ample room, under the existing system, for a large Majority of the Electors to find themselves in a woeful minority in the House. The only change for the worse, that I can think of, would be the method of "equal electoral Districts each returning one Member." Almost any other change would be a change for the better: but any system which, like the one I have here proposed, secures that the Majority of the Electors shall be duly represented, must necessarily do the same for the Minority.

CHARLES L. DODGSON.

28. Redistribution by Rule of Three (by G. A. Simcox)

[1884: Colindale]

❦

From Mr. G. A. Simcox we receive the following communication, suggested by Mr. C. L. Dodgson's letter which we printed on Saturday last:—

The very ingenious scheme of redistribution propounded by Mr. Dodgson seems open to one serious objection. Assuming it to be proved that justice requires electoral districts with not less than ten members, while no elector is to have more than one vote in one district, how is the average elector to be saved from throwing away his vote on a candidate who is safe without it? If the returning officers are to deduct the superfluous voting-papers by lot, and distribute them by fixed rules among other candidates of the same side as far as they will go, electors on each side will be fairly enough represented; but it does not follow that they will be represented by men of their own choice. And the case is no better if the action of the returning officer is to be forestalled by the instructions of some political committee.

The device of "ballotage" seems hard to apply. Are those electors, on both sides, who have already carried one or more candidates of their own way of thinking to vote again?

The prospect of getting 91 per cent. of the electorate directly represented is so attractive that one hopes there may be an answer to these difficulties. If not, perhaps it may be worth while to inquire whether Mr. Hare's scheme may not be simplified in another direction than that proposed by the Proportional Representation Society.

What we want a general election to tell us is, what following

St. James's Gazette, 17 October 1884, 3–4.

political leaders can command in the country for that Parliament. If we divided a general election into two stages, we might give up the first to answering this question. The whole process need not take longer than a general election takes in any country where "ballotage" is in force.

Supposing we decide with Lord Randolph Churchill to go by population alone, it would be simplest to treat the whole of the United Kingdom for this purpose as one constituency, and let the returning officers nominate all commoners of Cabinet rank, and such other commoners as they were required to nominate by so many thousand electors, to serve in the Parliament of the United Kingdom. Then let the electors vote in their separate constituencies for persons so nominated, giving each elector one vote in one constituency. When the returns came in the returning officers would declare, according to Mr. Dodgson's rules, how many supporters each leader was entitled to. In the meantime lesser politicians would be issuing addresses, holding meetings, and canvassing single constituencies in the usual fashion; but they would have to wait a little before they could be nominated. The returning officers would have much to do first: they would have to distribute the voters between the different constituencies; the largest constituencies would be taken first, where the local majority would be entitled to all the seats, and not unfrequently to one or two more. The minority and the overplus of the majority (the latter determined by lot) would be distributed among neighbouring constituencies of their own way of thinking: thus, for instance, the Reds of Oxfordshire might make up the quota of Oxford, and the Blues of Oxford and Banbury make up the quota of Woodstock. Every member would have the same number of constituents; it would not be necessary to disfranchise a single existing constituency; for the Irish in Great Britain would doubtless wish to vote for Mr. Parnell or his successor, so that the representation of Ireland would cease to be excessive, while at the same time every single loyal Irish vote would tell.

The constituencies being made up, the electors would then be summoned in each to elect one or more supporters of So-and-so. Candidates would be nominated, and in the larger constituencies electors would be able to make a fight for their favourite shade without risking the victory of their favourite colour. In the smaller constituencies there would, no doubt, be a risk that the candidates would be strangers to most of the electors, as they are in large constituencies now, though there would probably be more speaking and printing, and "nursing" constituencies would cease to pay. Legitimate local interests would not suffer: a member once returned would attend to them in order to make his local constituency a fortress of his party. The distinction of town and country need not be effaced: a red and blue "farmers' friend" would be always nominated in the first stage of the election, and when the labourers have votes there will be a red and blue "labourers' friend;" and it might be arranged that the surplus urban votes should be distributed in the first instance in towns of 40,000 and upwards, and the surplus county votes in towns of 10,000 and under.

If it were desired to give more weight to property than is given by allowing active citizens to qualify in many constituencies—if it were desired to make a vote in Middlesex more valuable than a vote in Midlothian, and a vote in Midlothian more valuable than a vote in Mayo, a vote in Surrey more valuable than a vote in Shropshire, and a vote in Liverpool more valuable than a vote in Limerick,—it would be possible to secure this much by dividing the United Kingdom into provinces about the size of Ulster, and assigning members to each in joint ratio of population and taxation. Such a division would be involved in any comprehensive scheme of local government. Birmingham, Dudley, and Wolverhampton have far more in common with each other than Birmingham with Warwick, Dudley with Evesham, and Wolverhampton with Lichfield.

In either form the scheme proposed would have two great advantages, if it proved practicable. It would entirely destroy the power of political committees to dictate to individual voters; it would make it impossible for local cliques to add new articles to a political creed. The supporters of local option or the opponents of vaccination would return a few hearty representatives, instead of forcing their shibboleth on the reluctant consciences of an increasing number of members for closely contested seats. Even Nonconformists would find themselves deprived of the weapons by which they abolished Church rates and carried the Burials Bill. There are two objections to the plan: it would throw very heavy work on the returning officers; and, if the Ballot Act is made permanent, it would be necessary to trust them as telegraph clerks are trusted now, for they would necessarily know in every election what they only know now when there is a scrutiny.

29. *Redistribution*

[1884: Colindale]

This letter was omitted in the LCH but is included in Roger L. Green's article, "Lewis Carroll and the *St. James's Gazette," Notes and Queries* (7 April 1945), 134.

❧

To the Editor *of the* St. James's Gazette.

Sir,—Mr. G. A. Simcox, in discussing my proposals (of Oct. 11) for Redistribution, asks "how is the average elector to be saved from throwing away his vote on a candidate who is safe without it?" This question does not belong to the subject of "Redistribution," but to that of "Parliamentary Elections," under which heading I fully discussed it in my paper of July 5, and there proposed that such votes should be at the absolute disposal of the candidate for whom they were given. I also discussed, but only to reject them, the other methods suggested by Mr. Simcox.

I am embodying both papers in a small pamphlet, which I hope to publish in a few days, and of which I shall be happy to send Mr. Simcox a copy.—I am, Sir, your obedient servant,

C. L. DODGSON.

Ch. Ch. Oxford, Oct. 20.

St. James's Gazette, 22 October, 1884, 6.

30. The Principles of Parliamentary Representation

[1884: LCH 168, 169; LCAT 443, 444: Lovett]

The first issue, for private distribution, is dated 23 October 1884; the expanded published issue carries the date 5 November 1884. In a 1970 article, Duncan Black wrote that in this pamphlet "Lewis Carroll presents the longest connected chain of reasoning in Political Science, apart from that given by Thomas Hobbes." Black goes on to say,

> From first to last there is no chink in the argument that each step is linked to the others by a strict logic. The argument has a mathematical structure and has all the rigour of mathematics without the mathematics appearing, save in a few pages where it emerges as a simple equation or an algebraic inequality . . . and it [the argument] could have been put into mathematical form only after 1928 when the first exposition of the 2-person zero-sum game was given by John von Neumann. This astonishing feature may be taken to indicate that the booklet incorporates something of Carroll's genius.[1]

The pamphlet was recently reprinted in McLean, McMillan, and Monroe, eds., *A Mathematical Approach to Proportional Representation: Duncan Black on Lewis Carroll,* 151–69, as well as in McLean and Urken, eds., *Classics of Social Choice,* 299–320.

PREFACE.

Through all the dust and din of the present controversy, four things, at least, are surely clear to all thinking men:—

First, that it would be an unmitigated evil to have a General

London: Harrison and Sons, 1884.

1. Duncan Black, "Evaluating Carroll's Theory of Parliamentary Representation," *Jabberwocky* 1 (1970), 19.

Election with the new Franchise, but without a new Distribution of Seats;

Secondly, that there would be no difficulty in avoiding all risk of such a catastrophe, *PROVIDED THAT* a clause were added to the Franchise-Bill, enacting that it "shall not be put into operation until a Redistribution-Bill has also been passed";

Thirdly, that there would be no difficulty in both parties agreeing to such a clause, *PROVIDED THAT* each felt secure against the other party obtaining an unfair advantage in the Redistribution;

Fourthly, that there would be no difficulty in making this secure, *PROVIDED THAT* some general principles, making it impossible for either side to obtain any such advantage, could be discovered and accepted by both parties.

It is in the profound conviction that such principles exist, and that they can be as clearly formulated, and as fully proved, as the principles of any other Science, that I venture to address these pages to all interested in the matter.

C. L. D.

Ch. Ch., Oxford, Nov. 5, 1884

CONTENTS

CHAPTER I.

Desiderata.

THE CHIEF *desiderata* seem to be as follows:—

(1) That each Elector should have the same chance of being represented in the House. (Under *any* system, *some* electors must be left unrepresented.)

(2) That each Elector, who is represented at all, should be represented by the same fraction of a Member. Or (which is the same thing) that each Member should represent the same number of Electors. Or (which is the same thing) that the number of Electors, needed to secure the return of a Member, should be uniform throughout the Kingdom.

(3) That the number of unrepresented Electors should be as small as possible.

(4) That the proportions of political parties in the House should be, as nearly as possible, the same as in the whole body of Electors.

(5) That the process of voting should be as simple as possible.

(6) That the process of counting the votes, and announcing the result, should be as simple as possible.

(7) That the waste of votes, caused by more votes being given for a Candidate than are needed for his return, should be as far as possible prevented.

(8) That the result of a local Election should depend as much

as possible on the wishes of the Electors in that District, and as little as possible on chance.

(9) That the Electors in a District should be, as far as possible, uninfluenced by the results of Elections in other Districts.

CHAPTER II.

Principles to be observed in forming electoral Districts, and in determining, for each District, how many members it shall return.

§ 1. *Number of Members in House*

There seems to be no sufficient reason, *a priori,* for any change in this particular. It would probably be best to take 660 as the number to be generally aimed at, though holding ourselves free to modify this as circumstances might require.

§2. *Number of electoral Districts; whether to be equal or unequal; &c.*

The two extreme cases are (1) to have as many Districts as Members, each to return one Member, in which case the Districts should of course be equal; (2) to form the whole Kingdom into one District.

In the first case (a method that has been much advocated) it is only a bare majority in each District who are represented. For it must not be supposed that all who vote for a Member are duly represented by him. If a District contains 20,001 Electors, so that 10,001 are enough to return a Member, all additional votes are absolutely wasted: hence only 10,001 Electors in that District are represented in Parliament; the other 10,000, whether they vote for the successful Candidate, or for a rival, or even if there be no contest at all, are unrepresented.

The injustice of this method may be illustrated from two points of view. Suppose a bare majority of the Electors to be of one party, and the rest of the opposite party; e.g. let 6-11ths be 'red' and 5-11ths 'blue.' Then, as a matter of abstract justice, about 6-11ths of the House ought to be 'red,' and 5-11ths 'blue.' But practically this would have no chance of occurring: if the 'reds' and 'blues' were evenly distributed through the Kingdom, a 'red' would be returned in every District, and the whole House would be of one party! Yet this distribution is, by the Laws of Probability, more likely than any other one distribution, and, the nearer the distribution to the most probably one, the nearer we come to this monstrous injustice.

The other way of looking at it is almost as telling. Suppose the House to have been elected, and that 6-11ths of the Members are 'red,' and 5-11ths 'blue': all we could learn from this, as to the views of the Electors, would be that 6-22ths (about 28 p.c. [percent]) are 'red,' and 5-22ths (about 23 p.c.) 'blue': as to the other 49 p.c., we should know absolutely nothing—if they were all 'red' (i.e. if 3-4ths of the Electors were 'red'), or all 'blue' (i.e. 7-10ths of the Electors 'blue'), it would make no difference in the House.

Taking this first extreme, then, as yielding the *maximum* of injustice which can be effected by arrangement of Districts, and observing that, if each District returned 2 Members, only 1-3rd of the Electors (on the assumption that each Elector has only one vote—an arrangement whose justice we shall hereafter prove) would be unrepresented, if 3 Members, only 1-4th, and so on, we see that the fewer and larger the Districts, i. e. the greater the number of Members which, on an average, each District returns, the fairer the result: till we come to the other extreme, where the whole Kingdom is formed into one District returning 660 Members, in which case only 1-661th of the whole body of Electors would be left unrepresented. A general Election, with so gigantic a District, would of course be impracticable: and probably Districts, returning 6 Members each, would be about as large as could be conveniently dealt with: but very small Districts should be, as far as possible, avoided.

I find, in the *Standard* for October 10, 1884, a very good instance of the injustice done by sub-dividing large electoral Districts. "The Birmingham Conservatives are, a Correspondent telegraphs, keenly discussing the Government Redistribution Scheme. The clause which apportions 6 Members to Birmingham gives much dissatisfaction in Conservative circles. It is contended that, if the borough is to be divided into three electoral Districts, each District to have 2 Members, the Liberals could so manipulate the voters as to be certain of returning the whole of the 6 Members." Now, assuming that each Elector is to have one vote only, the Liberals could only do this by mustering more than two-thirds of the votes in each District; i.e. they must be 67 p.c., or more of the whole body of Electors in Birmingham. But, if the three Districts were made one, it would need about one-seventh of the whole (i.e. 14 and 2-7ths p.c.) to return one Member. Hence 67 p.c. could only return 4 of the 6 Members: it would require 71 p.c. to return as many as 5; and they could not return all 6, unless they were 86 p.c. of the whole body.

Taking it as proved, then, that single-Member Districts should be in all cases avoided, and that all such should be grouped together, so as to form districts returning at least 2 Members each, and, wherever it is possible, 4 or 5 or even more, we need only add, as a general remark, that, the more we equalise the Districts, the more we equalise the chance that each Elector has of being one of those represented in the House. Thus, in a District, returning 2 Members, the chance is 2-3ds; with 3 Members, it is 3-4ths; and so on.

§3. *Formula for determining, for each District, how many Members it shall return.*

A preliminary question must here be asked, viz. are we to count population, or Electors only? I do not think it matters much which, as they probably vary nearly together, i.e. a District having twice the population of another would probably have twice as many Electors. The Formula can best be determined for the number of *Electors:* but if, in using it, the number of population be substituted, it will make no important difference in the result.

The formula will of course have to be modified for each case, if it be agreed to give political weight to differences in rateable property, or to the distinction between town and country voters: and for this purpose rules would have to be laid down.

Now, taking *'e'* to represent, for any one District, the number of Electors, and *'m'* the number of Members to be assigned to that District, and assuming that each Elector has only one vote, we require a formula giving m in terms of e. This formula must evidently be such as will secure that every Member in the House shall, as far as possible, represent the same number of Electors.

Now, whatever be the quota of recorded votes, which is necessary and sufficient, *before the poll is closed,* to make it certain that '*A*' will be returned, that is the number of Electors whom *A* will represent in the House. He cannot represent *less,* for this number is *necessary;* and he cannot represent *more,* for it is *sufficient,* so that all additional votes are superfluous. Let us call this necessary and sufficient quota '*Q*.'

Now, in order that *Q* may be *sufficient,* it must not be possible for *m* other Candidates to obtain *Q* votes each; i.e. (m + 1). *Q* must be greater than *e;* i.e. *Q* must be greater than $\frac{e}{m+1}$. Also, in order that *Q* may be *necessary,* it must be the whole number *next* greater than this fraction. Hence, approximately, $Q = \frac{e}{m+1}$; i.e. $m = \frac{e}{Q} - 1$.

This, then, is the formula required. An example will make it clear. Suppose the universal quota to be 6,000: then a District containing 50,000 Electors would have 7 Members assigned to it.

We have yet to find a formula for determining *Q*. Let 'e_1' be the number of Electors in District No. 1, 'e_2' the number in No. 2, and so on; let 'm_1' be the number of Members assigned to District No. 1, 'm_2' the number assigned to No. 2, and so on; also let '*E*' be the total number of Electors in the Kingdom, '*M*' the number of Members in the House, and '*D*' the number of Districts. Then we have

$$(m_1 + 1) \,.\, Q = e_1,$$
$$(m_2 + 1) \,.\, Q = e_2,$$
$$\&c.$$
$$\therefore\ (M + D) \,.\, Q = E; \text{ i.e. } Q = \frac{E}{M+D};$$
$$\therefore\ m = e \cdot \frac{M+D}{E} - 1.$$

§ 4. *Tables calculated by the preceding Formulæ.*

Let us suppose the 2,000,000 new Electors to be already enfranchised, thus making the total Electorate about 5,000,000. Let us further assume the number of electoral Districts to be 180, so that each will return, on an average, 3 and 2-3ds of a Member.

Let M = No. of Members in House = 660.
D = No. of Districts = 180.
e = No. of Electors in a District .
E = total No. of Electors = 5,000,000.
p = population in a District.
P = total population = 36,000,000.
Q = universal quota, to be aimed at.
m = No. of Members assigned to a District.

Then $\frac{E}{M+D} = \frac{5{,}000{,}000}{840}$ = about 6,000;

$$\therefore m = \frac{e}{6{,}000} - 1 \ldots\ldots\ldots\ldots (a)$$

It will be worth while to contrast with this the 'rough and ready' method of assigning Members in proportion to the number of Electors, so that m : e : : M : E. This gives us

$$m = e \cdot \frac{M}{E} = e \cdot \frac{660}{5{,}000{,}000} = \frac{e}{7{,}600} \ldots\ldots\ldots\ldots (b)$$

In the following Table, the second column gives the number of Members to be returned by a District, the first the number of Electors by Formula *(a),* and the third the same by Formula *(b).*

Table I

e, by (a)	*m*	*e, by (b)*
9,000		4,000
	1	
15,000		11,000
	2	
21,000		19,000
	3	
27,000		27,000
	4	
33,000		34,000
	5	
39,000		42,000
	6	
45,000		49,000
	7	
51,000		57,000
	8	
57,000		65,000
	9	
63,000		72,000
	10	
69,000		80,000

The numbers, in the first and third columns, have been calculated by giving to *m,* in the preceding Formulæ, the successive values one-half, 3-halves, 5-halves, &c. Hence we see that, by Formula *(a)*, a District containing between 9,000 and 15,000 Electors must have between one-half and 3-halves of a Member (i.e. must have *one* Member) assigned to it; and so on. If a district contained almost exactly 15,000, it could not fairly be determined, by this Table, whether it ought to return one Member, or two. In such a case, it would be best to change the boundaries of the District, so as to increase or diminish the number of Electors by 2,000 or so.

Comparing the results of the two Formulæ, we see that, for Districts whose population is about 27,000, it matters very little which Formula we use: but, for small Districts, Formula *(b)* assigns too many Members, and for large Districts, too few; e.g. 13,000 Electors ought to return only one Member—Formula *(b)* gives them 2; 60,000 ought to return 9—Formula *(b)* gives them 8.

We will now examine the effect of counting the population of a District, and not the Electors only.

Here, for $\frac{E}{M+D}$, we must substitute $\frac{P}{M+D}$;

i.e. $\frac{36{,}000{,}000}{840}$, i.e. about 43,000.

Hence Formula *(a)* becomes

$$m = \frac{e}{43{,}000} - 1 \;.\;.\;.\;.\;.\;.\;.\;.\;.\;.\;.\;.\;.\; (c)$$

Also Formula *(b)* becomes

$$m = e \cdot \frac{660}{36{,}000{,}000} = \frac{e}{54{,}500} \;.\;.\;.\;.\;.\; (d)$$

TABLE II

e, by (c)	m	e, by (d)	e, by (c)	m	e, by (d)
64,000		27,500	322,000		354,500
	1			7	
107,000		82,000	365,000		409,000
	2			8	
150,000		136,500	408,000		463,500
	3			9	
193,000		191,000	451,000		518,000
	4			10	
236,000		245,500	494,000		572,500
	5				
279,000		300,000			
	6				

Comparing this with Table I, we see that, provided only it be true that the number of Electors in a District is always about 5-36ths of the population, the substitution of number of population for number of Electors will suffice for all practical purposes; and, seeing that there is evidently a tendency to go by population, and that it is much more easy to take the population of a District than to estimate what will be the number of its Electors when the Franchise-Bill is passed, the first column of Table II. is probably the best to employ.

CHAPTER III.

Principles to be observed in conducting Elections.

§ 1. *Number of Votes each Elector may give.*

The two extreme cases are (1) to let each Elector give as many votes as there are Members to be returned by the District; (2) to let him give one vote only.

The effect of each of these methods, and of the intermediate methods which lie between them, will be best understood by considering the following Tables of percentages.

We will first find general formulæ for determining what number of Electors, in a given District, is necessary and sufficient to secure the return of one Candidate, of 2, of 3, &c.

Let e = No. of Electors in the District,
m = ... Members assigned to it,
v = ... votes each Elector can give,
s = ... seats it is desired to fill,
x = ... Electors required.

Also let it be assumed that an Elector may not give 2 votes to the same Candidate. (N. B. 'cumulative' voting is discussed at p. 27 [p. 191].)

Now, in order that x may be *sufficient* to fill s seats, it must be large enough to make it impossible for the other $(e - x)$ Electors to fill $(m + 1 - s)$ seats; since the two events are incompatible, so that, if the latter were possible, the former would be impossible.

To effect this, each of the s Candidates must have more votes than it is possible to give to each of $(m + 1 - s)$ rival Candidates.

In order that x may be *necessary,* it must be only *just* large enough for the purpose.

It will be necessary to consider the following 4 cases separately. Observe that $>$ means 'greater than,' $\ngtr$ means 'not greater than,' and $\therefore$ means 'therefore'.

Case *(a)* v is $\ngtr s$, and also $\ngtr (m + 1 - s)$;
Case *(b)* . . . . $> s$, but $\ngtr (m + 1 - s)$;
Case *(c)* . . . . $\ngtr s$, but $> (m + 1 - s)$;
Case *(d)* . . . .$> s$, and also $> (m + 1 - s)$.

In case *(a),* the x Electors can give vx votes, which, divided among s Candidates, supply them with $\frac{vx}{s}$ votes apiece. Similarly, the $(e - x)$ Electors can give $v.(e - x)$ votes, which, divided among $(m + 1 - s)$ Candidates, supply them with $\frac{v.(e-x)}{m+1-s}$ votes apiece. Hence we must have

$$\frac{vx}{s} > \frac{v.(e-x)}{m+1-s},$$

where v divides out;

$$\therefore x.(m + 1 - s) > se - sx;$$

$$\therefore x.(m + 1) > se;$$

$$\therefore x > \frac{se}{m+1}.$$

In case *(b),* each of the x Electors can only use s of his v votes, since he can only give *one* to each Candidate; hence the x Electors can only give sx votes, thus supplying s Candidates with x votes apiece. But the $(e - x)$ Electors can, as in case *(a),* supply $(m + 1 - s)$ Candidates with $\frac{v.(e-x)}{m+1-s}$ votes apiece. Hence we must have

$$x > \frac{v.(e-x)}{m+1-s};$$

$$\therefore x.(m + 1 - s) > ve - vx;$$

$$\therefore x.(m + 1 - s + v) > ve.$$

$$\therefore x > \frac{ve}{m+1-s+v}.$$

In case *(c),* the x Electors can, as in case *(a),* supply s Candidates with $\frac{vx}{s}$ votes apiece. But each of the $(e - x)$ Electors can only use $(m + 1 - s)$ of his votes: hence the $(e - x)$ Electors can only give $(m + 1 - s) \,.\, (e - x)$ votes, thus supplying $(m + 1 - s)$ Candidates with $(e - x)$ votes apiece. Hence we must have

$$\frac{vx}{s} > e - x;$$

$$\therefore vx > se - sx;$$

$$\therefore x \,.\, (s + v) > se;$$

$$\therefore x > \frac{se}{s + v}.$$

In case *(d),* the x Electors can, as in case *(b),* supply s Candidates with x votes apiece. and the $(e - x)$ Electors can, as in case *(c),* supply $(m + 1 - s)$ Candidates with $(e - x)$ votes apiece. Hence we must have

$$x > e - x;$$

$$\therefore 2x > e;$$

$$\therefore x > \frac{e}{2}.$$

Tabulating the results, we have the following formulæ.

	Data.	*Formulæ.*
(a)	$v \not> s$ $\not> m + 1 - s$	$x > \frac{se}{m + 1}$
(b)	$v > s$ $\not> m + 1 - s$	$x > \frac{ve}{m + 1 - s + v}$
(c)	$v \not> s$ $> m + 1 - s$	$x > \frac{se}{s + v}$
(d)	$v > s$ $> m + 1 - s$	$x > \frac{e}{2}$

By these formulæ the following Table is calculated. It shows, for a given District, what percentage of the Electors is necessary and sufficient to secure the return of *one* candidate, of 2, of 3, &c.

The 2nd line in the 3d section represents the well-known "three-cornered constituency." Observe (by comparing it with the next line) that it makes it too hard for a minority to fill *one* seat, and too easy for a majority to fill *all.*

Table III

No. of Members ret. by District.	No. of votes each Elector can give.	No. of Seats it is desired to fill. 1	2	3	4	5	6
1	1	51					
2	2	51	51				
	1	34	67				
3	3	51	51	51			
	2	41	51	61			
	1	26	51	76			
4	4	51	51	51	51		
	3	43	51	51	58		
	2	34	41	61	67		
	1	21	41	61	81		
5	5	51	51	51	51	51	
	4	45	51	51	51	56	
	3	38	43	51	58	63	
	2	29	34	51	67	72	
	1	17	34	51	67	84	
6	6	51	51	51	51	51	51
	5	46	51	51	51	51	55
	4	41	45	51	51	56	61
	3	34	38	43	58	63	67
	2	26	29	43	58	72	76
	1	15	29	43	58	72	86

In examining this Table, we notice, first, the uniformity of the *upper* line in each section (i.e. the percentages required when each Elector can give as many votes as there are seats to fill). Here, in every case, more than half the Electors must agree, in order to fill one single seat: but, when once this number have mustered, they have it in their power to fill *all* the seats! *'C'est le premier pas qui coûte.'*

This absurdity diminishes gradually, from line to line, as we look down each section; the lowest line (i.e. the percentages required when each Elector can give one vote only) being always the most reasonable. One of the most startling anomalies is the 4th line of the 6th section. Here we see that, out of 100 Electors, we must muster 34 in order to fill *one* seat: with four more Electors, we can fill the second seat: with five more, the third: but 'then comes the tug of war'; to win the fourth seat, we actually need *fifteen* more Electors!

Lastly, comparing together the lowest lines of the several sections, we notice that they gradually improve as we move down from section to section, requiring a smaller percentage to fill *one* seat, thus giving a minority a better chance of being represented, and a larger percentage to fill *all,* thus leaving a smaller number unrepresented. This last figure (the right-hand end of each lowest row) represents the percentage of the Electors in the Kingdom who would be represented in the House, supposing all the Districts similar to the one under consideration: and this percentage we find to rise, from 51 in the case of single-Member Districts, to 86 in the case of six-Member Districts.

The obvious conclusion is—let the Districts be as *large* as possible, and let each Elector give *one* vote only.

The effect, on the composition of the House, will be yet more clearly seen by considering the following three Tables, which are calculated on the assumption that, in any District, all proportions, between 'red' and 'blue,' are equally probable, and that 6-11ths of the House are 'red' and 5-11ths 'blue.' Table IV. gives

TABLE IV

Number of Members assigned to each District.	*Number of votes each Elector can give.*					
	6.	*5.*	*4.*	*3.*	*2.*	*1.*
1.	....	....	....	....	....	28
2.	....	....	....	....	28	37
3.	....	....	....	28	36	42
4.	....	....	28	35	40	44
5.	....	28	33	39	43	46
6.	28	32	36	40	44	48

TABLE V

Number of Members assigned to each District.	*Number of votes each Elector can give.*					
	6.	*5.*	*4.*	*3.*	*2.*	*1.*
1.	....	....	....	....	....	23
2.	....	....	....	....	23	31
3.	....	....	....	23	30	34
4.	....	....	23	29	34	37
5.	....	23	28	32	36	38
6.	23	27	30	34	37	38

TABLE VI

Number of Members assigned to each District.	Number of votes each Elector can give. 6.	5.	4.	3.	2.	1.
1.	....	....	....	....	....	49
2.	....	....	....	....	49	32
3.	....	....	....	49	34	24
4.	....	....	49	36	26	19
5.	....	49	39	29	21	16
6.	49	41	34	26	19	14

the percentage of the whole body of Electors represented by the 'red' Members, Table V. the percentage represented by the 'blue,' and Table VI. the percentage unrepresented:—

By inspecting the Tables, we see two things:—

First, that the fewer and larger the Districts, i.e. the greater the number of Members returned (on an average) by each District, the more equitable the result. This conclusion we have already arrived at, from general considerations. (See p. 6, line 1. [p. 180, para. 3, line 6.]) We observe, further, that the advantage, in fairness of result, increases rapidly at first and more slowly afterwards. For instance, in Table VI, if each Elector be allowed one vote only, the change from single-Member to two-Member Districts changes the percentage of unrepresented Electors from 49 to 32 (i.e. deducts about 1-3rd); whereas the change, from 5-Member to 6-Member Districts, only changes the percentage from 16 to 14 (i.e. deducts only 1-8th). The conclusion is that *the* important point is to have as few single-Member, and even as few 2-Member, Districts as possible; but that, when we have got as far as to Districts returning 4 or 5 Members each, it is hardly worth while to go further.

Secondly, we see that the fewer the number of votes (down to the least possible, viz. '*one*') that each Elector is allowed to give, the more equitable the result. We observe, further, that the advantage, in fairness of result, increases slowly at first and more rapidly afterwards. For instance, in Table VI, if 6 Members be assigned to a District, the change from 6 votes to 5 only changes the percentage of unrepresented Electors from 49 to 41 (i.e. deducts less than 1-6th); whereas the change from 2 votes to one changes it from 19 to 14 (i.e. deducts more than 1-4th). We observe, further, that the system of allowing each Elector as many votes as there are seats to fill produces, in *every* case, the same result, (the most inequitable that it is possible to produce by any variation in these data,) viz. that it leaves about 49 p.c. of the Electors unrepresented. The system (already discussed at p. 4 [p. 179]) of "equal electoral Districts, each returning one Member" is only a particular instance of this general law.

The method of 'cumulative voting' (where an Elector can give two or more votes to the same Candidate) will usually have no other effect than to increase the 'specific gravity'—so to speak—of a vote. Let each Elector have 4 votes, with permission to 'lump' them if he chooses, and in the end you will find most of the votes given in lumps of 4, and the result much the same as if each Elector had had *one* vote only.

The conclusion is that *the* important point is to let each Elector give *one* vote only.

§ 2. *Formula for determining, after the poll is closed, the quota of Votes needed to return a Member.*

By a process, exactly similar to that employed at p. 9 [p. 182], we may prove that, if 'r' be the number of recorded votes, and 'm' the number of Members to be returned, the quota must be just greater than $\frac{r}{m+1}$. For example, if 55,000 votes had been given, and the District had to return 6 Members, the quota needed to return one Member would be just greater than 7,857 and 1-7th: i.e., a Member, having 7,858 votes, would be returned. Similarly, anything just greater than 15,714 and 2-7ths would be enough (if the votes could be reckoned *en masse*) to return 2 Members: i.e., if 2 Members of the same party had 15,715 votes between them, both could be returned. We shall prove, further on, that such reckoning of votes is equitable and ought to be provided for.

This quota must be carefully distinguished from the one discussed at p. 9 [p. 182]. If a District, returning one Member, contains 10,001 Electors, the quota needed, *before the poll is closed,* to make it certain that 'A' will be returned, is 5001; bur if only 8,001 vote, the quota needed, *after the poll is closed,* to return him, is only 4,001. For the purpose of *assigning Members to a District,* it is fair to proceed as if *all* the Electors were sure to vote; but for the purpose of *returning Members,* we can count only the votes that are actually recorded.

§ 3. Method for preventing waste of Votes.

Assuming it to be agreed that each District is to return 2 or more Members, and that each Elector is to give one vote only, we have now to consider what is to be done when 2 or more Candidates of the same party have got, among them, enough votes to be returned, but when some have got more than the quota, and others less. It is obviously not fair that the party should fail in bringing in their rightful number of Members, merely by an accidental disarrangement of votes; but how to make an equitable transfer of the superfluous votes is by no means so obvious.

Various methods have been proposed for this: of which I will consider two:—

(1) "The Proportional Representation Society" proposes to let each Elector hand in a list of Candidates, marked in the order of his preference; and that his vote, if not required for his No. 1, should be transferred to his No. 2, and if not required for him, then to No. 3, and so on. One great objection to this method is the confusion it would cause in the mind of an ignorant Elector, who, though quite able to name his favourite Candidate, would be utterly puzzled if told to arrange 5 or 6 names in order of merit. But a much stronger objection is the difficulty of deciding to *which* of the remaining Candidates the surplus votes should go: e. g. if 8,000 be the quota needed to return a Member, and if 6,000 lists be headed *'A B,'* and 4,000 *'A C,' which* 2,000 are to be transferred? Mr. J. Parker Smith, in a Pamphlet entitled "Preferential Voting," says (at p. 2), "The course which is exactly fair to B and C is that the votes which are transferred should be divided between them in the same proportion as that in which the opinions of the whole number of A's supporters is divided." (This would require, in the above instance, that 3-5ths of the 2,000, i.e. 1,200, should be taken from the *'A B'* lists, and 2-5ths, i.e. 800, from the *'A C'* lists.) He adds, "This principle avoids all uncertainty, and is indisputably fair." He then proceeds to show that if, instead of counting and arranging the surplus votes, they be tak-

en "in a random order," the chances are very great that they will come out nearly in this proportion. And he further adds (at p. 4), that "the element of chance will not be of importance as between the different parties, but only as between different individual Candidates of the same party." Now all this rests on the assertion that this mode of dividing the surplus votes, whether effected by counting or left to chance, is "indisputably fair:" and this assertion I entirely deny. The following instance will serve the two purposes, of showing that this method may easily lead to gross injustice, and of showing that the difficulty may easily arise between candidates of opposite parties.

Take a town of 39,999 Electors, returning 3 Members, so that 10,000 votes will suffice to return a Member; let there be 4 'red' candidates, *A, B, C, D,* and one 'blue,' *Z;* and let there be 21,840 lists *"A B D,"* 10,160 *"A C B,"* and 7,999 *"Z."* There can be no shadow of doubt that, as a matter of justice, *A, B, C* ought to be returned, since there are more than two full quotas who put *'A B'* first, and, over and above these, more than one quota who put *'A C'* first. Let us see what, under the Society's present rules, would be the most probable result.

The 32,000 lists headed *"A"* are of two kinds, bearing to each other the ratio of the numbers 273, 127. Hence the certain event, if the lists are divided by rule, and the most probable event, if they are divided at random, is that the 10,000 lists, used in returning A, will contain 6,825 *"A B D"* and 3,175 *"A C B."* Erasing *"A"* from the remaining lists, we have now in hand 15,015 *"B D,"* 6,985 *"C B,"* and 7,999 *"Z"*; so that *B* is returned. Erasing *"B"* from the remaining lists, we now have 5,015 *"D,"* 6,985 *"C,"* and 7,999 *"Z";* so that *Z* is returned with a majority of more that 1,000 over *C*. And the 'reds' must derive what consolation they can from the reflection that their rejected Candidate really had 2,161 more supporters than the successful 'blue'!

While fully agreeing, then, with the Proportional Representation Society as to the propriety of allowing only one vote to each Elector, I think I have sufficiently proved the fallacy of its method for disposing of surplus votes.

(2) A mechanical method of recording votes was suggested, in a letter signed "F. R. C.," in the *St. James's Gazette* for Aug. 1.

Each Elector is to pass (unseen) through one of a set of turnstiles, (each Candidate having a separate turnstile), which will mechanically record his vote. The records are to be periodically examined, and the results placarded outside, in order that Electors, on seeing that a Candidate has already got votes enough to secure his return, may cease to vote for him. One is that, if the periods were short enough to prevent waste of votes, the inspection would destroy the secrecy of the ballot, as it would be known who had just voted, and the result of his voting would be at once placarded; whereas, if the periods were long enough to avoid this, time would be allowed for large waste of votes. Another is that, as the quota, necessary to return a Candidate, could not be fixed till the poll had closed, it would be impossible to know, during the Election, whether a Candidate had or had not received votes enough to secure his return. Another is that, if part of the machinery went wrong, so as (for instance) to record a total of votes greater than the number of Electors, the mistake could not (as it can with voting-papers) be rectified, but the Election would have to be held over again.

Having proved, then, that the method of arranged lists will not serve fairly to dispose of surplus votes, and yet that we cannot prevent such votes being given, we have now to find, if possible, a fair method for disposing of them. Clearly *somebody* must have authority to dispose of them: it cannot be the Elector (as we have proved); it will never do to refer it to a Committee. There remains *the Candidate himself, for whom the votes have been given.* This seems to solve the whole difficulty. The Elector must understand that, in giving his vote to A, he gives it him as his absolute property, to use for himself, or to transfer to other Candidates, or to leave unused. If he cannot trust the man, for whom he votes, so far as to believe that he will use the vote for the best, how comes it that he can trust him so far as to wish to return him as a Member?

§ 4. *Method for preventing the Electors in one District from being influenced by the results of Elections in other Districts.*

That Electors are liable to such influences may be proven both *a priori* and *a posteriori.* On the one hand, it is a tendency of human nature, too well-known to need proving, to surrender one's own judgment in order to be on the winning side. In the words of the immortal Mr Pickwick, "it's always best on these occasions to do what the mob do." "But suppose there are two mobs?" suggested Mr. Snodgrass. "Shout with the largest," replied Mr. Pickwick. On the other hand, no one, who has ever watched the progress of a General Election, can need to be reminded how obviously the local Elections of the later days have 'followed suit,' under the irresistible influence of those of the earlier days. "The secret of success," it has been well said, "is to succeed:" and there can be little doubt that the party, which fails in carrying a majority of the local Elections at first, is heavily handicapped during the rest of the contest.

Supposing it admitted that such an influence does exist in General Elections as now managed, and that it is an influence to be avoided, the remedy is not far to seek: let the local Elections be so arranged that all, or nearly all, the results may be announced at the same time.

This arrangement would no doubt be unwelcome to certain 'pluralists' who are now able to vote in several different Districts. Possibly, in such exceptional cases, voting papers might be allowed. But even if no remedy could be found, the justice of allowing one Elector to vote as if he were, "like Cerberus, three gentlemen at once," seems so doubtful that the objection hardly deserves serious consideration.

§ 5. *Conduct of Elections.*

The practical working of the principles, which have now been demonstrated, would be as follows:—When the poll is closed, let the total number of votes recorded be divided by the number of Members to be returned increased by one, and let the returning-officer announce the whole number next greater than the quotient as the quota needed to return *one* Member. Similarly, the whole number next greater than twice the quotient will be the quota needed to return *two,* and so on.

Let him further announce the number of votes for each Candidate, and also announce as "returned" any Candidate who has received the quota needed to return *one.* If there are still Members to return, let him appoint a time and place for all the Candidates to appear before him; and any two or more Candidates may then formally signify that they wish their votes to be clubbed together, and may nominate so many of themselves as can be returned by the votes so clubbed. They must of course include in their nomination any of themselves who have been already declared to be returned. Let the returning-officer add together the votes of these Candidates, and if the amount be not less than the necessary quota, let him declare to be duly returned the Candidates so nominated.

As an example, suppose that a District is to return 5 Members, and that there are 4 'red' Candidates, *A, B, C, D,* and 3 'blue,' *X, Y, Z.* Then the returning-officer might announce as follows:—

Votes given for

C	.	15,000
X	.	9,000
D	.	8,001
Z	.	8,000
B	.	7,500
A	.	6,500
Y	.	6,000

6 | 60,001
10,000 and 1-6th.

Quota needed to return

1 Member .	.	10,001
2 Members	.	20,001
3 Members	.	30,001
4 Members	.	40,001
5 Members	.	50,001

I hereby declare *C* to be duly returned.
Four vacancies remain to be filled.

(Signed) ______________________________

The Candidates might then appear before the returning-officer, and B, C, D might formally declare that they wished to club their votes; and, as the sum total of their votes is 30,501, they would be declared to be "returned": similarly, X, Y, Z might club their votes, naming X and Z as the Candidates to be returned; and, as the sum total of their votes is 23,000, X and Z would be declared to be "returned."

Such candidates would have to sign some such paper as the following:

We, the undersigned, for whom the recorded votes, as stated below, amount to ________, which is not less than ________, the quota announced as needed to return ____ Candidates, hereby declare that we desire the said votes to be clubbed together. And we nominate, as Candidates whom we desire to be returned by the said votes, in addition to ____________________, who have been already declared to be duly returned, ______________________________.

Signed,

Names.	*Votes.*
Sum total of votes	

This method would enable each of the parties in a District to return as many Members as it could muster the proper quota for, no matter how the votes were distributed. There would be no risk of a seat being left vacant through rivalry between two Candidates of the same party: an unwritten law would soon come to be recognised—that the one with fewest votes should give way. With Candidates of two opposite parties, such a difficulty should not arise at all: one or other of them could always be returned by the surplus votes of his own party. The only exception to this would be the occurrence (a very rare one) of an exact balance of votes. This might happen, even in the case of a single-Member constituency, if each of 2 Candidates got exactly half the votes. Of course, in such a case, somebody must give a casting-vote.

CHAPTER IV.

Final Summary.

The main points, which I claim to have made good in this little treatise, are as follows:—

(1) That electoral Districts should be so large as to return, on an average, 3 or more Members each: and that single-Member Districts should be, as far as possible, done away with.

(2) That Members should be assigned to the several Districts in such numbers that the quota, needed to return a Member, should be tolerably uniform throughout the Kingdom.

(3) That each Elector should give one vote only.

(4) That all votes given should be at the absolute disposal of the Candidate for whom they are given, whether to use for himself, or to transfer to other Candidates, or to leave unused.

(5) That the Elections in the several Districts should terminate, as nearly as possible, at the same time.

As a practical conclusion to this treatise, I venture to suggest the following ideal Schedule of General Resolutions, such as might fairly be agreed on by all parties, and thus tend to the peaceful termination of this deplorable controversy.

[N. B. The *numbers* here suggested are merely tentative, and capable of being modified *ad libitum.*]

General Resolutions.

1. The House shall consist of 660 Members.

2. There shall be 180 electoral Districts.

3. No District shall contain less than a population of 60,000, or more than 500,000.

4. A District, whose population is between 60,000 and 105,000, shall have one Member assigned to it; between 105,000 and

150,000, two Members; and so on, in accordance with the following Table:—

Population.	*Members.*
60,000	
	1
105,000	
	2
150,000	
	3
195,000	
	4
240,000	
	5
280,000	
	6
320,000	
	7
365,000	
	8
410,000	
	9
455,000	
	10
500,000	

5. If the population of a District be very near to one of the above-named numbers, its boundaries shall be altered so as to increase, or diminish, the population, by not less than 10,000.

6. If it be agreed to give political weight to differences in rateable property, or to the difference between town and country voters, this shall be done by modifying the number of Members assigned by the above Table.

7. The procedure at a local Election shall be as follows:—Each Elector shall give one vote only. When the poll is closed, the number of recorded votes shall be divided by the number of Members to be returned increased by one, and the returning-officer shall announce the whole number, next greater than the quotient, as the quota needed to return one Member; the whole number, next greater than twice the quotient, as the quota needed to return two Members; and so on. He shall also announce the number of votes recorded for each Candidate, and shall declare to be duly returned any Candidate who has obtained the quota. If any vacancies remain to be filled, he shall appoint a time when the Candidates shall appear before him, and any two or more of them may then formally signify their desire to club their votes, and may nominate, as Candidates to be returned by those votes, so many of themselves as the votes suffice for: provided always that they include, in such nomination, any of themselves who

have been already declared to be returned. And, if the sum total of the votes so clubbed be not less than the quota needed to return the Candidates so nominated, the returning-officer shall declare to be duly returned all of them who have not been already so declared.

8. The local Elections shall be so arranged that their results may be announced, as nearly as possible, at the same time.

INDEX.

31. The Principles of Parliamentary Representation. Supplement

[1885: LCH 172, LCAT 446: Lovett]

This pamphlet is reprinted in McLean, McMillan, and Monroe, eds., *A Mathematical Approach to Proportional Representation,* 169–72.

❦

Now that the public are beginning to realise the justice of the demand for "proportional representation," the day cannot be far off when they will understand the gross injustice (so clearly proved by Lord Salisbury in the *National Review* for October) of the "single-member" districts, and will recognise as true the main contention of the Society for Proportional Representation, that each district should return several Members, and that each elector should have *one* vote only.

May I, as one who has given much thought to this subject, point out a serious mistake which the Society is making in the details of its method, and which is in my belief greatly damaging its cause?

It is fairly obvious, and by this time pretty generally known, that, to obtain the quota of votes necessary to return a candidate, when each elector has one vote only, we must divide the total number of votes by the number of members to be returned plus one, and that the whole number, next above the quotient, is the required quota: e.g. if the district returns 3 members, and 4000 votes are recorded, we divide by 4, and the quota is 1001.

It is also obvious that it will often happen to a candidate to poll more votes than he needs, and the question arises, how are the spare votes to be utilised? The answer of the Society is "Let the

Oxford: E. Baxter, 1885.

voter mark on his paper his second-best man, his third-best, and so on: and, if his first man is already returned, let his vote be used for his second, and so on." This method is complicated and likely to puzzle voters: but such an objection might well be set aside, if only it were just.

But a second question arises. Suppose that A has votes to spare, and that some of the papers, headed A, have B as second-man, while others have C: which papers are we to transfer? To this the Society replies "The absolutely just method would be to count how many papers have B as second-man, and how many have C, and to maintain this proportion in the transferred votes: e.g. if 3-4ths of the whole set of papers, headed A, have B as second-man, then B ought to have 3-4ths of the transferred votes. But, if the votes are simply shuffled and drawn at random, the probability is that this proportion will be almost exactly secured: so that the above calculation may be dispensed with."

Thus, the Society is in effect making two assertions, both of which are demonstrably incorrect: one, that it is only when an elector's first-man is already returned that his vote would be used for his second-man; the other, that the Society's method for transferring spare votes would always secure a just result.

Let a constituency have to return 3 Members, and let 5 candidates stand, 3 Liberals, 1 Independent Liberal, and 1 Conservative.

Let 11999 voting-papers be filled up as follows:—

CHAMBERLAIN	4	4	2	1	4	—
GLADSTONE	1	2	1	2	2	—
GOSCHEN	3	3	4	4	1	—
HARTINGTON	2	1	3	3	3	—
NORTHCOTE	—	—	—	—	—	1
Nos. of papers	3030	2980	2020	1100	790	2079

Here the necessary 'quota' is 3000, since, if 3 candidates get 3000 each, a fourth can only get 2999.

Also it is clear that, as a matter of justice, Gladstone, Hartington, and Chamberlain ought to be returned, since there are 6010 electors who put Gladstone and Hartington as their first two favorites, and, over and above these, 3120 who put Gladstone and Chamberlain as their first two.

The First Count would give:—

Gladstone	....	5050
Hartington	....	2980
Northcote	....	2079
Chamberlain	....	1100
Goschen	....	790

Thus Gladstone is to be returned, with 2050 votes to spare, which must be divided between Hartington and Chamberlain in the proportion of 3030 to 2020, i.e. of 3 to 2; i.e. Hartington must have 1230 of them, and Chamberlain 820.

The Second Count would give:—

Gladstone	....	3000
Hartington	....	4210
Northcote	....	2079
Chamberlain	....	1920
Goschen	....	790

Thus Hartington is returned, with 1210 votes to spare, the whole of which must go to Goschen.

The Third Count would give:—

Gladstone	....	3000
Hartington	....	3000
Northcote	....	2079
Goschen	....	2000
Chamberlain	....	1920

What is to be done now? There is one seat yet to be filled, and no one has the necessary quota. Merely counting votes as they now stand would bring in Northcote, which we know would be unfair. The method of the Society in such a case would be (they tell me) to transfer to Goschen so many of Chamberlain's votes as would give him the necessary quota. But this also would bring in the wrong man.

Thus the Society's method not only excludes Chamberlain, who most undoubtedly ought to be returned; but it actually uses, for the purpose of returning Goschen, the votes of 1000 electors who prefer Chamberlain!

May I, in conclusion, point out that the method advocated in my pamphlet (where each elector names one candidate only, and the candidates themselves can, after the numbers are announced, club their votes, so as to bring in others besides those already announced as returned) would be at once perfectly simple and perfectly equitable in its result?

In the above instance, the returning-officer would announce as follows:—

"Gladstone	....	5050
Hartington	....	2980
Northcote	....	2079
Chamberlain	....	1100
Goschen	....	790

4 / 11999
2999 and 1-4th.

Quota needed to return 1 Member is 3000.
2 .... 6000.
3 .... 9000.

I hereby declare Mr. Gladstone to be duly returned.

Two seats remain to be filled."

Gladstone, Hartington, and Chamberlain would then club their votes, making 9130 votes, which would suffice to return all three.

C. L. DODGSON.

Ch. Ch., Oxford, Feb., 1885.

1. In *Postscript to Supplement* (item 32), Dodgson adds an erratum that the "1-4th should read 3-4ths."

32. The Principles of Parliamentary Representation. Postscript to Supplement

[1885: LCH 173, LCAT 447: Lovett]

This pamphlet is reprinted in McLean, McMillan, and Monroe, eds., *A Mathematical Approach to Proportional Representation,* 172–74.

❧

Objection has been taken to my statement on page 5 [of the *Supplement,* item 31; pp. 203–4] ("it is clear that, as a matter of justice, Gladstone, Hartington, and Chamberlain ought to be returned") on the ground that, of the 9920 Liberal electors, there are 6800 who prefer Goschen to Chamberlain, while there are only 3120 who prefer Chamberlain to Goschen. And it has been pressed upon me that, after all, Goschen is the right man to return, so that the Society's method does *not* break down in this instance.

Now first, we might almost on *a priori* considerations reject such a text as manifestly unfair. For does it not involve the using [of] an elector's voting-power *more than once?* We first let an elector exhaust his full voting-power in helping to return (say) Gladstone; and, after that, we allow his opinion to have weight in deciding between two other candidates. Is not this to abandon the principle, adopted by the Society, that each elector shall have *one* vote only?

But secondly, this test may be easily proved to be valueless, by a simple *reductio ad absurdum.*

Oxford: E. Baxter, 1885.

CHAMBERLAIN	4	4	2	1	3	—
GLADSTONE	1	2	1	2	2	—
GOSCHEN	3	3	4	4	1	—
HARTINGTON	2	1	3	3	4	—
NORTHCOTE	—	—	—	—	—	1
Nos. of papers	1826	1712	1826	1712	1910	3013

Let the 11999 voting-papers be filled up as follows:—

Gladstone	3652
Northcote	3013
Goschen	1910
Chamberlain	1712
Hartington	1712

The First Count would give:—

Thus Gladstone and Northcote are returned, and Gladstone's 652 spare votes must be equally divided between Chamberlain and Hartington.

Northcote	3013
Gladstone	3000
Chamberlain	2038
Hartington	2038
Goschen	1910

The Second Count would give:—

What is to be done now? There is one seat yet to be filled, and no one has the necessary quota.

Let us try the new test. And first, of course, we apply it to Chamberlain and Hartington. We find that

5448 prefer Chamberlain to Hartington;
3538 prefer Hartington to Chamberlain;

so that Chamberlain is clearly the victor.

Let us next apply it to Chamberlain and Goschen. We find

that

3538 prefer Chamberlain to Goschen;
5448 prefer Goschen to Chamberlain;

so that Goschen is clearly the victor, and we might perhaps rest satisfied that he is the right man to be returned.

Let us, however, in order to make assurance doubly sure, apply the test to Goschen and Hartington. We find that

1910 prefer Goschen to Hartington;
7076 prefer Hartington to Goschen!

This lands us in a hopeless circle: and the logical conclusion I believe to be that the proposed test is absolutely valueless.

The statement, thus objected to, may be more fully expressed as follows:—

The 6010 electors, who put Gladstone and Hartington as their first two favorites, have a clear *moral* right to return these two, as the muster more than two full quotas, and it is a mere accident (which they would have avoided had they known how the voting was going on) that they did not divide themselves so as to *secure* this result.

Now suppose them to have exercised this right, and that Gladstone and Hartington are returned. Then the 3120, who put Gladstone and Chamberlain as their first two favorites, would undoubtedly (Gladstone being now safe) all vote for Chamberlain. *He* therefore has also a *moral* right to be returned.

C. L. DODGSON.

Ch. Ch., Oxford, Feb. 1885.

Erratum in Supplement.

Page 7, line 10 from end, *for* 1-4th *read* 3-4ths.

33. Election Gains and Losses

[1885: LCH 145: Colindale]

❦

To the Editor *of the* St. James's Gazette.

Sir,—Will you allow me to present, to such of your readers as may be suffering from the present epidemic of *febris electoralis,* a simple formula for calculating the relative gains and losses of the several contending parties—a formula which will take account of a rather perplexing item in the *data,* viz. the change in the number of seats assigned to a constituency.

This change will not affect the *relative* gains and losses in any constituency where the seats are shared in the same relative proportions as before: *e.g.* if a town, which returned 4 Liberals and 2 Conservatives to the last Parliament, now returns 2 Liberals and 1 Conservative, there are no relative gains or losses. But if a town, which formerly returned 5 Liberals, 2 Conservatives, and 1 Independent, has lost 2 of its 8 seats, and now returns 4 Liberals, 1 Conservative, and 1 Independent, it might puzzle some of your readers to estimate the relative gains and losses. They might have a vague consciousness that the Independents, who did hold 1 seat in 8, and now hold 1 in 6, are rather better off, but *how much* they might be unable to say.

The formula is this. Let S_1 be the number of seats formerly assigned to the town, and S_2 the new number. Similarly let L_1 be the number of seats formerly held by Liberals, and so on. Then the Liberal gain is $(L_2 S_1 - L_1 S_2)$ divided by S_1. If this comes out *negative,* it is really a *loss.*

Thus, in the above example, the old set of numbers, S_1, L_1, C_1, I_1, are 8, 5, 2, 1, and the new set are 6, 4, 1, 1. Hence the Liberal "gain" is (4 x 8 – 5 x 6) divided by 8, *i.e.* one-fourth; the Conservative "gain" is (1 x 8 – 2 x 6) divided by 8, *i.e. minus* one-half; and

St. James's Gazette, 4 December 1885, 6.

the Independent "gain" is (1 x 8 – 1 x 6) divided by 8, *i.e.* one-fourth.

Thus the Conservatives have lost half a seat, which has been shared equally between the Liberals and the Independents.—I am, Sir, your obedient servant,

LEWIS CARROLL.

December 3.

Political Humor

The Transvaal War: Signing the terms of peace with the Boers at O'Neil's Farm, near Prospect Hill Camp, March 21, 1881. President J. H. Brand of the Orange Free State, seated at the right, is signing the treaty; the two figures beside him are Sir Fredrick Sleigh Roberts (behind Brand), representing the British government, and General Sir Evelyn Wood, the commander of British Forces in the Transvaal. Both men are parodied in Dodgson's poem "Who Killed Cock Robin?" (item 35).

Introduction

Dodgson's diary entry of 24 November 1868 gave his reason for sending a letter to the *Oxford University Herald* (item 34) about the election in Woodstock, a town less than ten miles northwest of Oxford. In the *Diaries* Green wrote that this letter, which he reprinted, represented perhaps the only occasion when Dodgson used his sense of humor to political account. Green was correct for his time; however, "Who Killed Cock Robin" (item 35), a parody in verse that Dodgson most probably wrote in 1882, is a second occasion; it was first published in 1972.

Dodgson's diary entry for 24 November reads, "An account of the Woodstock Election has appeared in the *Oxford Chronicle*—written by a Liberal, but so charmingly candid as to the brutal behaviour of the Liberal electors, that I thought it fair subject for a letter to the *University Herald*."[1]

On the next day he recorded in his diary that he wrote another letter, to the *Standard;* it was prompted by his reading of an article in *The Times* about the defeat of Gladstone in (South) Lancashire, the district he represented as a Liberal Member of the House of Commons. He also sent an anagram for William Ewart Gladstone: "Wilt tear down *all* images?" But neither piece was published.

Dodgson signed the Woodstock letter "A Liberal of the Liberals," perhaps to continue to the end the irony the letter represents. The winner of the election was the Conservative, Henry Barnett; the loser was the Liberal, George Charles Brodrick, who made several unsuccessful attempts to enter Parliament.

As Green notes in his interspersed comments, Dodgson is quoting in his letter, "the ridiculous Liberal 'interpretation' from the *Oxford Chronicle* . . . weigh[ing] each accusation in the balance of his own logical sense of humour. . . . After which ironical revelation of Conservative courtesy and Liberal intolerance and bad manners, Dodgson signed himself 'A Liberal of the Liberals.'" Green adds that Van Amburgh, whose feats Dodgson cites in his letter, was a well-known lion tamer.[2]

The writer of the letter to the *Oxford Chronicle* makes it appear, in each of the four accusations he describes, that the Conservatives were responsible for the hootings, the cheering, the threatening acts, and the "unprece-

1. Green, *Diaries,* 275; the letter is reprinted on 275–76.

2. Ibid., 275–76. Green misspelled Brodrick's name in his transcription of the letter.

dented display of heroism," when, as Dodgson shows, the Liberals were actually responsible for these inappropriate behaviors. This approach, turning an argument around to expose fallacious reasoning, Dodgson used again in his letter of 4 August 1883 (item 8) where he turned Cavendish's argument around, and in his letter of 7 August 1884 (item 26), where he turned around Chamberlain's metaphor.

Dodgson wrote "Who Killed Cock Robin?" as a political parody, inspired by the Transvaal War, later called the first Anglo-Boer War, of December 1880 to March 1881. It is the only politically inspired poem Dodgson composed. The British had annexed the Transvaal in 1877. After an armed revolt by the Boers and their proclamation of a new republic in December 1880, Britain restored the independence of the Transvaal in the form of internal self-government. Each four-line stanza of Dodgson's poem, which was probably written in 1882, contains the name of a political figure associated with this conflict.

The eight names are:

Willy: William Ewart Gladstone, Prime Minister for the second time in 1880–1885.

Childers: Hugh Culling Eardley (1827–96), Secretary of State for War, 1880–1882, later Chancellor of the Exchequer.

Quaker Bright: John Bright (1811–1889), cabinet member in Gladstone's government, who approved the re-establishment of autonomy of the Transvaal in 1881.

Roberts of Cabul: Sir Fredrick Sleigh Roberts (1832–1914), later Earl Roberts of Kandahar, Pretoria, and Waterford, a specialist in colonial warfare and commander in India. When the British lost three major battles in the Boer Rebellion during February 1881, the last at Majuba Hill on the 27th, Roberts, who was then on leave in England, was dispatched to South Africa.

Kimberly: John Wodehouse (1826–1902), First Earl of Kimberly, Colonial Secretary for the second time from 1880 to 1882; later Indian Secretary.

Evelyn Wood: Sir Henry Evelyn Wood (1838–1918), specialist in colonial warfare and the commander who signed the treaty making peace with the Boers.

Cairns: Hugh McCalmont (1819–1885), First Earl Cairns, Lord Chancellor under the Conservative Prime Minister Benjamin Disraeli in 1868 and again from 1874 to 1880, and a distinguished lawyer.

Selbourne: Sir Roundell Palmer (1812–1895), created Earl of Selbourne in 1882; he served as Lord Chancellor from 1872 to 1874 and again from 1880 to 1885 under Gladstone.

Sir Fredrick Sleigh Roberts (1832–1914), later Earl Roberts of Kandahar, Pretoria, and Waterford, by John Singer Sargent, 1906.

Sir Henry Evelyn Wood (1838–1918), by Sir Leslie Ward, 1879.

Sir Roundell Palmer (1812–1895), later Earl of Selbourne, by James Malcolm Stewart, 1889.

The dating of this poem in the *Lewis Carroll Handbook* and in Shaberman and Crutch, *Under the Quizzing Glass*[3], is incorrect. Palmer was made Earl in 1882, so the poem could not have been written before then.

Many of Dodgson's political letters, while not entirely in a humorous vein, also contain sections that display their author's penchant for humor. Certainly the discussion of purity of election as an attainable utopian goal in the opening of the letter bearing that title (4 May 1881; item 14) is an example.

3. R. B. Shaberman and Denis Crutch, *Under the Quizzing Glass: A Lewis Carroll Miscellany* (London: Magpie Press, 1972), 42.

Humor also runs through the short letter Dodgson wrote on cloture (23 March 1882; item 15), where he introduced the *perpetuum mobile,* a clock that can wind itself up whenever it runs down. He used this principle to parody the parliamentary scene by describing the antics of Mr. Pyke and Mr. Pluck.

The postscript to Dodgson's letter titled "Proportionate Representation" (19 May 1884, item 20) , in response to William Carr Sidgwick, includes a short humorous poem.

In these public political letters, we see how Dodgson used humor to focus attention on political issues that he considered were being handled illogically. Dodgson had a relentlessly logical mind, yet he could present his arguments with a touch of humor to dissolve the underlying animosities that attend the making of important political decisions. Perhaps it is this interplay between logic and humor that best illuminates the sincerity and unselfishness of Dodgson's motives in writing his letters and pamphlets to promote justice and fairness as the most desirable goals to achieve in matters affecting the public.

34. Woodstock Election

[1868: LCH 66: Colindale]

This letter bears the unique signature, "A Liberal of the Liberals." It is reprinted in Green, *Diaries,* 275–76.

❦

To the Editor of the "Oxford University Herald."

Sir,—With your well-known impartiality, you will not, I trust, object to admit a Liberal communication to your columns. The proceedings at the recent election at Woodstock were so remarkable, and reflect so deep a discredit on the Conservative cause, that a sense of honour should compel even a Conservative paper to give publicity to them, if only as a warning to others of that misguided faction.

The following account appeared in the 'Oxford Chronicle' of Saturday last, and I am sure the eloquent writer will not object to my quoting it 'in extenso':—

"Having been present as a spectator at the Woodstock election during the whole of Tuesday, I should be glad if you would allow me the use of your columns to state one or two significant facts which may be interesting to the public. At the declaration of the result of the poll, the successful candidate, Mr. Barnett, endeavoured in vain to address the crowd. Not a word was audible amidst the hootings and execrations which greeted him. The defeated candidate, Mr. Brodrick, was received with enthusiastic cheering, and listened to in perfect silence. The successful candidate had to be escorted at every appearance in public by twenty or thirty policemen, and even then seemed hardly secure from personal violence. His unsuccessful rival walked without a single

Oxford University Herald, 28 November 1868, 10.

person attending him through the middle of the cheering crowd. Throughout the whole time I did not hear one shout for Barnett or one groan for Brodrick. In what sense, Sir, may I ask, is Mr. Barnett to be considered to 'represent Woodstock?'"

Facts like these, Sir, speak for themselves: but, with your permission, I will offer a few remarks 'to point the moral and adorn the tale.' The real origin of the scandal, the true cause of the cowardly conduct of the Conservative majority is not far to seek. What but ducal influence could have so far degraded the spirit of true-born Britons, and banished the cabbage-stalks and dead kittens, the natural weapons of freemen? But enough on this painful theme: let us turn to the account of the actual proceedings.

We are told, Sir, that the successful candidate, Mr. Barnett, *"attempted in vain to address the crowd. Not a word was audible amidst the hootings and execrations which greeted him."* I cannot, Sir, tell you in words how refreshing to my ears were those manly voices! Though Tory tricks, aristocratic art, and the brute force of numerical superiority, had turned the day against that noble and enlightened minority, I seemed to hear in those voices the knell of a dying monster, the crashing downfall of the rotten fabric of Conservatism!

Mark, however, the contrast when the defeated candidate, Mr. Brodrick, comes forward. He *"was received with enthusiastic cheering, and listened to in perfect silence."* I do not, of course, suppose that the Conservative electors were hypocrites enough to join in the enthusiastic cheering; such depths of baseness have not yet, let us hope, been reached, even in degenerate Woodstock. But that he should be *"listened to in perfect silence"!* Sir, my blood boils within me at the thought. What! That a set of electors, with lungs in their bodies and breath in their lungs, should listen to a political opponent *"in perfect silence"!* It is too mean, too pitiful for belief: "execrations," possibly, their vocabulary may have been deficient in, (though even these they might have picked up, with attention, from their Liberal brethren), but surely they might have hooted!

But we have not yet nearly reached the depths of this abyss of infamy. The successful candidate, we are told, *"had to be escorted at every appearance in public by twenty or thirty policemen, and even then seemed hardly secure from personal violence."* This is as it should be: else what are fists meant for in 'Merrie Englande'? Arguments may fail to convince the Conservative blockheads; even hootings and execrations may be unheeded by such crass intellects as theirs: but the 'one, two,' delivered from the shoulder, is a mode of reasoning that the dullest cannot ignore—it is a thick skull indeed that is insensible to a brickbat!

And now, Sir, for the contrast—Look on this picture, and on this. *"His unsuccessful rival walked without a single person attending him through the middle of the cheering crowd."* Sir, the feats of Van Amburgh pale before this unprecedented display of heroism. His experience of the tender mercies of the gallant Liberal electors towards the Conservative candidate had doubtless prepared him for very different conduct: he felt that he was courting danger—that from that hostile crowd he could scarcely expect to emerge without a torn coat, a black eye or two, and possibly a broken head. And for the first few yards of his perilous march no doubt he moved on with beating heart, with fists clenched, and elbows squared ready for the combat. But he little knew the cowards among whom he went! Not a man dared to lay a finger on him: with bowed heads and bated breath the poltroons sneaked away wherever his manly form was seen. If the indignation of his soul could have found vent in words, might he not in some such sort as this have apostrophised those lily-livered minions?—

"Conservative cravens, where are ye? Brodrick, the son of Brodrick, dares you to the fray. Have ye voices, only to vote with—and are political fights to be waged only in the polling-booth? What is demonstration to a dig in the ribs? Is there any reasoning like rotten eggs? What, not one shout for Barnett? Not one groan for Brodrick! And you call yourselves Englishmen? O tempora, O mores!"

The writer asks, in conclusion, *"in what sense is Mr. Barnett to be considered to represent Woodstock?"* Let Oxford, Liberal Oxford, make reply. So long as Woodstock is degraded by a voiceless, heartless, Conservative majority, who can neither hoot, pelt, nor even execrate their foes, we must with shame confess that Mr. Barnett only too truly represents them. *But* if the noble band of Liberals, whose prowess I have here recorded, should ever become the majority—then indeed, to represent so fine a phase of political enthusiasm, no Barnett, no Brodrick, may we not add no English gentlemen whatever, can be found fully and really competent!

—I am, Sir, your obedient servant,

"A LIBERAL OF THE LIBERALS."

Nov. 24, 1868.

35. *Who Killed Cock Robin?* *A MS. Political Parody*

[1882?: LCH 145a: Woking]

A poem consisting of eleven four-line stanzas written in violet ink in Dodgson's hand, probably in 1882, and sent to Mrs. E. L. Shute on 18 February 1887. Mrs. Shute eventually gave it to the Dodgson family. No diary entries refer to this piece.

Edith Letitia Hutchinson Shute (1854–1952) was the wife of Richard Shute, Student and Tutor of Christ Church, who died in 1886. Dodgson met her for the first time on 2 November 1882[1] and they became good friends.

The poem was first published in Shaberman and Crutch, *Under the Quizzing Glass: A Lewis Carroll Miscellany,* 42–43, where 1881 is incorrectly given as the presumed publication date.

❦

Who caused the Boer Rebellion?
  "I," said the people's Willy,
  "With my speches [*sic*] all so silly:
I caused the Boer Rebellion".

Who sent out reinforcements?
  "I," said Childers, blandly:
  "And I did it very grandly:
I sent out re-inforcements".

Who advised surrender?
  "I," said Quaker Bright:
  "For I never mean to fight:
I advised surrender."

1. Green, *Diaries,* 410; see also 423.

Who went out to lead them?
  "I," said Roberts of Cabul:
  "And was made an April-fool.
I went out to lead them."

Who tried negotiation?
  "I," said Kimberly, sadly:
  "And I did it very badly:
I tried negotiation."

Who signed the treaty?
  "I," said Evelyn Wood,
  "Tho' I never thought I could.
I signed the treaty."

Who spoke up against it?
  "I," said Cairns, profoundly:
  "And I gave it to them roundly:
I spoke up against it."

Who said 'twas honorable?
  "I," said Selbourne glib,
  "Though I knew it was a fib.
I said 'twas honorable."

Who cried 'Shame!' upon it?
  "We," say Whig & Tory,
  "Who care for England's glory:
We cried 'Shame!' upon it."

Who approved it strongly?
  "We," say all the Rads
  And the mean-spirited cads.
"We approved it strongly."

Who will pay the piper?
  "I," says poor John Bull:
  "For, whoever plays the fool,
I always pay the piper!"

Appendix

The Value of Redistribution: A Note on Electoral Statistics

Robert Arthur Talbot Gascoyne-Cecil, Lord Salisbury

[1884: Princeton]

❧

The obtrusion of statistics upon the readers of the *National Review* requires some apology, though I hope to confine the offence within endurable limits. My main object in appealing to figures is to refute a calumny which has been directed, with lavish reiteration, against the Conservative Party during the last two months. It is said that we are dishonest in the account we give of our own wishes and motives; that we are insincere in professing to accept the Franchise Bill, if coupled with redistribution; that we really dread both franchise and redistribution, and are only desirous of delay. Mere denials, however emphatic, do not diminish the confidence with which this false charge is repeated. Perhaps I may convince some of those who make it of its emptiness, if I show them by figures that we should have no cause, for Party reasons, to dread enfranchisement coupled with a fair redistribution—even if the strictest numerical principles were its only guide. I believe that the statistics in our possession show that the householders of Great Britain in town and county, if the proportion of Conservatives and Liberals among them could be exactly reproduced at Westminster, would elect a House of Commons much more favourable to us than that which sits there now; and that, therefore, we have every motive to desire extension of the county franchise, under as fair an apportionment of seats as can be obtained. It can also, I believe, be shown, by figures, that extension without redistribution would aggravate, certainly to some extent, and perhaps very seriously, the artificial and unjust disadvantage

National Review, October 1884, 145–62.

to which we are at present subjected; and that, therefore, our resistance to a one-sided Reform Bill is no mere move of Party tactics; it is dictated by the strongest instincts of self-preservation.

I have seen such strange opinions attributed to myself, and deduced from what I have said by such singular logic, that I may be pardoned for explaining—before I go further—not only what I do mean, but also what I do not mean. Because I deal only with numbers, I do not mean that a Redistribution Bill should take account of no other than numerical considerations. I shall dwell on the injustice which minorities would suffer by the mutilated legislation which has been proposed; but I do not mean that they would be the only sufferers: I am dealing with only part of a large case. I do not mean in these few pages to offer, or to suggest, any legislative project; for I think that proposals for legislation on such a subject would come more usefully from Ministers of the Crown, who can command the information necessary for the elaboration of practical provisions. More especially, I am not proposing a plan for equal electoral districts. I say this, because I shall have to make some use of the first four rules of arithmetic; and I have observed that when any speaker in the course of an argument refers to arithmetical considerations, the proper reply to him, according to the controversial usage of the hour, is, "Oh! you are in favour of equal electoral districts." Now, as I shall presently show, equal electoral districts would, in most communities, not attain the object I desire to recommend. They proceed exclusively on the system of direct territorial representation, to the exclusion of virtual representation altogether; and I doubt much whether any mechanism can be found to give anything like an exact copy in Parliament of the wishes of the people, which does not make use of the principle of virtual representation. What is true of equal electoral districts is true, to a great extent, of many of the less sweeping plans which are in vogue. They are apt to have this grave defect, that they seem to be constructed on no other principle than that of advancing by steps, more or less hesitating, towards an equal electoral division. To cut off a certain number of small boroughs at the bottom of the list, and to add a corresponding number of new large constituencies at the top, is assumed to be the only mode of operation possible to the reformer; and a moderate measure seems to differ from a drastic measure only in the number of the small boroughs that are so effaced. But there is no security whatever that a true representation will be the issue of such a process. A sensible removal of the inequalities of representation must, no doubt, be one of the effects of any redistribution; and in remedying the inadequate representation under which some great districts of the kingdom suffer, it will mitigate a very real grievance. But a Reform Bill which does not tend to reproduce with fidelity the balance of opinion in the country, wholly misses the main object at which it should be aimed. Even equal electoral districts may be so devised that they will produce injustice as great as the most grotesque anomalies could achieve. Indeed, in a community where opinions are profoundly divided, such a result of a purely numerical system would be highly probable. These are two sets of circumstances, completely different, in which equal electoral districts would cause a flagrant misrepresentation of the people. First suppose the case of a province—let us say in Belgium—consisting of Catholics and Liberals, in the proportion of eight of the one to nine of the other; and suppose the population to be so well-mixed and stirred together, that in each part of the province the same proportion of the two parties is accurately preserved. It is obvious that in such a case the Catholics would be completely effaced by a system of equal electoral districts. In every constituency, no matter how you divided them, the Liberals would be in the majority, and would return every single member; and the representation of the province would be wholly Liberal. The Catholics of the province would be as entirely deprived of any share in the government of their own country as if they were a subject race. If by some military revolution they were entirely deprived of Parliamentary institutions, they would be neither worse nor better off—so far as their representation was concerned—than they had been under Parliamentary institutions.

But the same result might spring from an arrangement of the two populations of an exactly opposite kind. Suppose another province of Belgium, in which the Liberals inhabited a large city lying in the centre of the province, while the Catholics had exclusive possession of the country round. Let the electors be in the same proportion of about eight Catholics to nine Liberals—say, roughly, 400,000 Catholics to 450,000 Liberals—and suppose there are seventeen seats to be disposed of. A symmetrical legislator arises profoundly impressed with the beauty of equal constituencies and accurate divisions. He proposes that seventeen lines should be drawn from the centre of the city to the borders of the province, so distanced that each of the triangular figures or compartments thus described should contain 50,000 voters. Nothing would appear superficially more fair, more regular, more exactly in accordance with the demands of a rigid equality. But each of these equal electoral divisions would contain, in round numbers, 24,000 Catholics and 26,000 Liberals, and the representatives would belong exclusively to the latter party; and the Catholics would be as entirely outside the right of representation, would be as completely paying taxes which they had no share in voting, and obeying laws made by their bitterest enemies, as if they belonged to a subjugated province.

The object of adducing extreme cases of this kind, is not, of course, to suggest that in this exact form they are likely to occur in practice, but to point out how far the unequal action of equal electoral division may conceivably extend, and how little limit there is, except that of pure chance, to its unjust operation. The necessity of guarding against this danger becomes more imperative in proportion to the increasing regularity and unbroken level of the franchise. The apparent symmetry tends to mask the misrepresentation which, if the community be sharply divided into two in matters of creed or in material interest, equality of division is apt to produce. And the last illustration is not so entirely foreign to our practical experience as may at first sight be thought. Suppose the Liberal city, instead of being collected into a great central nucleus, is scattered in towns and urban patches over each of the supposed electoral districts, and you have a state of things not inaptly representing the condition in which many an English county will find itself if the new voters are divided into constituencies by existing boundaries. The urban voters will be so marshalled that, upon questions which divide the two, they will in many districts wholly silence the agricultural minority, whose right to vote, as Mr. Mill says, will be converted into a right to be out-voted.

The ordinary and plausible answer to these considerations is that however theoretically sound they may be, they are in practice fortuitously remedied; that the parties into which the population is divided chance to be so disposed geographically, that the domination of one party in one region is, in sufficient proportion, balanced by the domination of the other party in another region. This ground was strongly held by Mr. Bright, in the discussions on the Minority clause in 1867; and he used to point to the instance of Liverpool, whose steady Toryism went far to counterpoise the unvarying Liberalism of Birmingham. This answer is practically sufficient if it rests on a sufficient basis of fact. If it be indeed true that the minorities effaced in one district are so balanced by the effacement of opposite minorities in another district, that, on the whole, the true dimensions of each party in the nation are accurately reproduced in their representative assembly, it is undoubtedly a very interesting case of providential compensation. But is it the fact? Does this balance exist even under the present system? Will there be any remnant of such a balance if the county suffrage shall be extended without redistribution, and the tenant-farmer vote, which unquestionably does now operate as an element of counterpoise to disproportion and inequality elsewhere, shall be entirely submerged?

These questions lie at the root of the present controversy. The statistics seem to me to show that the balance does not exist; and that on the hypothesis the most adverse to the Conservative Party, the householders in this island are much more Conservative than those who represent them in the House of Commons. If this be the fact, it should protect from charges of insincerity those who are claiming that the extension of the county franchise shall be accompanied by a measure which will make the House of Commons a more faithful mirror of the opinions of the people. If it can also be shown that enfranchisement within existing boundaries will not only not tend to this result, but will cause the reflection of the mirror to be more distorted and more untrue than it is at present, the Conservatives who have resisted this aggravation of existing evils should be acquitted of having acted on any trivial or temporary motive. The new justification of his policy which Mr. Gladstone has learned from Birmingham is that enfranchisement is a good in itself, even if no redistribution occurs to make it better. This cannot be; unless it is a good to provide an electoral system which shall misrepresent the opinions of the nation.

I will leave Ireland out of the account; for the questions in issue there are wholly different, and would require to be separately treated. And I will take the date of the General Election in 1880, as the most recent period at which we have full information concerning the opinion of the electors. The date will not be challenged as one unduly favourable to the Conservatives. The question, then, is, what was the true strength of the two parties among the householders of Great Britain, in county and town, in April 1880? We know the opinion of the householders of the towns, for the poll-book is there to tell us. We know also the opinion of the county electors under the present law. But what would have been the view of "the two million"—the householders in the counties—if they had had the vote? Different men will form very different estimates of the state of opinion in this vast multitude, according to their temperament or the political prepossessions from which they argue. Some think the county householders will be nearly as Conservative as the present county electors—especially if they are reinforced by that faithful army of lodgekeepers and gamekeepers whom Mr. Gladstone, with a condescension of which he is never weary of reminding us, has admitted into the ranks of capable citizens. Others, on the contrary, hold that Liberalism will be as powerful among the householders of the counties as it has hitherto been among the householders of the towns. There is something to be said for both views, according as the industrial or the agricultural portion of England is under consideration. The experience of some of the widely extended boroughs in which there is a large rural area, such as Shoreham, Wilton, Eye, and Wenlock, goes to show that the agricultural householder does not differ in his politics from the present electorate of the rural counties. On the other hand, the strong Liberalism developed by the boroughs which were created out of urban districts in the counties by the Act of 1867, such as Hartlepool, Middlesborough, and Dewsbury, shows that such localities are not distinguished in sentiment from the older boroughs in the same neighbourhood. But though, under the light of these examples, estimates may vary much, according to the proclivities of the enquirer, there are limits on each side to the range of possible hypothesis. The most sanguine Radical does not expect that the new county voters will, as a whole, be more Liberal than their brother householders in the towns. The most optimist Conservative does not venture to hope that, as a body, they will be more Conservative than the existing county voters. Setting aside eccentricities of opinion, the field of reasonable conjecture may safely be bounded at either end of these two assumptions. Guided by them, let us enquire what, in either case, would have been the composition of the House of Commons if the county householders had been enfranchised, and the constituencies had been arranged in such a manner that the strength of parties among the members should be exactly the same as the strength of parties among the electors.

Let us first proceed upon the assumption that the householders in the counties of each division would vote exactly like the householders in the towns of that division: that is to say, that there would be the same proportion of Conservatives and Liberals among them. In order to find what the Parliamentary result of this supposition would be, we must ascertain for each division what per-centage of the aggregate votes polled in the contested boroughs was given to each side, and then apply the per-centage to the number of members which that division would have in proportion to its population. Fortunately for my purpose, contests in the boroughs were almost universal in 1880, so that the contests furnish a broad basis for induction. Out of 220 boroughs in Great Britain, only twenty-one were uncontested; and of these, Liverpool had a contest two months before, and thirteen others had contests at one time or other during the present or the last Parliament. In every case I have taken the highest number polled on each side as the strength of that side. In Birmingham and Glasgow it has, of course, been necessary to halve the numbers polled for all three Liberal candidates taken together.

For the purpose of fixing the number of members to which, on the hypothesis of a proportional representation, each division would be entitled, I have taken the figures furnished for the counties by Mr. Henry Bernard in his very useful pamphlet on Redistribution. They are obtained by dividing the population of each county by the number of 54,242—a number which is the result of dividing the population of the United Kingdom by the number of borough and county members in the House of Commons. One member, consequently, is allowed for each 1/643 of the population. In publishing these figures, Mr. Bernard expresses an opinion in favour of adopting a rigid electoral equality among all counties in the United Kingdom; and he negatives very summarily the idea of meeting any portion of our difficulties by increasing the members of the House of Commons. In employing his figures for a statistical purpose, I must guard myself very distinctly from being thought to accept his legislative views; but the arithmetical data which he has brought together are well worthy of careful examination.

I have grouped the counties according to the divisions of the Registrar-General, except that I have not put Monmouthshire into Wales.

The South-East Division includes Kent, Sussex, Surrey, Berkshire, and Hampshire. All the boroughs in the division, being thirty-two in number, were contested, except Hythe and Sandwich; and for these I have used the figures of 1874. The division includes the Metropolitan boroughs of Gravesend, Greenwich, Southwark, and Lambeth. The aggregate of votes given was as follows:—

	Aggregate number of votes in boroughs.	
	Conservative.	Liberal.
South-Eastern Division	77,068	79,014
Per-centage	49•4	50•6

2. The South-Western Division includes Cornwall, Devon, Dorset, Somerset, and Wilts. It contains thirty-one boroughs, in all of which there were contests in 1880, except in Tavistock, which has never been contested by a Conservative, and Frome, for which I have taken the figures of 1876. The division contains no large city, for Bristol is counted in Gloucestershire:—

	Aggregate of votes in contested boroughs.	
	Conservative.	Liberal.
South-Western Division	26,136	28,825
Per-centage	47•55	52•45

3. The South Midland Division includes the counties of Middlesex, Buckingham, Oxford, Hertford, Bedford, Cambridge, Huntingdon, and Northampton. It contains twenty boroughs, all of which were contested in 1880, except Huntingdon and Wycombe, for which I have taken the figures of 1884 and 1883. This division includes the cities of London and Westminster, and the Metropolitan boroughs of Marylebone, Chelsea, Hackney, Finsbury, and Tower Hamlets:—

	Aggregate of votes given in boroughs.	
	Conservative.	Liberal.
South Midland Division	90,447	103,943
Per-centage	46•53	53•47

4. The Eastern Division contains the counties of Norfolk, Suffolk, and Essex. Besides the city of Norwich, this division only contains seven boroughs, all of which were contested:—

	Aggregate of votes in boroughs.	
	Conservative.	Liberal.
Eastern Division	13,704	15,219
Per-centage	47•4	52•6

5. The West Midland Division includes the counties of Gloucester, Monmouth, Hereford, Shropshire, Warwick, Worcester, and Stafford. Besides Birmingham and Bristol, it includes twenty-eight boroughs, at all of which there were contests in 1880, except at Walsall and Wednesbury, for which I have taken the figures of 1874, and Cirencester, for which I have taken those of 1878:—

	Aggregate of votes in boroughs.	
	Conservative.	Liberal.
West Midland Division	77,017	116,091
Per-centage	39•9	60•1

6. The North Midland Division includes the counties of Lincoln, Derby, Leicester, Rutland, Nottingham. It contains only ten

boroughs, which were all contested. But of these, Derby was scarcely contested seriously, so that the Conservative per-centage is unduly low:—

	Aggregate of votes in boroughs.	
	Conservative.	Liberal.
North Midland Division	23,645	43,246
Per-centage	35•35	64•65

7. The North-Western Division includes Lancashire and Cheshire. There are nineteen boroughs in it, all of which were contested in April 1880, except Liverpool, which had been contested two months before, and Bury, for which I have taken the figures of 1874:—

	Aggregate of votes in boroughs.	
	Conservative.	Liberal.
North-Western Division	116,281	125,823
Per-centage	48•03	51•97

8. The Yorkshire Division. In this division, which consists only of the county of York, there are nineteen boroughs, all of which were contested:—

	Aggregate of votes in boroughs.	
	Conservative.	Liberal.
Yorkshire Division	68,489	114,022
Per-centage	37•5	62•5

9. The Northern Division consists of the four northern counties, Northumberland, Cumberland, Westmoreland, and Durham. It contains fifteen boroughs. All of them were contested in 1880, except Morpeth, for which I have taken the figures of 1874. It is the only contest which has taken place in that borough since the Reform Bill of 1832:—

	Aggregate of votes in boroughs.	
	Conservative.	Liberal.
Northern Division	24,607	54,615
Per-centage	31•06	68•94

10. Wales. In the Principality contests were comparatively fewer. There are fourteen Parliamentary boroughs, and of these

Beaumaris, Carnarvon, Cardigan, and Swansea were uncontested in 1880. But Beaumaris and Swansea were contested in 1874, and Carnarvon in 1832, and I have taken the figures of these elections. Cardigan has not been contested since 1855.

	Aggregate of votes in contested boroughs.	
	Conservative.	Liberal.
Wales	20,206	30,332
Per-centage	39•98	60•02

11. Scotland. It would have been more convenient to have divided Scotland so as to have presented the Highlands and the Lowlands separately. But the system of contributory boroughs, which does not respect the county boundaries, makes such a division very difficult. It would have been impossible to draw a line which would separate the counties into two groups, without mutilating a Parliamentary borough. Scotland contains twenty-two boroughs, of which seventeen were contested in 1880. For Montrose and Paisley I have used the figures of 1874 and 1884. Inverness, Stirling, and Wick have not been contested by Conservatives for many years past.

	Aggregate of votes in contested boroughs.	
	Conservative.	Liberal.
Scotland	44,010	116,049
Per-centage	27•4	72•6

If the per-centages thus obtained are multiplied into the number of members assignable to each division under a strictly numerical system, we shall have the precise constitution of the House of Commons that would reflect faithfully the condition of political opinion among the people—always on the assumption with which we are now dealing, that the county householders and the borough householders each contain the same proportion of Conservatives. The numbers of members assignable to each division are taken from Mr. Bernard. The following table gives the result. The fourth column is obtained by multiplying the second and third, and dividing by 100; the fifth column, by taking the fourth from the third.

Districts.	*Per-centage of Conservative Borough Voters 1880.*	*Total Numbers of Members under Numerical System according to Bernard's Tables.*	*Computed Conservative Proportion.*	*Computed Liberal Proportion.*
South East	49•4	68	34	34
South West	47•55	35	17	18
South Midland	46•53	76	35	41
Eastern	47•4	26	12	14
West Midland	39•9	60	24	36
North Midland	35•35	31	11	20
North Western	48•03	76	37	39
Northern	31•06	30	9	21
Yorkshire	37•5	53	20	33
Wales	39•98	25	10	15
Scotland	27•4	69	19	50
		549	228	321

The Liberal majority in Great Britain in 1880—setting aside University members—was 128. If household suffrage in counties had existed in 1880, with an absolutely fair apportionment of seats, even on an assumption so adverse to the Conservatives as that which I have made, the majority would only have been 93. In other words, the Conservatives would have been stronger on every division by thirty-five. It is not necessary for me to examine in detail the effect on our recent political history which a difference of 35 votes in the House of Commons, in favour of the Conservatives, would have produced. It is enough to say that that dissolution, which we desire as a measure both of justice and of safety, would already have taken place.

Now let us take the opposite hypothesis. We have made the assumption most unfavourable to the Conservatives; and the conclusion to which it leads us is that the Conservative strength is short, by 35 votes, of the number that should legitimately belong to it. Let us make the other assumption—that which is most favourable to the Conservatives. Let us assume that the new county voters will vote precisely on the pattern of those who have the county franchise now. To ascertain how a House of Commons, chosen on this hypothesis, would be composed, it will be necessary to number, in separate columns, those elected by the counties and those elected by the boroughs. For we assume that the boroughs will continue to vote as they did in 1880. Therefore, the right strength of parties among their members must be found by multiplying the per-centages already ascertained into the number of members assignable in each division to the boroughs in proportion to their population. But for the county members under this hypothesis a new per-centage must be found, calculated from the votes which the present county electors gave in 1880. The computation is a little less trustworthy than that which concerns the boroughs, because contests were less general; for of 127 county constituencies in Great Britain, 32 were uncontested. In ten of these cases, I have been able to use the figures of contests which took place in this or the last Parliament. Of the remaining

Table I.

Division.	*Aggregate of County Votes, 1880.*		*Conservative Per-Centage.*
	Conservative.	*Liberal.*	
1. South Eastern	46,500	34,418	57•5
2. South Western	16,317	15,121	51•9
3. South Midland	30,865	24,737	55•5
4. Eastern	22,765	19,431	53•95
5. West Midland	41,113	38,736	51•49
6. North Midland	27,093	25,535	51•48
7. North Western	47,447	43,575	52•13
8. Northern	23,419	26,092	47•30
9. Yorkshire	38,938	43,237	47•4
10. Wales	15,128	20,448	42•52
11. Scotland	27,574	32,224	46•11

22, 2 are split seats, 8 are Liberal, and 12 are Conservative. The effect, therefore, of the withdrawal of these constituencies from the calculation is, so far as it goes, adverse to the Conservatives; but it probably makes little difference.

The members assigned, according to Mr. Bernard's figures, to each division, are, in the following tables, assigned respectively to the counties and boroughs, in proportion to their population.

The upshot, then, of these computations is as follows: If we believe the county householders to be as Liberal as the householders of the towns, we are weaker now in Parliament by thirty-five votes than we should be with a true distribution and the proposed enfranchisement. If we believe the county householders to be as Conservative as the present county electors, we are now weaker by eighty-nine votes than we should be with a true distribution and the proposed enfranchisement.

An objection may be taken to this mode of looking at the matter, that I am assuming too rigid a division between Liberal and Conservative; that there is a moveable intermediate body which swings to one side or the other, as it may be impelled by its opinion on the passing events or passing statesmen of the day, and cannot be ranged permanently under either flag. This is no doubt the fact—though this transferable quantity is much smaller than is generally assumed, as may be evident from the fact that the last election, sweeping as it seemed to be, was turned by some two thousand persons. But the defect suggested is undoubtedly inherent in these, as in all statistical computations which concern human beings. And therefore, a prediction, for any particular occasion, can never be safely founded on them; for it may be falsified by any passing gust of feeling. But there are very strong elements of stability in both political parties, arising out of religious persuasion, local or family tradition, and material interest; and these are changed by processes so slow that for our purpose they may be taken as permanent. Moreover, it must be borne in mind that I have selected the dissolution of 1880 as my moment of comparison; and the Liberal flood which ran at that time swept away in its rush everything that was loose and friable, and left nothing of the Conservative formation but the bare rock.

Another objection may plausibly be raised on the ground of

TABLE II.*							
Col. 1	*2*	*3*	*4*	*5*	*6*	*7*	*8*
	Conservative Per-centage.		*Members assigned to*		*Computed Proportion of Total.*		*Total Members assigned by Bernard.*
Division.	*Boroughs.*	*Counties.*	*Borough Popula-tion.*	*County Popula-tion.*	*Conser-vative*	*Liberal.*	
1. South Eastern	49•4	57•5	32	36	37	31	68
2. South Western	47•55	51•9	11	24	18	17	35
3. South Midland	46•53	55•5	25	51	38	38	76
4. Eastern	47•4	53•95	4	22	13	13	26
5. West Midland	39•9	51•49	31	29	28	32	60
6. North Midland	35•35	51•48	9	22	14	17	31
7. North Western	48•03	52•13	36	40	37	39	76
8. Northern	31•06	47•30	13	17	12	18	30
9. Yorkshire	37•5	47•4	26	27	22	31	53
10. Wales	39•98	42•52	9	16	10	15	25
11. Scotland	27•4	46•11	30	39	26	43	69
			226	323	255	294	549
						255	
			Liberal majority			39	

Real Liberal majority of 1880 = 128: Conservative gain on the assumption made, 89.

the impracticability or difficulty of obtaining this perfectly fair redistribution. No arrangement, it may be said, has yet been proposed, which could be relied upon to give at Westminster an exact reflection, in reduced proportions, of the political divisions of the nation. It may be so; but no such assertion can be made with confidence, for the effort has never been really made. Excepting the enactment as to three-cornered constituencies, inserted by

*Columns 4 and 5 are equal to column 8; so are columns 6 and 7.

Amounts in col. 6 = $\frac{\text{col. 2} \times \text{col. 4}}{100} + \frac{\text{col. 3} \times \text{col. 5}}{100}$

Lord Cairns in the last Reform Bill, which was necessarily scanty and tentative, no provision having this end directly in view has been placed on the Statute Book since Parliamentary Reforms commenced. It is doubtful whether this clause can be usefully carried further; but the cumulative vote in School Board elections has worked satisfactorily: and material redress might be afforded by good boundary provisions, by giving to urban and rural populations a fairer relative representation than they have now, and by a recourse, when it is needed, to Mr. Cobden's principle of single-membered constituencies. But I am not engaged in drawing a Reform Bill. I am concerned with its object; and wish that Reform Bills should rather be judged by the end they achieve than by their manner of effecting it. The object at which every measure of the kind should aim, and to which, in its degree, it should approach, is the perfect representation of the interests, the opinions, and the divisions of the nation; of minorities as well as majorities; of interests which are weak, as well as of those which are strong. That a complete solution of the problem may be difficult, I do not deny. But I am convinced that we may arrive much nearer to it than we stand now. The interest of agriculture is suffering a serious wrong by the existing arrangements; and the middle classes in some of our great towns have much cause to complain of an effacement, which at present, perhaps, is only a theoretical injury, but which tends to become more practical every year. We are never likely to reach an ideal state of things in this, or any other respect; it may cost much effort to attain even to a condition of substantial redress; but the indispensable condition of any remedy is that the extent of the evil should be recognized. And at least we may avoid the error of making it worse—a result which would undoubtedly be produced by a mutilated Reform Bill.

I have shown why the Conservatives have no cause to dread the proposed enfranchisement, if it be coupled with a redistribution which is even moderately just towards interests which, by the existing arrangement, are submerged. I have now to show that they have very cogent reasons for objecting to the omission of redistribution altogether. How many county seats now held by Conservatives will fall, if, with the enlarged franchise, the present boundaries of borough and county be maintained? That is the question we have to solve. The answer must, of course, depend on the assumption which we make with respect to the political views of the county householders. If we believe that they will vote as the present electors do, it is obvious that no change will be made by their admission to the present county registers. If we take the opposite extreme, and assume they will vote like the already enfranchised householders in the towns of their respective districts, the following table gives the losses which (calculating on the polls of 1880) omission of redistribution would inflict on the Conservatives.

That I may not seem to be a prophet of evil, I must observe that I do not put forward this issue as a probable event, but rather as the limit of what may reasonably be thought possible, in the way of loss, on the least favourable assumption.

The number of probable new voters is found by taking 79 per cent. of the houses in the county and deducting the existing resident voters. That proportion is the one in which houses now are found to furnish voters in the towns.

To these must be added five divisions where a Liberal headed the poll, but the second seat was not contested by a Liberal—Carmarthenshire, W. Cumberland, N. Northamptonshire, N. Staffordshire, S. Leicestershire. On this assumption, therefore, the total loss to the Conservatives by enfranchisement without redistribution would be 47 seats, counting 94 votes on a division. On the same assumption, they are already weaker by 35 than, according to the numerical strength of their party in the country, they should be.

I need not say that I do not give these computations as in any sense a prediction of the future. The elements of variation and uncertainty, which no computations can ever approximately measure, are too large to make a forecast possible; and its place if it were attempted, would probably be somewhere between the extreme suppositions I have mentioned, and not at either limit. But these figures do show the momentous significance of the question whether we are to have a redistribution or not; and whether, if we have one, it is to be fair. They show that whatever the influence of the Conservative Party may be, whatever meas-

	Probable Number of New Voters.	Per-centages of Conserva-tives in Boroughs of Divi-sions.	Estimated Number (by Per-centages in last Column) of		Esti-mated Majority of Liberal New Voters.	Conser-vative Majority at the Election of 1880.	Seats transferred.
			Conser-vative New Voters.	Liberal New Voters.			
Bucks	14,315	46•53	6,661	7,654	993	166	1
Mid-Cheshire	13,256	48•03	6,366	6,890	524	*326	1
Essex, E.	17,544	47•4	8,316	9,228	912	392	2
Essex, S.	24,983	47•4	11,842	13,141	1,299	517	2
Essex, W.	14,271	47•4	6,764	7,507	743	*625	1
Lancashire, S.W.	39,658	48•03	19,048	20,610	1,562	*1,239	1
Leicester, N.	11,249	35•35	3,977	7,272	3,295	695	2
Lincoln, S.	10,768	35•35	3,806	6,962	3,156	938	2
Lincoln, N. (1881)	11,300	35•35	3,995	7,305	3,310	471	2
Monmouth	16,327	39•9	6,514	9,813	3,299	513	2
Norfolk, N. (1879)	15,767	47•4	7,473	8,294	821	490	2
Norfolk, W.	15,260	47•4	7,234	8,026	792	367	2
Northumberland, N.	7,129	31•06	2,214	4,915	2,701	654	2
Nottingham, N.	17,017	35•35	6,015	11,002	4,987	*10	1
Nottingham, S.	8,968	35•35	3,170	5,798	2,628	1,046	2
Shropshire, S.	6,919	39•9	2,761	4,158	1,397	757	2
Somerset, W.	12,581	47•55	5,982	6,599	617	219	2
Stafford, W.	11,827	39•9	4,719	7,108	2,389	779	2
Suffolk, E.	21,173	47•4	10,036	11,137	1,101	753	2
Wiltshire, N.	9,634	47•55	4,581	5,053	472	*50	1
York, E. R.	15,111	37•5	5,666	9,445	3,779	1,220	2
York, N. R. (1882)	18,344	37•5	6,879	11,465	4,586	386	1
Ayr, N.	8,262	**38•14	3,151	5,111	1,960	45	1
Ayr, S.	8,904	38•14	3,396	5,508	2,202	247	1
Inverness	9,671	†27•4	1,650	8,021	6,371	29	1
Dumbartonshire	6,037	‡30•	1,811	4,226	2,415	9	1
Haddingtonshire	3,707	§37•3	1,263	2,444	1,181	92	1
					Total loss		42

* One seat only.

** Per-centage taken from Ayr burghs.

† " " " Scottish burghs generally.

‡ " " " Kilmarnock burghs.

§ " " " Haddington burghs.

ure of success or failure awaits them, a just solution of the question of redistribution means to them a difference in their favour of some hundred votes in the House of Commons. This result does not depend on the truth of either hypothesis, or of any more moderate supposition lying between them. It accrues in any case. If the best is true, and the new county electors think like the old, then we are at this moment weaker by 89 votes than we ought to be. If the worst is true, and the county householders think like the householders in the towns, then we are at this moment 35 weaker than we justly should be, and we shall lose under the existing boundaries 47 seats, counting 94 votes, into the bargain. If there be no fair redistribution, be our party prosperous or unlucky, it appears that in either case we shall be defrauded of from 89 to 130 votes to which, on the mere principles of numerical representation, we should have an indefeasible right. It hardly seems that any issue of the present controversy which could possibly occur would be worse for us than this, or more unjust to the cause we represent. Mr. Gladstone's doctrine, "Enfranchisement is a good in itself," might be a sound one if the divisions into which the new voters are to be arranged were just. By fastening the new enfranchisement on to the old distribution, he practically claims the right so to parcel out his new voters that the Conservatives amongst them shall be effaced.

The argument I have followed proceeds on the assumption that no system of distribution is completely just which does not, formally or virtually, give to the minority a representation corresponding to its actual weight. This contention is generally resisted by the Radical Party, whose doctrine is essentially despotic. In their language freedom means little more than the right of the majority to choose an absolute ruler. No views of distribution which would make the minority at Westminster as strong as it is in the country will find much favour in their eyes. Mr. Lefevre, in arguing against the rights of the minority, even borrows the phrase with which the Duke of Wellington defended the state of things that existed before 1832—"How is the Queen's Government to be carried on?" According to this view, the only function of popular election is to provide the master. When he is found, the less he is impeded by the criticisms of a minority the better.

Such a doctrine implies a belief on the part of those who hold it that the party to which they belong will generally be uppermost, and is not likely to be welcome to their opponents, who have not that ground for admiring it. But, apart from the natural disinclination of a minority to surrender all power of self-defence, there are, in the present drift of the political struggle, dangers ahead, which give an especial value to the rights of a minority. A dozen years ago, Lord Beaconsfield epigrammatically divided his indictment against his opponents into two counts, "plundering and blundering." In doing so he marked a great change which had come over political warfare in recent times. Formerly, it was in most cases only "blundering" that an Opposition had to deal with. Occasionally there were wide divergences of principle; but the ordinary work of an Opposition was to convince the country that the Ministers were guilty of mistaken aims and incompetent administration, and the obvious and indeed only cure they had to recommend was that they should be allowed to try their hands and prove their own superiority. This is the essential function of an Opposition under a system of party government, and must remain so as long as party government exists. Perhaps it tends to justify the old definition of party, "the madness of the many for the profit of the few"; but the mechanism can be worked in no other way. It is not possible to remedy the blunders of a Government, except by changing the men who compose it. But in addition to this primary duty, the shifting of political issues has imposed upon the Conservative Opposition a totally different function, which can be fulfilled, at least to a considerable extent, even when a change of Government is impracticable. They have to prevent "plundering," as well as to remedy "blundering"; and the performance of this duty interests their followers throughout the country quite as much as the leaders in the House. When a Radical Government, now-a-days, comes into power, with a strong majority at its back, a feeling spreads itself abroad among all sorts of people who belong to any class electorally weak, similar, at least in kind, to that which is felt in a Turkish province on the announcement that a new Pasha has been appointed. They know that the process of "conveyance" is about to begin. Whether they be land-owners, or ship-owners, or belong to an old corporation, or are members of an endowed Church, they look forward to the future with misgiving, for they know that reform, of the predatory species, is in the air. To this portion of the Conservative party—a very large one—it is not of so much importance to displace the Government, or at least it is not indispensable for them to do so. Much of the safety, which is their chief desire, can be secured by the existence of a strong minority. A Government bent on plundering seldom polls its whole strength in the House of Commons. A certain—though small—portion of every majority is accessible to argument, especially on this subject, and a strong Conservative Opposition can usually prevent any serious wrong from being done. The calm and moderate legislation of the Liberal Parliaments of 1837, 1847, and 1859, show the enormous advantage which a strong Opposition may confer on the Conservative interests of the country. Under the influence of bye-elections, a gleam of moderation gilded the declining years even of the Parliament of 1868. Such moderate Parliaments are not to be looked for if the new Liberal plan for the suppression of minorities is allowed to succeed. A fair redistribution—that is to say, a recognition according to their true strength, so far as possible, of all interests in the country—is needed, not so much to decide the race for office, as to maintain, and indeed to restore, that equable temperature which, for many generations before 1868, was one of the distinctive features of our legislation.

SALISBURY.

Selected Bibliography

Abeles, Francine F. "Ranking by Inversion: A Note on C. L. Dodgson." *Historia Mathematica* 6 (1979), 310–17.

______. "C. L. Dodgson and Apportionment for Proportional Representation." *Ganita-Bhāratī* 3 (1981), 71–82.

______. "The Mathematical–Political Papers of C. L. Dodgson." *In Lewis Carroll: A Celebration,* edited by Edward Guiliano, 195–210. New York: Clarkson N. Potter, 1982.

______. "Power in Decisions Among Multiple Alternatives." *Journal of Information & Optimization Sciences* 5 (1984), 43–48.

______, ed. *The Mathematical Pamphlets of Charles Lutwidge Dodgson and Related Pieces.* New York: Lewis Carroll Society of North America; distributed by the University Press of Virginia, 1994.

______. "Charles L. Dodgson, Mathematician." In *Yours very sincerely, C. L. Dodgson (alias "Lewis Carroll"): An Exhibition from the Jon A. Lindseth Collection of C. L. Dodgson and Lewis Carroll,* 44–53. New York: The Grolier Club, 1998.

______. "Charles L. Dodgson's Version of Pari-Mutuel Betting." *The Carrollian* 3 (1999), 30–36.

Arrow, Kenneth. *Social Choice and Individual Values.* New York: John Wiley, 1951; 2d edition 1963.

Baily, W. *Proportional Representation in Large Constituencies.* London: Ridgway, 1872.

Balinski, Michel L., and H. Peyton Young. "Criteria for Proportional Representation." *Operations Research* 27 (1979), 80–95.

______. *Fair Representation.* New Haven, Conn.: Yale University Press, 1982.

Bartholdi, J., C. A. Tovey, and M. A. Trick. "Voting Schemes for Which It Can Be Difficult to Tell Who Won the Election." *Social Choice and Welfare* 6 (1989), 157–65.

Benians, E. A., *et al. The Cambridge History of the British Empire.* Cambridge: Cambridge University Press, v. III, 1959.

"The Berol Collection of Lewis Carroll: A Preliminary Checklist." Typescript compiled by John Frost. New York: New York University Library, 1981.

Black, Duncan. "Discovery of Lewis Carroll Documents." *Notes and Queries,* February 1953, 77–79.

______. *The Theory of Committees and Elections.* London, U.K.: Cambridge University Press, 1958. Reprint, 1968.

______."The Central Argument in Lewis Carroll's 'The Principles of Parliamentary Representation.'" *Papers on Nonmarket Decision Making* 3 (1967), 1–17.

______. "Lewis Carroll and the Theory of Games." *American Economic Review* 59 (1969), 206–15.

______."Lewis Carroll and the Cambridge Mathematical School of P.R.; Arthur Cohen and Edith Denman." *Public Choice* 8 (1970), 1–28.

______. "Evaluating Carroll's Theory of Parliamentary Representation." *Jabberwocky* 1 (1970), 19–21.

Campbell, Donald E. "Realization of Social Choice Functions." *Econometrica* 46 (1978), 171–80.

Clark, Anne. *Lewis Carroll: A Biography.* New York: Schocken Books, 1979.

Cohen, Morton N., ed. *The Letters of Lewis Carroll.* 2 vols. New York: Oxford University Press, 1979.

______. *Lewis Carroll. A Biography.* New York: Knopf, 1995.

Collingwood, Stuart Dodgson. *The Life and Letters of Lewis Carroll.* London: T. Fisher Unwin, 1898.

d'Hondt, Victor. *La répresentation proportionelle des partis par un électeur.* Ghent, Belgium, 1878.

______. *Système pratique et raisonné de représentation proportionnelle.* Brussels: Muquardt, 1882.

Doron, Gideon. "The Hare Voting System is Inconsistent." *Political Studies* 27 (1979), 283–86.

Doron, Gideon, and R. Kronick. "Single Transferable Vote: An Example of a Perverse Social Choice Function." *American Journal of Political Science* 21, (1977), 303–11.

Doyle, Jon, and Michael P. Wellman. "Impediments to Universal Preference-Based Default Theories." In *Knowledge Representation,* edited by Ronald J. Brachman *et al.,* 97–128. Cambridge, Mass.: MIT Press, 1992.

Droop, H. R. *On Methods of Electing Representatives.* London: Macmillan, 1868.

Dummett, Michael. *Voting Procedures.* Oxford: Clarendon Press, 1984.

Farquharson, Robin. *Theory of Voting.* Oxford: Blackwell, 1969.

Fishburn, Peter. "A Comparative Analysis of Group Decision Methods." *Behavioral Science* 16 (1971), 538–44.

______. *The Theory of Social Choice.* Princeton: Princeton University Press, 1973.

______."Condorcet Social Choice Functions," *Society for Industrial and Applied Mathematics Journal of Applied Mathematics* 33 (1977), 469–89.

Fishburn, Peter, and Steven J. Brams. "Kyzywsky's Paradoxes of Preferential Voting." Bell Telephone Laboratories, Murray Hill, N.J., and New York University, 1981. Photocopy.

Gardner, Martin. *The Universe in a Handkerchief.* New York: Copernicus, 1996.

Goodacre, Selwyn H. "An Enquiry into the Nature of a Certain Lewis Carroll Pamphlet." *The Book Collector* 27 (1978), 325–42.

Green, Roger L., ed. *The Diaries of Lewis Carroll.* 2 vols. New York: Oxford University Press, 1954.

______."Lewis Carroll and the *St. James's Gazette." Notes and Queries.* 7 April 1945, 134–35.

Guiliano, Edward, ed. *Lewis Carroll: A Celebration.* New York: Clarkson N. Potter, 1982.

Hare, T. *The Election of Representatives, Parliamentary and Municipal: A Treatise.* London: Longmans Green, 1859.

Hemaspaandra, Edith, Lane A. Hemaspaandra, and Jörg Rothe. "Exact Analysis of Dodgson Elections: Lewis Carroll's 1876 Voting System is Complete for Parallel Access." *Journal of the Association for Computing Machinery,* 44 (1997), 806–25.

Hoag, C. G. and G. H. Hallett. *Proportional Representation.* New York: Macmillan, 1926.

Humphreys, J. H. *Proportional Representation.* London: Methuen, 1911.

Huntington, E. V. "The Mathematical Theory of the Apportionment of Representatives." *Proceedings of the National Academy of Science* 7 (1928), 123–27.

______. "The Apportionment of Representatives in Congress." *Transactions of the American Mathematical Society* 30 (1928), 85–110.

Imholtz, August A. Jr., and Charles Lovett. *In Memoriam: Charles Lutwidge Dodgson 1832–1898. Obituaries of Lewis Carroll and Related Pieces.* New York: Lewis Carroll Society of North America, 1998.

Johnson, W. "Isaac Todhunter (1820–1884): Textbook Writer, Scholar, Coach and Historian of Science." *International Journal of Mechanical Science* 38 (1996), 1231–70.

Jones, Andrew. *The Politics of Reform 1884.* London: Cambridge University Press, 1972.

Kinnear, Michael. *The British Voter: An Atlas and Survey Since 1885.* Ithaca, N.Y.: Cornell University Press, 1968.

Knuth, Donald E. *The Art of Computer Programming,* vol. III: Sorting and Searching. Reading, MA: Addison-Wesley, 1973.

Kuhn, Harold W., ed. *Classics in Game Theory.* Princeton, N.J.: Princeton University Press, 1997.

Lakeman, Enid. *How Democracies Vote.* London: Faber and Faber, 1974.

Lewis, Alain A. "On Effectively Computable Realizations of Choice Functions." *Mathematical Social Sciences* 10 (1985), 43–80.

Lovett, Charles. *Lewis Carroll and the Press: An Annotated Bibliography of Charles Dodgson's Contributions to Periodicals.* New Castle, Del. and London: Oak Knoll Press in association with the British Library, 1999.

Lubbock, Sir John. *Representation.* London: Swan Sonnenschein, 1885.

Lutz, Cora E. *Essays on Manuscripts and Rare Books.* Hamden, Conn.: Archon, 1975.

Marshall, James G. *Minorities and Majorities; Their Relative Rights. A Letter to the Lord John Russell, M.P. on Parliamentary Reform.* London: James Ridgway, 1853.

McLean, Iain, and Arnold B. Urken, eds. *Classics of Social Choice.* Ann Arbor: University of Michigan Press, 1995.

McLean, Iain, Alistair McMillan, and Burt L. Monroe, eds. *A Mathematical Approach to Proportional Representation: Duncan Black on Lewis Carroll.* Boston: Kluwer Academic Publishers, 1996.

Miller, Nicholas R. "A New Solution Set for Tournaments and Majority Voting: Further Graph-Theoretical Approaches to the Theory of Voting," *American Journal of Political Science* 24 (1980), 68–96.

Mitchell, J. C. "Electoral Strategy under Open Voting: Evidence from England 1832–1880." *Public Choice* 28 (1976), 17–32.

Packel, Edward. *The Mathematics of Games and Gambling.* Washington: Mathematical Association of America, 1981.

Saari, Donald. "Mathematical Structure of Voting Paradoxes, I: Pairwise Votes." *Economic Theory* 15 (2000), 1–53.

______. "Mathematical Structure of Voting Paradoxes, II: Positional Voting." *Economic Theory* 15 (2000), 55–102.

Sen, K.A. *Collective Choice and Social Welfare.* San Francisco: Holden Day, 1970.

Seneta, Eugene. "Lewis Carroll as a Probabilist and Mathematician." *Mathematical Scientist* 9 (1984), 79–84.

Seymour, Charles. *Electoral Reform in England and Wales [1915]. The Development and Operation of the Parliamentary Franchise 1832–1855.* Hamden, Conn.: Archon Books, 1970.

Shaberman, R. B., and Denis Crutch, eds. *Under the Quizzing Glass: A Lewis Carroll Miscellany.* London: Magpie Press, 1972.

Stern, Jeffrey, ed. *Lewis Carroll's Library.* New York: Lewis Carroll Society of North America, 1981; distributed by the University Press of Virginia.

Straffin, P. D. *Topics in the Theory of Voting.* Boston: Birkhäuser, 1980.

Taylor, Robert N., compiler. *Lewis Caroll at Texas: The Warren Weaver Collection and Related Dodgson Materials at the Harry Ranson Humanities Research Center.* Austin: The University of Texas, 1985.

Todhunter, Isaac. *A History of the Mathematical Theory of Probability from the Time of Pascal to That of Laplace.* 1865; reprint, Bronx, N.Y.: Chelsea, 1965.

Wakeling, Edward, ed. *The Oxford Pamphlets, Leaflets, and Circulars of Charles Lutwidge Dodgson.* Charlottesville: University Press of Virginia, 1993.

______. *Lewis Carroll's Diaries.* 5 vols. Luton, U.K.: Lewis Carroll Society, 1993–99.

Williams, S. H., F. Madan, R. L. Green, and Denis Crutch. *The Lewis Carroll Handbook.* Folkestone, U.K., and Hamden, Conn.: Dawson and Archon, 1979.

Index